ZAIRE

ZAIRE

Continuity and Political Change in an Oppressive State

Winsome J. Leslie

Westview Press
BOULDER • SAN FRANCISCO • OXFORD

Westview Profiles/Nations of Contemporary Africa

Published in 1993 in the United States of America by Westview Press, Inc., 5500 Central Avenue, Boulder, Colorado 80301-2877, and in the United Kingdom by Westview Press, 36 Lonsdale Road, Summertown, Oxford OX2 7EW

Library of Congress Cataloging-in-Publication Data
Leslie, Winsome J.
  Zaire : continuity and political change in an oppressive state /
Winsome J. Leslie.
    p.   cm. — (Westview profiles. Nations of contemporary Africa)
  Includes bibliographical references and index.
  ISBN 0-86531-298-2
  1. Zaire—Politics and government—1960–   . 2. Zaire—Economic
conditions.   3. Despotism—Zaire—History.   I. Title.   II. Series.
DT658.L46   1993
967.51—dc20   92-46921
                                                                                          CIP

Printed and bound in the United States of America

 The paper used in this publication meets the requirements
of the American National Standard for Permanence of Paper
for Printed Library Materials Z39.48-1984.

10   9   8   7   6   5   4   3   2   1

Contents

Tables and Illustrations

Acknowledgments

Writing a book is in many ways a collaborative effort, and I would like to express my appreciation to all those who participated in this project. A special word of thanks must go to Thomas Callaghy for encouraging me to contribute to the Westview Profiles. Larry Bowman offered invaluable editorial insights for which I am grateful, and Barbara Ellington, Mick Duffy, and the staff at Westview Press are to be applauded for their untiring assistance on so many phases of this manuscript.

My deepest appreciation goes to all the individuals, including Zairians, who graciously granted me confidential interviews. Certain aspects of the book could not have been written without them. My thanks go to Maria de Santis for her assistance with graphics, to Bill Hezlep for his first-rate work in cartography, and to Ulrich Boegli for the contemporary map of Zaire. I express my gratitude to Don Fitzpatrick for his help with obtaining information on Zaire at the United Nations, to Abu Kari for access to Zairian newspapers and other current information on Zaire, to Felipe Tejeda for information on Zairian music, and to Learned Dees for graciously granting me permission to use his photographs.

Dianne Roberts and Harold Young provided critical comments on earlier drafts of the manuscript, and for this I thank them. A special word of appreciation goes to T. Michael Peay for his friendship and for providing substantive feedback on several chapters. Thanks to my parents and sister for their love and support and, finally, to my grandmother for all the intangible ways in which she enriched my life. This book is dedicated to her.

Winsome J. Leslie

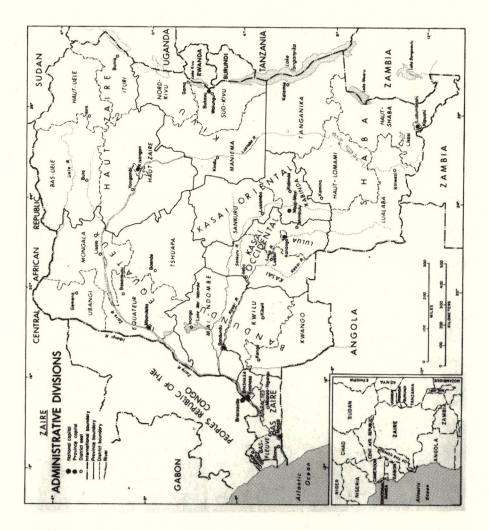

ADMINISTRATIVE DIVISIONS

● National capital
● Province capital
○ District seat
——— International boundary
——— Province boundary
——— District boundary
~~~ River

ZAIRE

Introduction

On June 30, 1990, the Republic of Zaire, formerly the Belgian Congo, celebrated thirty years of independence. The country first emerged on the international stage when Africa was partitioned by the European powers at the Berlin Conference of 1884. After more than one hundred years as a political entity, Zaire still captures international attention.

Zaire has had a turbulent past. The country has experienced foreign conquest, colonial exploitation, and finally—in 1960—independence hastily engineered by the Belgians. The postcolonial period between 1960 and 1992 has reflected this legacy: Violent upheaval and tenuous stability on the political front have been coupled with brief periods of growth in the midst of general economic decline. Although it is potentially one of the richest countries in Sub-Saharan Africa, given its vast natural resource endowments, the fortunes of the majority of Zaire's citizens have not improved. Nevertheless, Zairians have shown an amazing resilience and a determination to survive and cope, often against tremendous odds.

Over time, there has been a fundamental element of continuity between the contemporary state and its past. The country still remains vulnerable with respect to foreign penetration and influence over the economy. Colonial economic and political structures remain, albeit adapted to modern realities, as traditional life and customs continue. Furthermore, Zaire has been ruled by one president, Mobutu Sese Seko Kuku Ngbendu Wa Za Banga, for over twenty-five years. In the view of the major Western powers, this rule has provided a powerful element of stability over time, but the oppressive, authoritarian nature of the regime has had an adverse impact on socioeconomic welfare. These threads of continuity in turn have implications for the future evolution of the Zairian state and the larger society as well as for the country's ability to function from a position of strength in the international economy. Prospects for change are inevitably shaped by the past and present. In the

1

broad overview of Zaire presented in this book, contemporary trends, linking present realities to the historical development of the state, are examined.

In physical terms Zaire is an imposing country. Lying in the heart of Africa across the equator, it is the third-largest country on the continent with respect to territorial size, covering approximately 2.3 million square kilometers. The fifth-largest country in terms of population, with an estimated 35.8 million people as of 1990, Zaire is divided into eleven administrative regions: Bas Zaire (or Lower Zaire), Kinshasa (the capital, which has the status of a region), Bandundu, Équateur, Haut Zaire (Upper Zaire), Kasai Oriental (Eastern Kasai), Kasai Occidental (Western Kasai), Nord Kivu (North Kivu), Sud Kivu (South Kivu), Maniema, and Shaba (see map on page xii; prior to 1990 Nord Kivu, Sud Kivu, and Maniema were subregions of Kivu). Population growth has increased significantly in recent years, averaging 3 percent annually, and has surpassed the growth of national income. As a result, gross national product (GNP) per capita has been declining according to official estimates. Forty-seven percent of the total population is under fifteen years of age; this age distribution and the high population growth together have put additional strains on the social welfare system. Average population density is generally low, although there is considerable variation between regions (from 8 inhabitants per square kilometer in Équateur to 266 in Kinshasa). By contrast, urbanization rates are high, with 39 percent of the total population living in urban centers. Kinshasa alone has approximately 3 million inhabitants, or about 10 percent of the total population.

The geography of the country is dominated by the Zaire river system. The river itself is 4,700 kilometers long, but with its tributaries there are 15,000 kilometers of navigable waterway. It originates near the Zambian border and crosses the equator twice as it winds its way toward the Atlantic. During the precolonial period, settlement patterns followed the water course fairly closely, and the distribution of subsequent economic activity was based on the use of the river as a transport system. This dependence still exists. The many falls and rapids along the course of the river provide one of the largest sources of hydroelectric power in the world, with an estimated potential of 100,000 megawatts.

Several geographic regions, containing varied natural vegetation, can be identified. The Central Zaire Basin, also known as the *cuvette* (shallow bowl), is located just northeast of Kinshasa and extends as far as Kisangani. The *cuvette* constitutes about one-third of the country's land area and includes about 1 million square kilometers of equatorial forest, a large portion of which is swamp. Elevations here average about 400 meters. The Southern Uplands area, also about one-third of Zaire's territory, extends southward from the *cuvette* toward Shaba, then northward into the Kivu region. Elevations in this region reach as high as 1,000 meters in the southeast, with a mixture of woodlands and savanna grasses at lower elevations and higher plateaus and low mountains in Shaba.

Western Zaire is an extension of the Southern Uplands that falls sharply to a narrow coastal area at Matadi. On the country's northern borders, the Northern Uplands region is largely savanna, with average altitudes reaching about 600 meters. Finally, the Eastern Highlands in the Kivu and Shaba regions contains the highest and most rugged terrain, with mountain ranges that vary from 1,000 to more than 5,000 meters. The region extends approximately 1,500 kilometers from Lake Mobutu Sese Seko (formerly Lake Albert) in the north to the area below Lubumbashi, Zaire's second largest city. The Ruwenzori Mountains (mountains of the moon) between Lakes Mobutu Sese Seko and Idi Amin Dada (formerly Lake Edward) are the highest in Africa, with spectacular and unusual vegetation. There are also active volcanoes north of Lake Kivu in the Virunga Mountains. Rainfall is abundant throughout the country, but with Zaire's location across the equator, the dry season (November through March) in the northern third of the country corresponds to the rainy season in the remaining two-thirds. Most of the country experiences high temperatures and humidity throughout the year, with the least variation in temperature occurring in the equatorial forest.

Zaire is exceptionally rich in mineral resources. Reserves of copper, cobalt, zinc, lead, manganese, platinum, cadmium, germanium, silver, and gold can be found in Shaba. This province boasts about 15 percent of the world's copper reserves. Until 1986, when it was surpassed by Australia, Zaire was the world's largest producer of industrial diamonds. Diamond deposits are found largely in Kasai Oriental and Kasai Occidental. Tin can be found in upper Shaba and Kivu, and gold mines are located in Haut Zaire and parts of Kivu. In the early 1970s bauxite was discovered in Bas Zaire, oil deposits were found offshore near Angola, and natural gas was discovered in the Lake Kivu region. There are also unexploited shale and geothermal deposits, uranium, and untapped solar energy potential. In agriculture, Zaire produces a variety of crops, both for export (oil palm, coffee, tea, and cotton) and for local consumption (cassava, maize, rice, and bananas). The country is capable of being self-sufficient in food, but this self-sufficiency has yet to materialize in the postindependence period.

Abundant natural resources and the accompanying possibilities for development have to be placed in a context of the country's historical beginnings when the political and economic configurations of the state were established. In Chapter 1 the impact of early foreign influences on the Zairian state—and particularly the precedents set for the exploitation of the country's natural resources—are discussed. Methods of exploitation crystallized under Belgian colonial rule, establishing a dual economy—an industrial sector linked to external capital coexisting with a rural sector focused on subsistence and plantation agriculture. This arrangement persists intact after three decades of independence. On the political front the Belgians instituted repressive centralized rule to facilitate control over the vast territory. This control was relinquished when the country was abruptly granted independence in 1960, leaving Zaire unprepared for postcolonial realities. Regional and ethnic tendencies largely held in check by colonialism clashed in the face of a fragile Western-style parliamentary system inherited from Belgium, plunging the country into five years of chaos.

After assuming the presidency in 1965, Mobutu Sese Seko quickly adopted the centralizing, oppressive aspects of Belgian rule as part of his own political consolidation process, which culminated in the creation of a one-party state. In Chapter 2 the key elements of this strategy, which have included political mobilization around an artificially created ideology (Mobutuism) as well as repression, are examined. Meanwhile, political strains on the system have come from internal and external opposition to the regime; the opposition has become persistent and more open, particularly since 1990.

The interaction between state and society is reviewed in Chapter 3. Zaire consists of over 200 ethnic groups, which themselves have impacted and have been influenced by changes within the Zairian polity over time. There are also cross-cutting affiliations based on class and religion, which have created cleavages within the state. Additional factors, such as unequal access to education, have affected social mobility and male-female roles in society. Finally, rapid urbanization and the accompanying rural stagnation have resulted in declining living standards and diminished well-being for Zairian citizens.

These hardships have been aggravated by an ongoing economic and debt crisis. In Chapter 4 the historical antecedents of the economy are explored, as well as various aspects of the current decline. Since its beginning, external actors have directly and indirectly helped shape economic and political outcomes in Zaire. Chapter 5 contains an examination of Zaire in the wider international arena as well as a discussion of the limits to and the Machiavellian nature of Mobutu's diplomacy. In conclusion, the implications of the colonial and Mobutuist legacies for Zaire's future are assessed in Chapter 6, which focuses on the prospects for and problems of political and economic reform.

1

The Historical Setting

The configuration of the modern Zairian state is a direct result of cross-cutting influences in its history. Vestiges of traditional societies can still be found in the contemporary state. External powers, from the Portuguese to the Arabs and finally the Belgians, exploited what became known as the Congo for economic gain. These early foreign contacts in turn profoundly impacted and fragmented precolonial society and culture, shaping ethnic, sociopolitical, and class relations while effectively incorporating the Congo into the global economic system as a producer of primary products. These conditions set the stage for the economic and political dislocations that have been characteristic of the postcolonial period.

EARLY KINGDOMS AND
THE IMPACT OF FOREIGN EXPLOITATION

The Congo's first recorded contacts with the external world were with fifteenth-century Portuguese explorers. In 1482 Diogo Cão discovered the mouth of the Congo River, giving it the name *zaire*, a misspelling of *nzadi*, the Kikongo term for river.[1] Cão established contact with the Kongo people, one of the major ethnic groups in the area (refer to Map 3.1). The Kongo kingdom at that time stretched from northern Angola to the north bank of the Congo River, in the area now known as Bas Zaire. The kingdom, with its capital at Mbanza Kongo, had a well-established centralized system of government; it was divided into six provinces, each administered by a local governor appointed by the king. Within each province Kongo district chiefs governed in their respective areas, and at the village level headmen were accountable to the district chiefs. The king was elected from the male descendants of the individual who had conquered the area. Although he was a member of the aristocracy and appeared to have absolute power, the king was in fact subject to the control of a council of elders who could depose him. Further limits

5

came from the district chiefs, whose authority was conferred by tradition rather than by the political system. The kingdom had a hierarchical system of tribute. The village headman received tribute from his people; he in turn gave payments to the district chief; the provincial governor took tributes from the district chiefs. Finally, a portion of each governor's receipts went to the capital for the king. Payment of tribute determined one's standing in the political hierarchy.[2] One notable feature of the kingdom was the king's absolute control over currency—shells found only in the royal fishery.

Portugal soon established formal diplomatic relations with the Kongo kingdom, leading to mutual socioeconomic exchanges. On the one hand, the Kongo were noticeably influenced by Catholicism as well as Portuguese customs, and many were converted to Christianity. On the other hand, Portugal's close ties with the Kongo greatly facilitated development of the slave trade in the region. Slaves purchased from the Kongo provided cheap labor for plantations on nearby Portuguese islands and, subsequently, the Americas. Over time, with the spectacular growth in the trade in response to growing demand, conflict developed between the Portuguese and the Kongo over this issue. The focus on the capture of slaves led to the depopulation of vast areas of Kongo territory, increasing warfare and border raids against neighboring tribes. Furthermore, the Kongo also fought among themselves over the activities of slave traders in the interior who sought allies among the various factions vying for Kongo kingship. In the final analysis, the slave trade undermined political authority and created social stratification in the kingdom. By the early seventeenth century, friction over access to land developed with the neighboring colony of Angola, founded by the Portuguese in the mid-sixteenth century. This friction culminated in open conflict that effectively destroyed Kongo military and economic power and, indeed, the kingdom itself.

Other major empires existing in the Congo at the time of the Kongo people—the Luba and the Lunda, for example—were similarly affected by developments of the period.[3] At its height, the Luba kingdom stretched from Lake Tanganyika in the eastern part of the Congo to the southern part of what became Katanga province (now Shaba). It is said to have been founded about the fifteenth century by a Bantu chief, Nkongolo Mukulu. By the seventeenth century, however, a number of Luba subgroups had migrated westward into Kasai province. The Luba state was also highly centralized. Groups of villages were organized into chiefdoms, several of which constituted a province under a provincial chief appointed by the king. Provinces in turn made up the kingdom. This political structure was subsequently adopted in areas bordering

Luba territory when former chiefs established themselves outside the kingdom.

The Lunda empire grew out of a kingdom formed by a brother of the reigning Luba king at the beginning of the seventeenth century. Lying in the southwest corner of the Congo, the Lunda settlements extended from Katanga province into neighboring Angola. The trading opportunities that arose because of the presence of the Portuguese on the Angolan coast were an important factor in the emergence of the Lunda state. There were striking similarities between the organization of the Lunda state and that of the Luba, but the Lunda generally sought to integrate conquered peoples into their empire. As a result, their political system influenced a vast area in the southern Congo until well into the nineteenth century. The collection of tribute was a central aspect of the Lunda empire and served to maintain the lines of political control that extended from the royal capital. It was this collection of tribute that fostered the transformation of the Lunda from a pyramidal to a hierarchical authority structure.[4] An important feature of the system was the organization of political posts. The successor to an office inherited his predecessor's title, as well as his status, name, and kinship relations. In the eighteenth century the Lunda expanded into Luba territory in search of manpower for their agricultural activities. Later they became actively involved in the ivory trade, establishing collection points and administering the trade in much the same way that the Kongo did with the trafficking of slaves.

It was partly this ivory trade that brought the Arabs into Central Africa from the East African coast. A lucrative caravan trade involving Arab traders began in the nineteenth century at about the time Portuguese influence in the lower Congo was declining. Initially the Arabs came in small groups, forming alliances with local chiefs to purchase slaves, copper, and ivory. Soon the Arabs began to raid Luba lands for slaves. This led to severe disruption of the Luba way of life, as Arab traders and Luba chiefs resorted to slave trading and trafficking of guns. Unlike the Portuguese, the Arabs were not interested in political ties with the local peoples but chose to focus exclusively on profits and trade. Nevertheless, with their continued expansion inland, they unwittingly established an administrative system. Certain Arab chiefs controlled large territories and as a result had a considerable influence over local tribes. The most famous of these chiefs, Mohammed Ben Junna ("Tippo-Tip"), became powerful enough to be considered the "king" of the region between Stanley Falls (just south of what is now Kisangani) and Lake Tanganyika. Arab activities had an important impact on local politics and customs in the eastern Congo. Traditional institutions were destroyed, and the establishment of formal trading centers in the area initiated regular contacts between different ethnic groups. The introduction of Swahili, which was to become one of the Congo's official languages, as well as the influence of Islam became common points of reference, integrating peoples from various tribes. These influences would persist long after the Arabs withdrew.[5]

EXTERNAL PENETRATION AND DOMINATION

Although the activities of the Portuguese and Arabs irreversibly altered and eroded traditional Congolese society, the most lasting and perhaps the most devastating impact came from the Belgians.[6] King Leopold II of Belgium came to focus on the Congo because of Henry Stanley's famous journey down the Congo River to the Atlantic Ocean in the 1870s. Leopold's desire for an overseas empire had not materialized in the Far East, so he turned his attention to the one area on the African continent that was relatively unknown and unexplored. With the other European powers preoccupied elsewhere in Africa, Leopold formed the Comité d'Études du Haut Congo (Survey Committee for the Upper Congo), later known as the Association Internationale du Congo (International Association of the Congo), and commissioned Stanley to conduct further explorations along the Congo River. Under the guise of humanitarianism and scientific exploration, the area quickly became the personal property of the king, and the 1884 Berlin Conference between the European powers on the partition of Africa formally acknowledged Leopold's jurisdiction over the Congo. At the time, it was widely assumed that European powers could freely annex African territory as long as the consent of a certain number of African chiefs had been obtained. The Association Internationale du Congo was recognized by the conference as an independent entity with its own flag. It became the Congo Free State in 1885. In turn, Leopold agreed "on paper" that activities in the Congo Basin would be regulated according to principles such as freedom of navigation and trade, suppression of the slave trade, and improvement of the socioeconomic condition of the local population.

Leopold's commercial ambitions in the Congo soon became paramount, and the desire to make the Free State a lucrative venture brought his agents there into open conflict with the local population. The focus was on the extraction of resources, the unification of the territory through military conquest, and the economic destruction of preexisting kingdoms.[7] Initially the Free State sought reconciliation with Arab traders in the east. Tippo-Tip agreed to recognize the rights of the Free State between the area of Banana (the point at which the Zaire River enters the Atlantic Ocean) and Stanley Falls. However, state merchants soon began to compete with the Arabs to monopolize the ivory trade. Open warfare between the Free State and the Arabs subsequently erupted, with Congolese fighting on both sides, resulting in significant loss of life. The Free State's superior military forces easily overwhelmed the Arabs and forcibly incorporated the eastern regions into Leopold's domain.

The king was represented in the Congo by a governor-general. The country was divided into fifteen districts, each headed by a commissioner. This arrangement ignored ethnic boundaries and reduced or eliminated the authority of local chiefs. The aim was the creation of a unified territory, even at the cost of the destruction of existing polities. The raison d'être of the Free State was the extraction of resources. In the pursuit of profit, Leopold devised a restrictive system of land ownership under which Europeans in the Congo had to register their landholdings, leaving all unowned lands and their products the property of the Free State. The Congolese were barred from collecting rubber and ivory except for sale to the state. Existing trading posts were closed to further consolidate the state's trading monopoly.

Such centralized control sparked protests by Belgian government officials and private companies, and Leopold accordingly permitted private exploitation of one-third of the unowned lands beginning in 1892, reserving another one-third as his private domain. Commercial companies were licensed as agents of the state and given long-term monopolies over the resources of vast areas in return for sizable tax payments. Directly contrary to the Berlin agreement, the state held majority shares in these companies. Moreover, the well-being of the indigenous population was subordinated to the pursuit of profits. By suppressing commercial activity, the Free State destroyed old trading centers and market networks and fragmented traditional sociopolitical institutions at the clan and village levels.

Accounts soon reached Europe from missionaries and commercial agents describing abysmal conditions in the Congo and the brutal methods used by *chefs de poste* (state agents) and concessionary company representatives to collect rubber and ivory. Payment of taxes to the state by the companies was used as a rationale for demanding impossibly high production quotas from the local population. Congolese were taken en masse from their native villages and forced to work for seven-year periods under the supervision of *capitas* (headmen) from different tribes. Both the *chefs de poste* and the *capitas* had a vested interest in the system, as their compensation was directly related to production levels in their territories. Accordingly, brutal methods—floggings, torture, and execution—were employed when villagers could not meet their assigned quotas. *Capitas* were often required by their supervisors to produce the right hands of individuals they had killed as proof that they had administered the appropriate punishment. Leopold belatedly appointed a commission of inquiry that visited the Congo in 1904; as a result of the commission's report, limited reforms were instituted in 1906. However, by that time the wave of international criticism had heightened against the Leopoldian regime; and as the Free State had become increasingly profitable, domestic pressure grew in Brussels for Belgian annexation of the territory. The Free State formally became a Belgian colony in 1908.[8]

The blatant exploitation of human and natural resources fostered by the Free State left a bitter legacy in relations among various ethnic groups. This mutual suspicion and animosity made it difficult to achieve political and administrative cohesion during the early colonial period. Although perhaps the more offensive and obvious abuses of the Free State were abolished, there was a basic continuity between the goals of Belgian colonialism and those of the Free State.[9]

In the Belgian Congo, policy was dominated by an attitude of benevolent paternalism. One writer puts it succinctly:

> The Belgian system was frankly paternalistic. Colonial officials prided themselves on their accomplishments in the fields of housing, health care, and primary education. They saw no need for experiments in self-government; they had no intention of granting independence in the foreseeable future. The Congolese, they explained, were "like children" and would need years and years of tutelage.[10]

It is therefore not surprising that the Belgians gave no thought to an independent Congo until it was virtually thrust upon them.

Until the 1950s Belgian rule was based on the principle of "native autonomy," according to which the Congolese colonial government was subject to direction from Brussels through the Ministry of the Colonies. The Congo was governed under the Colonial Charter of 1908, which granted the king legislative authority. Limits were placed on his power by the Belgian Parliament, which also controlled the colonial budget. On a local level, in the Congo itself, institutions were allowed some measure of independence. The central government based in the capital of Leopoldville was headed by a governor-general (the king's representative), and a government council served as an advisory body. Administrative ordinances issued by the governor-general had the force of law. In the spirit of *dominer pour servir* (ruling in order to serve) the Belgians felt that their "civilizing process" was one that should be implemented from above. Economic, social, and moral development was the order of the day. Political advancement was to be postponed until it was determined that the Congolese had reached a sufficient level of "maturity." Accordingly, the state and the large concessionary companies, along with the Catholic missions operating in the Congo since the coming of the Portuguese, formed a triumvirate with mutually reinforcing roles that sought to fulfill Belgian colonial objectives.[11]

To the Congolese the Colonie Belge was alien and larger than life. By the 1920s its hegemony extended to the far reaches of the Congo through highly effective administrative and coercive instruments of the state. The Belgians put in place an elaborate system of administration based on central and local governments. As in the Leopoldian era, powerful chiefs who extended their authority over large areas were either forced into submission or neutralized by undermining their power through the appointment by the Belgians of new chiefs and local officials. The Congo was initially divided into four provinces and then in 1933 into six: Lower Congo (with a capital in Leopoldville), Équateur (Coquilhatville), Orientale (Stanleyville), Katanga (Elisabethville), Kasai (Luluabourg), and Kivu (Bukavu) (see Map 1.1). The provinces were divided into districts, which were subdivided into territories. Katanga and Orientale operated fairly independently of the central government, owing to their particularly strong provincial governments. This independence frustrated efforts at administrative and economic cohesion throughout the colonial period, and it was one factor that brought secessionist tendencies to the surface in both areas immediately after independence in 1960.

During the years of Belgian rule, the boundaries of districts and territories were redrawn several times as dictated by administrative concerns, although after reforms in 1933 some attempt was made to incorporate tribal divisions. Nevertheless, the entire process only underscored the artificial nature of the system. Predictably the Congolese had no role in the central government until after World War II. Indeed, by 1960 there were an estimated 10,000 Belgian civil servants in the various organs of government, including the army, whereas educated Congolese held only subordinate clerical posts.

At the local level administrative control of the native population was based on the Belgian interpretation of Congolese traditional political organization. Initially in rural areas the administrative units were the *chefferie* (district) and *sous-chefferie* (subdistrict) made up of small villages headed by chiefs recognized by colonial district commissioners. Chiefs were given administrative and judicial powers and were paid a salary in direct proportion to the size of their *chefferies*. Subject to European control, chiefs became more concerned with enforcing colonial policy than with reaffirming tradition. By 1921 the number of *chefferies* that were administratively too small had proliferated to such an extent that they were organized into larger units called *secteurs* (divisional districts), also ruled by traditional chiefs. Urban areas were divided into *cités indigènes* (native towns)—small African urban centers, with no administrative

MAP 1.1   Republic of the Congo, 1960

infrastructure—governed by a *chef de cité* (town leader) and *centres extra-coutumiers*, African quarters in larger towns organized administratively in a manner similar to the *chefferies*. The net result of this vast system was an undermining of traditional chiefly authority. Custom was recognized and respected only at the level of the *chefferie*, even though tribal chiefs had been entrusted with the welfare of entire tribes in precolonial times.[12]

The colonial state intruded on traditional life in other ways. Under the Colonial Charter the central government in Brussels made the Belgian colony responsible for financing its own expenditures. The Congo had to be profitable, and therefore by the 1920s large financial and commercial conglomerates were firmly entrenched in the local economy, developing the mineral and agricultural sectors with the blessing of the state. State action provided cheap labor to support these activities through direct coercion, through labor recruitment with the cooperation of tribal chiefs, and indirectly through the taxation of all adult males, forcing them to seek wage employment. More specifically, in agriculture, forced cultivation was promulgated by law in 1917 to ensure adequate production of both export crops and a low-cost food supply for the local market. Peasants had to devote at least sixty days per year to the cultivation of crops dictated by the colonial government, and state officials were given authority to impose this policy through fines or imprisonment. Labor conscription also occurred for large infrastructure projects such as construction of the railway linking the interior of the country to the Atlantic coast at Matadi. Not surprisingly, many areas in provinces such as Katanga and Leopoldville saw significant decreases in population at this time. Population movements were also tightly controlled through forced resettlement. Congolese were required to carry identity cards, listing name, place of residence, and civil status. It is estimated that in 1924 9 million Africans were registered out of a native population of 10.5 million.[13] This level of regulation was unparalleled in colonial Africa at the time.

As a result of all these restrictions, the Colonie Belge soon became known as Bula Matari, a phrase used decades earlier to refer to the explorer Henry Stanley, meaning "he who breaks rocks." In the colonial context it evoked the image of an all-powerful state, forcibly imposing its will on the local population, regulating every aspect of colonial life, and crushing all resistance to its policies.[14] To traditional societies such as the Lunda, colonial rule primarily meant limits on long-distance trade, taxation, forced labor recruitment for road-building, and the cultivation of unfamiliar cash crops—in sum, interference with their way of life. This negative image could not be overcome by the greater availability of consumer goods, improved economic and educational opportunities, and better health services.[15]

Catholic and Protestant missionary activities in the Congo often worked in tandem with state policies. Overall, Christian missionary activity had a profound impact on traditional life in the Congo. Both Protestants and Catholics were eager to eradicate what they viewed as "heathen" native customs, although the Catholics were far more intrusive in terms of their methods. Whereas Protestants recruited evangelists from the local Congolese population to act as intermediaries between the church and traditional society, the Catholics focused on entire communities, uprooting prospective converts (mostly children) from their areas and organizing separate settlements under the supervision of the mission. This effort created what became known as the *ferme chapelle* (church farm) system, an attempt to establish "a new society" through isolation from traditional influences. Protests from Belgium led to the abandonment of this system in favor of mass evangelization using Congolese catechists. On the local level the catechist was a political, social, and religious force in the village. He was the link between the villager and the strange European world of the colonizer, an adviser to the village chief. It was hoped that as a representative of the Catholic mission his presence would modify the demands of local administrators. Although both Catholic and Protestant missionaries became involved in evangelical as well as educational activities, Catholics undertook a broader range of projects, including agriculture. Crop cultivation by converts produced an additional source of revenue for the missions to supplement operating costs.[16]

Besides its evangelical role, the church had a vital welfare function with extensive involvement in education and health. Government health efforts were supported by the Christian missions and philanthropic organizations. The missions were already established in the rural areas, often in places inaccessible to official medical services. With respect to education, Catholic and Protestant mission schools subsidized by the colonial government were the norm until 1954, when the first public schools were opened, just six years before independence. Prior to this time the government subsidized a large part of the operating costs of mission schools, particularly those affiliated with the Catholic church. The state often encouraged missions to develop remote areas that the government was either unwilling or unable to develop. Education was a natural part of the religious conversion process, as individuals had to learn to read in order to understand the Bible and other religious texts. The state itself encouraged the establishment of mission schools to teach basic skills in order to provide a pool of trained workers for state institutions. Protestants and Catholics held different views on the question of church involvement in education. The Protestants firmly believed in the separation of church and state and had to adjust their beliefs to the idea of missionary education in a colonial setting. The Catholics, however, were convinced that education was an important responsibility of the church to be undertaken with the financial support of the state. Furthermore, the development of Catholic schools soon became an imperative for the missions in order to counteract the significant Protestant presence in the Congo.[17] In time Catholics had a virtual monopoly over education in the colony. Overall, the missions with their intimate daily contacts with Congolese touted their own version of the colonizer's *mission civilatrice* (civilizing mission), creating tensions between the imperatives of tradition, on the one hand, and Western mores, on the other.[18]

Access to education beyond the primary school level was largely denied to the Congolese until the late 1940s. Prior to that time, relatively small numbers of students were allowed to go on to specialized vocational schools—the only option besides a seminary education. It was felt that advanced education would only serve to politicize the Congolese, creating desires for assimilation and undermining the existing colonial system. More specifically, the Belgian government believed in the concept of gradual development, in which all Congolese would advance at the same pace, preempting the emergence of a class that would prove a threat to Belgian rule.[19]

TOWARD INDEPENDENCE

The immediate post–World War II period brought new challenges to bear on Belgian colonialism. There were fortunate Congolese who had been granted access to education beyond the elementary level, primarily in mission schools. Referred to as *évolués* (civilized individuals) by the Belgians, this group began to question their true role in the Belgian system, demanding equal treatment with Europeans. In general, Belgian colonialism reinforced the principle of European authority and African subordination. In practice the result was the effective separation of the Congolese and Belgian communities with respect to education, social services, and access to economic opportunities. Such inequality in turn was reinforced by the legal system. The European population in the Congo was subject to statutory law based on Western legal principles, whereas the "natives" were governed by customary law—in effect, the Belgian interpretation of traditional mores.

Évolués insisted on better educational opportunities for Congolese as a whole. From their perspective this was an important issue. Although a few Catholics saw the need for higher education outside the seminaries, the majority of the missionaries failed to support the demands of this new elite. The migration from rural to urban areas, accelerated by the war, went against the aims of the missionaries, who sought to create religious converts committed to remaining in the rural areas where they could spread the faith and be isolated from the corruptive influences of the city.[20] In the urban centers the increased population, with only a primary education, merely fueled existing social problems.

Internal pressures for change were matched by initiatives on the international front. An anticolonialism movement under way in the United Nations called for independence and self-determination for all colonized peoples. It became clear to officials in Brussels that the colonial state was under siege; and although it was apparent that emancipation of the Congolese would have to come in the future, Belgium needed to control the process. This control could come only if social mobility and economic well-being were immediately available to the indigenous population within the colonial framework.

Accordingly, the Belgian notion of the *mission civilatrice* gave way to the idea of a Belgo-Congolese community, which was an attempt to reconcile *évolué* demands and the desire on the part of the local European population to retain its privileges. Nevertheless, the effort involved no meaningful reforms in the existing colonial structure. Running in tandem with this new strategy was a significant expansion in social services (health and education) along the lines of the welfare state (see Table 1.1).[21] The Fonds du Bien-Être Indigène (FBEI; Native Welfare Fund) was established to fund projects in the health sector. Furthermore, all mining, industrial, agricultural, and commercial companies operating in the Congo were legally obligated to provide medical attention for their workers. Services were often extended free of charge to the surrounding community. This period also saw the formulation of a Ten-Year Plan for development of the Congo by the Belgian government. In the area of health, plans were unveiled for a countrywide network of medical units. Each of the 138 territories (administrative units with an average of 100,000 inhabitants) would have a government medical-surgical center run by two doctors in its main town; the center would support a network of rural dispensaries.

In 1948 educational reforms were implemented that sanctioned secondary education for Congolese for the first time. A full six-year secondary program was instituted, which nevertheless effectively separated education for the white elite from that of the Congolese. Natives would study under a program known as *le régime congolais* (the Congolese program), which was less academic and more loosely based on the Belgian system than *le régime metropolitain* (the metropolitan program) offered to the European students. Educational reform also distinguished between technical education and higher education for the elite. The end of this segregated system of education came only in 1958, in response to demands by the *évolués* for access to the same opportunities as the Belgians.[22]

University education and, more specifically, the establishment of a full-fledged university in the Congo continued to be resisted until the mid-1950s, when a few students were allowed to attend the University of Louvain in Brussels. Prior to this change, missions were not free to send their students to study abroad. The University of Louvanium was formally established at Kimuenza, on the outskirts of Leopoldville, in 1954 following sustained pressure by Catholic missionaries, and the University of Elisabethville came into being two years later. Indeed, Zaire is one of the few African countries in which university education was started by

TABLE 1.1
Public Health in the Belgian Congo, 1946 and 1956

Category	1946	1956
Population (mil.)	n.a.	12.8
Population density (inhabitants per sq. km)	n.a.	9.42
Average birth rate (per 1,000)	n.a.	35.0
Average death rate (per 1,000)	n.a.	21.6
General hospitals	190	293
Dispensaries (government and private)	1,078	1,953
Doctors		
Government/semipublic bodies	191	340
Missions	40	81
Companies	99	158
Private practice	18	64
Pharmacists		
Government	4	16
Companies	12	46
Dentists		
Government	2	16
Private	13	28
Nurses	574	1,084
Public health officers	317	581
Congolese medical staff[a]	2,329	4,600
Inhabitants per one doctor	36,400	20,000

[a] Includes medical assistants, male nurses and assistant nurses, public health assistants, and midwives.

Source: Hygiene and Health Group, Ministry of the Belgian Congo and Ruanda-Urundi, Public Health in Belgian Africa (Brussels: INFORCONGO, 1958), pp. 18, 23-24.

the church. By December 1958 there were 248 Congolese at Lovanium and 42 Congolese at Elisabethville. A third university was formed with Protestant support in Stanleyville (Kisangani) in 1963, after independence.

In the mid-1950s the *évolués* began to make insistent calls for independence. In part, the notion of self-government was triggered by the writings of a Belgian law professor, A.A.J. Van Bilsen, who in 1955 published a thirty-year plan for the political emancipation of Belgian Africa. As a result, the first Congolese political manifesto endorsing the Van Bilsen plan appeared in *Conscience Africaine*, a Congolese journal expressing the views of the *évolués*, followed by a more aggressive counterproposal formulated by the Alliance des BaKongo (ABAKO; BaKongo Alliance), an ethnic association of the Kongo, demanding immediate independence. At the same time, Belgian political parties founded *amicales* (fraternal associations) in the Congo with membership open to *évolués* as well as Europeans. Although *évolués* played no important roles in such organizations, in many instances the organizations provided them with their first introduction to politics in the Western European tradition.

Fledgling Congolese political organizations developed during the 1950s along ethnic lines in the context of existing urban ethnic associations.[23] During the colonial period urbanization had taken place fairly rapidly with substantial migration from the rural areas to the towns. Ethnically based organizations were created to promote culture and offer mutual support in the face of close interactions with other ethnic groups. Ethnic polarization occurred with urbanization and the resulting competition for social, economic, and political status. Polarization was further reinforced by ethnic organizations. Two such associations—the ABAKO and Lulua Frères (Lulua Brotherhood)—were particularly effective in the political arena. The formation of ABAKO in 1950 was an attempt to restore the Kongo to preeminence in Leopoldville. The Kongo felt threatened by migrant peoples upriver collectively known as the Ngala, after the language they spoke (Lingala). Although the city of Leopoldville was on the fringe of their territory, the Kongo believed they had a right to social leadership there. With the standardization of Lingala, the Kongo feared that this group would usurp their predominant role. The Lulua Frères sought to improve the socioeconomic situation of the Lulua because of a fear of domination by the Luba in Luluabourg.[24] Within four years of its founding in 1951, the organization had branches in all the major mining centres in Katanga, as well as in the neighboring territories of Angola, Northern Rhodesia, Congo-Brazzaville, and Burundi. Other points of polarization could be found in Bukavu, the capital of the Kivu region, between the Kusu and the Shi.

In the face of growing politicization of the Congolese, the traditional triumvirate of state, church, and large conglomerates in the Congo steadily disintegrated. As the Catholic church in Leopoldville looked to the future, it found it expedient not only to Africanize the clergy but also to firmly support Congolese independence in order to preserve and expand the presence of the church in the Congo. This action effectively distanced the church from state policies. The large companies operating in the Congo took a different approach, supporting state policies on the independence issue, on the one hand, and making financial contributions to Congolese political organizations, on the other.

In 1958 President Charles de Gaulle gave a moving speech from Congo-Brazzaville offering independence to the French colonies in Africa, an announcement that further strengthened calls for self-determination from Leopoldville. At the same time, the colonial state was progressively losing administrative control in various parts of the Congo, including the Leopoldville region. Passive resistance to state policies and a refusal to compromise on the independence issue became widespread. By 1959 the Belgians were given some indication of the extent of Congolese nationalist feeling when riots broke out in the capital. Belgian political leaders were completely overwhelmed by these events. Suggestions of a military intervention to reimpose order, which were proposed by Europeans in the Congo, were dismissed when a major campaign got under way in Belgium against such intervention. Evidently the Belgian government quickly lost confidence in the future of the Congo as a viable colony but proved incapable of constructing a coherent plan for decolonization.[25] By 1960 Belgium had hastily convened a Roundtable Conference to discuss Congolese independence. Plans were made in earnest to establish a Western-style parliamentary democracy in the new state. Elections were set for May that year, with independence to follow in June, and a new draft constitution, the Loi Fondamentale (Fundamental Law), was drawn up and passed by the Belgian Parliament.

The first Congolese municipal elections, called for by the government reforms in 1957, provided the only initial opportunity for serious political organization. Political mobilization had to be achieved rapidly, so there was no time to develop ideologies or political philosophies with which to win support. Existing ethnic organizations therefore became the vehicles for mobilization, resulting in the formation of dozens of political parties based largely on ethnic loyalties. After the 1959 riots the pace of decolonization accelerated and attempts were made to create nationally based parties. Three such organizations emerged: the Mouvement National Congolais (MNC; National Congolese Movement) headed by Patrice Lumumba, with its base of support in Orientale province—Lumumba's birthplace—and Kasai; ABAKO, led by Joseph Kasavubu, with strong support in Leopoldville and the Bas Zaire region; and the Parti National du Progrès (PNP; National Progressive Party), a coalition of tribal-based parties backed by traditional chiefs and led by Paul Bolya, with its center of support in Équateur.

Voting during the May 1960 elections took place along ethnic lines. Lumumba's party gained a narrow victory with only 24 percent of the Assembly's 137 seats, underscoring the fragmentation that existed in party affiliations. As a result, it was necessary for him to enter political alliances with other parties, such as ABAKO, to form a government. This situation created an uneasy compromise between Lumumba and Kasavubu, who had represented opposing views within the Congolese independence movement. Lumumba was subsequently made prime minister, and Kasavubu was appointed as president of the Congo.

In the Congolese political mosaic, Lumumba symbolized the "radicals" who were committed to obtaining "authentic" independence in both the political and economic spheres and stressed nonalignment on the international front. The radicals enjoyed grass-roots support. Other prominent members of this group included Antoine Gizenga and Pierre Mulele, who played important roles in the immediate postindependence period. Kasavubu belonged to the "moderates," who enjoyed the support of the Belgians, other Western governments, and the politically conservative multinationals in the Congo. Political figures such as Moise Tshombe, Albert Kalonji, Joseph Ileo, Cyrille Adoula, and Joseph Mobutu were also part of this group.[26] The PNP was also a "moderate" party supported by the Belgian administration in the Congo. Hence it was not surprising that the PNP favored close cooperation with Belgium after independence. This association with Europeans proved to be a liability and cost the PNP crucial votes in the 1960 elections. In contrast, ABAKO formed tactical alliances with several political parties in Kasai and Katanga that improved its showing in the elections.

INDEPENDENCE AND CHAOS

Independence Day on June 30, 1960, was a momentous occasion. King Baudouin of Belgium and Gaston Eyskens, the Belgian prime minister, were in attendance to transfer the reins of power to the Congolese leadership. The king made a solemn speech in which he reviewed Belgium's contribution to the development of the Congo. President Kasavubu responded in typical diplomatic fashion with kind words and gratitude. Patrice Lumumba, however, broke the conciliatory mood with a more forthright speech, denouncing Belgium's policy of slavery and oppression in the Congo since 1908. This speech injected a feeling of foreboding into the festivities and underscored the fact that beneath the veneer of stability were divisive issues that had been ignored in the rapid decolonization process.

Independence brought the First Republic into being. The Loi Fondamentale superimposed a parliamentary model on a people with no tradition of political organization in the Western sense. Colonialism had
crystallized ethnicity but controlled overt confrontation. Ethnic loyalties
were strengthened when political parties were hastily formed in the few
months before independence. The electoral campaigning opened up the
prospect of political self-determination for all ethnic groups for the first
time, and it is in the campaigning that the seeds of regionalism were
sown.

Indeed, the fragile stability achieved with nationhood was undermined by a Congolese army mutiny less than a week after Independence
Day. It had become clear to soldiers in the Force Publique (Public Army)
that self-determination would not mean greater Congolese control over
the military. Demanding promotions, pay increases, and dismissal of
Belgian army commander General Emile Janssens, the army rank and file
imprisoned their Belgian officers and demonstrated in Leopoldville.
What began as a local incident fanned the flames of discontent throughout the country, provoking violent upheavals and precipitating a series of
events known internationally as the Congo Crisis. The mutiny led to a
hasty decision to Africanize the Force Publique—but not before the situation had severely deteriorated, resulting in countrywide attacks on the
European population. With the rapid departure of Belgian army com-
manders, the Force Publique was totally ineffective in the midst of the
chaos. Many Belgians left the Congo at this time; and because of their
strong presence in business, industry, and commercial agriculture, the exodus did irreparable damage to the economy. The predominantly Belgian
white population, which had totaled 110,000 in 1959 and fallen to approximately 80,000 at independence, fell dramatically to 20,000, the majority
of whom were in Katanga province.[27]

Continued instability in the Congo prompted Belgian military intervention, ostensibly to protect the European population; but from the
point of view of the Congolese government, this action violated national
sovereignty. Accordingly, the Congolese government broke diplomatic
relations with Belgium and appealed to the United Nations Security
Council to provide military assistance and to secure the withdrawal
of Belgian troops. Lumumba's and Kasavubu's request to the United
Nations unwittingly brought the crisis to center stage, precipitating
strategy formulations at the highest levels among the key external players—
the United States, the Soviet Union, Belgium, and the United Nations
itself. In the West the situation in the Congo was seen in strategic terms
rather than as an issue of sovereignty and territorial integrity. Clare
Timberlake, U.S. ambassador to the Congo, saw unrest in the Congo as
providing an opportunity for so-called radicals to take over the govern-

ment, bringing this mineral-rich and strategically located Central African country into the Soviet sphere of influence.[28] For his part, UN Secretary-General Dag Hammarskjöld viewed the matter in geopolitical terms as a crisis ripe for superpower intervention and therefore a threat to international peace and security. It was his view that Lumumba and Kasavubu had further complicated the crisis by breaking diplomatic relations with Belgium and threatening to approach the Soviet Union directly for assistance.

In the heated UN debate, the Belgian government indicated it would recall its forces only after the arrival of UN troops in the Congo. Meanwhile the province of Katanga, center of copper and cobalt mining activity in the Congo, seceded under the leadership of Moise Tshombe with the unofficial support of Belgium. Brussels apparently stopped short of formal recognition in order not to cause irreparable damage to its relations with the central government in Leopoldville. On the one hand, Katanga was the center of major Belgian investments in the Congo and needed to be protected from Soviet "influence." On the other, official recognition would alienate Belgium not only in the Congo but in the more moderate African states whose troops made up the UN peacekeeping force. Nevertheless, the presence of Belgian troops in Katanga virtually ensured the survival of the Tshombe regime. The Belgians disarmed forces loyal to the government in Leopoldville, and Belgian military assistance further strengthened Tshombe's regime. Finally, in contrast to the situation in the rest of the Congo, Belgian officials in Katanga were instructed by Brussels to remain at their posts. Their presence insulated the Katangan economy from the debilitating effects of the Congo Crisis.[29]

Lumumba—facing a divided cabinet, rivalry with Kasavubu, and an ineffective army—tried to secure Western support and became increasingly dependent on UN forces to topple the Tshombe regime in Katanga. In effect, he saw the United Nations as a surrogate for the Congolese government, but the organization saw itself in a tenuous position. On one level, the United Nations was mainly concerned with avoiding a larger world crisis; on another level, it was motivated by a desire to preserve its structure and credibility for future peacekeeping operations. These opposing positions led to frequent disagreements between Lumumba and UN officials led by Secretary-General Dag Hammarskjöld. Impatient with the lack of effective Western support and UN "impartiality," Lumumba appealed to the Soviets for military assistance, thereby alienating the West as well as what little support he had in Leopoldville. With what was seen as Lumumba's pro-Communist stance, attempts began in earnest to overthrow him.

September 1960 saw the collapse of the parliamentary regime established under the Loi Fondamentale. President Kasavubu fired Lumumba and established a new government with Joseph Ileo as prime minister. However, Lumumba managed to regain support at a joint session of parliament. The standoff between Kasavubu and Lumumba was complete. Before the appointment of Ileo could take effect, army chief of staff Colonel Joseph Mobutu staged a peaceful military coup, announcing that the army was neutralizing both Lumumba and Kasavubu and appointing a Collège des Commissaires (College of Commissioners) to serve as the provisional government. The Collège consisted of recent Congolese university graduates as well as students studying in Belgium whom Mobutu asked to return home. The new student government made it clear that it did not intend to seize power but would run the administration only long enough to give the various political factions time to reach agreement.[30]

Lumumba defied Mobutu's efforts to arrest him by placing himself under UN protection. He was subsequently captured by the army on his way to Stanleyville, where his supporters were in power. Shortly after Lumumba's arrest, Antoine Gizenga, a staunch Lumumba supporter and a leader of the Parti Solidaire Africain (PSA; African Solidarity Party), proclaimed Stanleyville the legal capital of the Congo. While Gizenga's forces consolidated their control over the northern and eastern parts of the country, plans to assassinate Lumumba crystallized. He was removed from the prison at Thysville in January 1961, on the pretext of returning him to power, and flown to Elisabethville, the capital of the "independent" Katanga province, where he was killed by the forces of his rival Tshombe shortly after landing.[31]

At the time of Lumumba's death, the Congo seemed irreversibly fragmented. There were two capitals—Leopoldville and Stanleyville— each claiming to be the legitimate capital of the country; and Katanga and Kasai had seceded under the leadership of Moise Tshombe and Albert Kalonji, respectively. Each area had its own armed forces and, except for Kasai, a group of international supporters. After fierce diplomatic maneuverings and with UN encouragement, three Roundtable meetings were held in 1961 between the various factions to negotiate a settlement for reunification. Talks focused on whether the Loi Fondamentale was a viable constitutional basis for unification. With respect to political organization, the secessionist government of Katanga favored a confederal structure, whereas the central government in Leopoldville favored centralization. The most concrete result of these meetings was an agreement to convene a parliament representing all groups to bring about a solution to the government crisis. The session was dominated by the Stanleyville and Leopoldville coalitions; representatives from Katanga failed to attend. In spite of this obvious setback, a compromise was found in a new

government headed by Cyrille Adoula. Adoula was not too closely asso-
ciated with the political landscape in either Leopoldville or Stanleyville,
although he had served as minister of interior in the Ileo government.

This apparent rapprochement was almost destroyed by Gizenga
when he returned to Stanleyville and unsuccessfully tried to reassert
control by reactivating rebel dissidence. His efforts were thwarted by
the authorities in Leopoldville, and he was arrested and sent into exile.
The question of unification with Katanga proved to be more difficult. A
series of discussions between Adoula and Tshombe early in 1962 produced an impasse over the question of the relationship between Katanga
and the capital. The international community, led by the United States,
was convinced that settlement of the issue of Katanga was crucial to
stability in the Congo as a whole. As a result, international actors—
including Belgium—were prepared to bring pressure to bear on Tshombe
to accept a settlement. As arbiter in the crisis, the UN took a tough position, presenting a nonnegotiable formula known as the U Thant Plan under which the UN would formulate a federal constitution for the Congo.
Proposals were outlined providing for Katangan representation in the
central government, amnesty, and the equitable distribution of foreign
exchange earnings and tax revenues between the province and Leopoldville. Economic sanctions would be speedily applied against Katanga if
the plan was rejected. At the same time, acting under a Security Council
resolution approving the use of force to end the secession, the UN troops
moved swiftly to remove all unauthorized expatriate personnel from the
province. This action resulted in the expulsion of hundreds of mercenaries and political advisers and UN occupation of key areas. Tshombe
clearly saw no options and relinquished control.[32]

The end of the Katanga secession in January 1963 did not quiet unrest in the Congo. The new Adoula government continued to experience
domestic opposition despite having stripped Gizenga and Tshombe of
their political power. Political fragmentation was once again assured with
the decision to increase the number of provinces from six to twenty-one.
With this move, made in the absence of a national base of support, the
fledgling central government in Leopoldville unwittingly gave significant control to the provinces. A Comité Nationale de Libération (CNL;
National Liberation Committee), made up of individuals loyal to the
Lumumba ideal and committed to the forcible overthrow of Adoula, was
established in Brazzaville. This group included the Gizenga faction of the
PSA and a part of the Lumumba faction of the MNC. Finally, Pierre
Mulele, minister of education in the Lumumba government and a former
key figure in the PSA, returned to the Congo in 1963. He immediately
began to organize an opposition movement in Kwilu, his home province.
Unable to stem the tide of opposition, Adoula resigned shortly after the

UN force left the Congo in 1964. According to one account, the Adoula government was basically a puppet regime, influenced by the U.S. embassy in Leopoldville and responsive to pressures exerted by Mobutu and his Binza Group. At that time the Binza Group controlled the key posts in government: the military, the security police, internal affairs, foreign affairs, and the national bank.[33]

Moise Tshombe was brought back from exile by President Kasavubu to lead a new government. However, Mulelist forces, encouraged by Soviet and Chinese diplomats, began attacking government installations in Kwilu province. Violence quickly spread across the country. Attacks were launched against Kinshasa from Brazzaville, a haven for the Adoula regime's opponents, but the eastern Congo was the focus of the most serious insurrections. Rebels captured Stanleyville in September 1964 and proclaimed the creation of a revolutionary government under the leadership of Christophe Gbenye, who had been a major MNC/Lumumba leader there. A "reign of terror" ensued in which thousands of educated Congolese were killed because of their "reactionary" ideas. With the army—renamed the Armée Nationale Congolaise (ANC; Congolese National Army)—still ineffective, Tshombe called on his former Katanga gendarmes and recruited white South African and Rhodesian mercenaries to lead them. Since the rebels were holding several hundred expatriate hostages as shields to halt army advances into Stanleyville, the United States and Belgium mounted what became known as the Stanleyville Rescue, code-named Dragon Rouge. The Belgian-American parachute operation began at dawn on November 24, 1964, and in a few hours the first army-mercenary divisions arrived in Stanleyville. Within five days about 2,000 Europeans had been evacuated and the town retaken by government and Belgian-American forces.[34]

Kasavubu soon came to consider Tshombe as a dangerous and formidable opponent. As head of a new political coalition—Convention National Congolaise (CONACO; National Congolese Assembly)—which held a majority in parliament, Tshombe could emerge the victor in the upcoming presidential elections. He was therefore fired and Evariste Kimba appointed as his successor. Before Kimba could officially take up his post as prime minister, General Mobutu, assured of Western backing, intervened once more and seized power on November 24, 1965.

Mobutu's astute political coup thus marked the end of the First Republic. In the eyes of the Congolese, the independence experience had so far been disappointing. Political power had been denied under Belgian colonialism, although in the final years of Belgian rule socioeconomic welfare of the masses had been improved. In the preindependence euphoria of the late 1950s, political candidates had given the impression that independence would bring a new millennium in which economic prosperity and political self-determination would go hand in hand. This outcome was not achieved because of the rapid development of political fragmentation fostered by cross-cutting ethnic factionalism and social stratification, which had to some extent been controlled by the colonial government. Furthermore, the new political elite of the First Republic were viewed as black versions of the colonizer who had retained the same privileges and in similar fashion had appropriated the resources of the state. In this scenario the riots that precipitated Mobutu's takeover were as much a result of ethnic competition as a call for genuine Congolese independence. Mobutu stated categorically that he would act as interim leader of the Congo for only five years to restore national unity and order, after which free elections would be held. Nevertheless, he moved swiftly to consolidate his rule and, as of 1993, is still in power.

NOTES

1. Throughout the book, I refer to Zaire as the Congo for periods prior to 1971. At that time the country became known officially as the Republic of Zaire by presidential proclamation.

2. David Birmingham, *Central Africa to 1870* (London: Cambridge University Press, 1981), p. 27. Some writers claim that patron-client relations in Africa began with tribute systems such as this.

3. For analyses of the development of the Congo kingdom and its interaction with the Portuguese, see *Zaire: A Country Study*, 3d ed. (Washington, D.C.: American University, 1979), pp. 12–20; and James Duffy, *Portuguese Africa* (Cambridge: Harvard University Press, 1959), cited in René Lemarchand, *Political Awakening in the Belgian Congo* (Berkeley: University of California Press, 1964), p. 315, note 2.

More generally, for a very comprehensive study of the ethnic groups in the precolonial period, see Jan Vansina, *Introduction à L'ethnographie du Congo*, Éditions Universitaires du Congo (Brussels: Centre de Recherche et d'information Socio-politiques [CRISP], 1966). See also Robert Cornevin, *Histoire du Congo: Des origines préhistoriques à la Republique Démocratique du Congo* (Paris: Éditions Berger-Levrault, 1970).

4. Edouard Bustin, *Lunda Under Belgian Rule: The Politics of Ethnicity* (Cambridge: Harvard University Press, 1975), p. 227; *Zaire: A Country Study*, pp. 20–22.

5. Lemarchand, *Political Awakening*, pp. 28–30.

6. Literature on the Belgian period is quite extensive. The first section, "The Historical Setting," of the Selected Bibliography lists some of the better-known works. For data as well as maps on the Belgian Congo in the 1950s, see *Belgian Congo*, vol. 2 (Brussels: Belgian Congo and Ruanda-Urundi Information and Public Relations Office, 1960).

7. Bogumil Jewsiewicki, "Zaire Enters the World System: Its Colonial Incorporation as the Belgian Congo, 1885–1960," in *Zaire: The Political Economy of Underdevelopment*, ed. Guy Gran (New York: Praeger, 1979), pp. 34–36.

8. In 1890 Leopold himself had given Belgium the right to annex the Free State after ten years in exchange for a government loan. Five years later, after violating the agreement and mortgaging part of the territory, he signed a treaty ceding the Free State to Belgium. However, Belgium was not prepared to assume the responsibility of a colony at that time. *Zaire: A Country Study*, pp. 30–32.

9. René Lemarchand cites a Belgian observer writing in 1919 who claimed that the goals of Belgian colonial policy were consistent with those of the Free State and that under the guise of "philanthropy" the policy of the colonial government still resulted in the "debasement of a race, not its emancipation." Alexandre Delcommune, *L'Avenir du Congo Belge Menacé* (Brussels, 1919), quoted in Lemarchand, *Political Awakening*, p. 36.

Although the colonial government employed different administrative methods, there was remarkable continuity with the Free State in terms of attitudes and assumptions regarding the aims of colonization, as well as a basic similarity with respect to policies adopted to fulfill these aims. See Lemarchand, *Political Awakening*, pp. 36–37.

10. Madeleine Kalb, *The Congo Cables* (New York: Macmillan, 1982), p. xxi.

11. Marvin D. Markowitz, *Cross and Sword: The Political Role of Christian Missions in the Belgian Congo, 1908–1960* (Stanford: Hoover Institution Press, 1973), p. 105; Crawford Young, *Politics in the Congo: Decolonization and Independence* (Princeton: Princeton University Press, 1965), pp. 10–18, 59–72.

12. Lemarchand, *Political Awakening*, pp. 55–74; Bogumil Jewsiewicki, "Zaire Enters the World System," p. 38; Georges Brausch, *Belgian Administration in the Congo* (London: Oxford University Press, 1961), pp. 42–43; Roger Anstey, *King Leopold's Legacy* (London: Oxford University Press, 1966), pp. 47, 60–61.

13. Robert Cornevin, *Le Zaire* (Paris: Presses Universitaires de France, 1972), p. 73.

14. Crawford Young and Thomas Turner, *The Rise and Decline of the Zairian State* (Madison: University of Wisconsin Press, 1985), pp. 30–37; Richard Sandbrook, *The Politics of Africa's Economic Stagnation* (London: Cambridge University Press, 1985), p. 54.

15. Bustin, *Lunda Under Belgian Rule*, p. 234.

16. Markowitz, *Cross and Sword*, p. 15; Lemarchand, *Political Awakening*, pp. 123–125.

17. Markowitz, *Cross and Sword*, pp. 52–53. The Catholics also secured control over schools of multinational firms in the Congo during the 1920s. These schools were established to guarantee a skilled labor force. They received subsidies from the companies for their services. Ibid., pp. 60–62.

18. Ibid.

19. Ibid., p. 105.

20. Eyamba G. Bokamba, "Education and Development in Zaire," in *The Crisis in Zaire: Myths and Realities*, ed. Nzongola-Ntalaja (Trenton: Africa World Press, 1986), pp. 195–196.

21. Young and Turner, *Rise and Decline*, pp. 38–39. For insights into political developments in Belgium at the time and their impact on the Congo, see Brausch, *Belgian Administration in the Congo*, pp. 63–68.

22. Bokamba, "Education and Development," pp. 197–198.

23. The stages in the development of Congolese nationalism cannot be elaborated here. See, for example, Young, *Politics in the Congo,* pp. 273–306; Anstey, *King Leopold's Legacy,* pp. 122–142; Lemarchand, *Political Awakening,* pp. 167–190.

24. Although culturally and linguistically the Lulua and Baluba are virtually identical, after the arrival of the Europeans in the nineteenth century, the Lulua sought to distinguish themselves from the Baluba groups who facilitated the colonizing process in northern Kasai. As such, they came to consider themselves a different tribe. Lemarchand, *Political Awakening,* p. 270. See also Crawford Young, *The Politics of Cultural Pluralism* (Madison: University of Wisconsin Press, 1976), pp. 173–174.

25. Brausch, *Belgian Administration in the Congo,* p. 72; Young, *Politics in the Congo,* pp. 140–161.

26. They were known at the time as the Binza Group. Nzongola-Ntalaja, "The Continuing Struggle for National Liberation in Zaire," *Journal of Modern African Studies* 17, no. 4 (1979), pp. 595–596.

27. Young, *Politics in the Congo,* p. 321. The Congo Crisis is complicated and is not dealt with at length here. For excellent analyses of events and the political maneuverings between the various actors, see Kalb, *Congo Cables*; Colin Legum, *Congo Disaster* (Baltimore: Penguin Books, 1961); Catherine Hoskyns, *The Congo Since Independence* (London: Oxford University Press, 1965); Helen Kitchen, *Footnotes to the Congo Story* (New York: Walker, 1967). More specifically on the role of the UN, see Rajeshwar Dayal, *Mission for Hammerskjöld: The Congo Crisis* (Princeton: Princeton University Press, 1976); Conor Cruise O'Brien, *To Katanga and Back* (New York: Simon & Schuster, 1962); Ernest W. Lefever, *Crisis in the Congo: A United Nations Force in Action* (Washington, D.C.: Brookings Institution, 1965); Ernest W. Lefever and Wynfred Joshua, *United Nations Peacekeeping in the Congo, 1960–64: An Analysis of Political, Executive and Military Control,* vols. 1–4 (Washington, D.C.: Brookings Institution, 1966). Detailed documents and correspondence describing events during the period can be found in *Les Dossiers du C.R.I.S.P.* for the years 1960–1965, compiled by Benoît Verhaegen and collaborators (Brussels: CRISP, and Princeton: Princeton University Press).

28. Kalb, *Congo Cables,* p. 7.

29. Michael G. Schatzberg, *Mobutu or Chaos? The United States and Zaire, 1960–1990* (New York: University Press of America, 1991), pp. 11–12.

30. Jean-Claude Willame, "The Congo," in *Students and Politics in Developing Countries,* ed. Donald K. Emmerson (New York: Praeger, 1968). The Collège soon fell apart owing to its large size (thirty-nine members) and inexperience. In spite of its initial declaration, many members soon began to maneuver for political power. Finally, the Collège had no solid base of support or effective power and was soon shaken by political events, namely, the assassination of Lumumba.

31. Kalb, *Congo Cables,* pp. 157–158, 175–196. For the role of the CIA in Lumumba's death see Stephen Weissman, "CIA Covert Action in Zaire and Angola: Patterns and Consequences," *Political Science Quarterly* 94, no. 2 (Summer 1979), pp. 267–269; and John Stockwell, *In Search of Enemies: A CIA Story* (New

York: Norton, 1978). For a pro-Lumumba view see Thomas Kanza, *The Rise and Fall of Patrice Lumumba* (Cambridge: Schenkman, 1977). Valuable insights on Lumumba himself can also be gained from Jean Van Lierde, ed., *Lumumba Speaks: The Speeches and Writings of Patrice Lumumba, 1958–1961*, translated from French by Helen R. Lane (Boston: Little, Brown, 1972).

32. Young, *Politics in the Congo*, pp. 337–343.

33. Nzongola-Ntalaja, "Continuing Struggle," p. 598.

34. See Fred E. Wagoner, *Dragon Rouge: The Rescue of Hostages in the Congo* (Washington, D.C.: National Defense University Research Directorate, 1980); David Reed, *111 Days in Stanleyville* (New York: Harper & Row, 1965). For a fascinating analysis of the rebellions in the Congo, see Crawford Young, "Rebellion and the Congo," in *Protest and Power in Black Africa*, ed. Robert I. Rotberg and Ali A. Mazrui, pp. 969–1011 (New York: Oxford University Press, 1970).

2

The Zairian Polity

On April 24, 1990, after much fanfare, President Mobutu announced what would in effect be the birth of the Third Republic with the abolition of the single-party state and the creation of a multiparty democracy. Leadership of the government would be relinquished to a prime minister, and Mobutu himself as president would be "above politics" in his new capacity as "referee" of the political process.[1] This installment in Mobutu's strategy of statecraft drew widespread international attention, as it would mean a major reconstruction of the Zairian state created and honed by its president over the previous twenty-five years. In response to prior demands for a multiparty system, Mobutu had consistently evoked the precolonial image of the supreme village chief, stating categorically that there could be only one leader and one party in Zaire. Nevertheless, in true Machiavellian fashion, he opted to change course to ensure political survival.

In order to put Mobutu's announcement and subsequent events in context, we must consider the process of political consolidation under his regime, noting elements of continuity with Zaire's past. Over time, centralization, political mobilization around an artificially created ideology, and repression have been key characteristics of the state. Meanwhile there have been major political strains on the system from rapidly escalating internal and external opposition to the president.

CONSOLIDATION AND THE RISE
OF THE SINGLE-PARTY STATE

Political and Administrative Centralization

After Mobutu assumed power in 1965, he quickly asserted control over the state. Stressing the need for discipline and law and order after the political chaos and destruction of the multiparty democracy during

31

the first five years of independence, he progressively dismantled the institutional remnants of the First Republic.[2] Leaders in the former government and opposition figures were either co-opted into the new government, isolated from their base of support, or eliminated.

In an early demonstration of the new regime's ruthlessness toward dissent, Mobutu encouraged opponents to return to Zaire by promising amnesty. However, when Pierre Mulele, leader of the 1964 Kwilu rebellion, returned from Congo-Brazzaville, he was publicly executed. A few months prior to this event, four former cabinet ministers from the First Republic were publicly hanged in an affair known as the Pentecost Plot. Evidently they had tried to initiate plans for the overthrow of the regime, and Mobutu clearly wanted to send a message to the Zairian people that opposition to his program would not be tolerated.

In one of his first acts as president, Mobutu began the process of destroying or weakening political participation. All political activities were immediately banned. The new prime minister, Leonard Mulamba, was initially given the responsibility of creating a representative government that would include each of the twenty-one provinces and the city of Kinshasa. The emphasis was to be on rebuilding the country, and the phrase *Retroussons les manches* (Let's roll up our sleeves) became the government slogan.

These efforts were soon abandoned, however, and political power was progressively centralized in the office of the president, which came to have direct responsibility for national defense and control of the security forces. A state of emergency was proclaimed. During this time Mobutu abolished the decisionmaking role of parliament by assuming the power to rule by decree, which had the force of law. The office of prime minister suffered a similar fate in 1966, and it soon became clear that official policy would be initiated solely by the president.

In effect, like the Belgians before him, Mobutu reverted to a form of centralized administration. This recentralization was soon extended to the provinces to prevent a resurgence of tribal activity. Within the first few months of the Mobutu regime, six of the twenty-one provincial governors were charged with corruption and removed from office. The number of provinces was reduced to eight, and provincial assemblies were stripped of their legislative powers and made purely consultative bodies. Provincial governors became administrative officials of the central government under the jurisdiction of the Ministry of Interior, and local police forces were nationalized. In this search for authority and control over the fragmented Zairian state, Mobutu was establishing an authoritarian form of rule, which would be personalized and supported by an extensive coercive apparatus.

The Popular Movement of the Revolution

As part of the consolidation and legitimization process, Mobutu created a new political organization in 1967, the Mouvement Populaire de la Révolution (MPR; Popular Movement of the Revolution), to replace all existing parties. The precursor to the MPR was the allegedly apolitical Corps des Volontaires de la République (CVR; Volunteer Corps of the Republic) formed in 1966 to foster support for the new regime and to mobilize the public for national reconstruction. Its theme, based on its acronym, proclaimed *conscience nationale, vigilance and reconstruction* (national consciousness, vigilance and reconstruction). CVR sections and subsections, which had been established throughout the country, were simply absorbed into the MPR.

The new institution had no popular roots but was simply imposed from above. In many respects it was not designed to be a party at all but merely a propaganda arm of the presidency. The president himself referred to the MPR as "a movement which reflect[ed] people's desire to speak with one voice" and "a revolutionary force" representing "a complete break from foreign ideas and practices."[3] The official party policy statement, the *Manifesto de N'Sele* published on May 19, 1967, stressed political and economic independence for Zaire and revolutionary transformation based on a "unique" Zairian model. According to party statutes, all Zairians were automatically members of the MPR by virtue of birth and therefore had an obligation to defend the revolution. The party defined its principal purpose as mobilization of the population in order to educate citizens politically, inform them of government programs, and to enlist their active support in Zairian development.

During this early period the nationalist theme was predominant, in both the political and economic realms. In the drive toward centralization, the image of Lumumba as a national hero was utilized as a unifying theme, and Mobutu sought to identify with his nationalist principles. In political terms, "nationalism" was touted as an alternative to both "communism" and "capitalism." On the economic front, major steps were initiated to exercise control over the large multinational companies operating in Zaire. By 1971 nationalism had given way to "authenticity" as the official party doctrine. According to MPR officials, Zaire would pursue development in the context of "tradition" and on the basis of its ancestral heritage. Nevertheless, the various aspects of this "tradition" that would serve as the guiding principle for the state were not clearly articulated. The new "ideology" was presented in cultural terms as an attempt to recapture "the spirit of Zaire" destroyed during the colonial period. As part of this process, the Democratic Republic of the Congo was renamed the Republic of Zaire, and cities and towns were appropriately changed.

A new Nationality Law came into effect, under which all nationals had to replace their Christian names with authentic Zairian names or automatically lose their citizenship. Mobutu himself relinquished his birth name, Joseph-Desiré Mobutu, to become Mobutu Sese Seko Kuku Ngbendu Wa Za Banga.[4]

The MPR consisted of three organs at the national level: the Congress, presided over by the president; the Political Bureau of nine ex officio members and six others appointed by the president; and the National Executive Committee. MPR committees were established at every territorial level, and all existing interest groups as well as public and private institutions—unions, schools, the press, church groups—were incorporated under the MPR umbrella.

The First Extraordinary Congress of the MPR was held in May 1970, at which time the role of the party was formalized as the supreme institution and sole party of the Republic. Between 1970 and 1974 steps were taken to end the dualism between state and party structures, with the progressive fusion of party and state. In 1972 the Council of Ministers, the highest government institution, was abolished and replaced by the Executive Council, which had the same governmental role but functioned as an institution of the MPR. In effect, the party absorbed the decision-making power of the state at the national level; but with respect to implementation, by and large the state structures remained intact. At the provincial level, where the party structure had not yet taken hold, the state administration absorbed the party. State administrators took over all party functions.[5]

With the fusion of party and state declared complete in 1974, a major reshuffle of the Political Bureau was announced, and membership was expanded to include representatives from the military, judiciary, and the university. A new constitution gave Mobutu the leading position as chief of state and president-founder of the party with full and direct control of all major party and state institutions: the Political Bureau; and the Executive, Legislative, and Judicial Councils. In addition, a party school—the Makanda Kabobi Institute—was created to provide ideological training, and a new doctrine—Mobutuism—was unveiled as the official ideology.

Mobutuism: Personalized Rule and Ideology

Mobutuism, as originally conceived, is based on the teachings, declarations, and thoughts of the president found scattered in various speeches. Rather than a coherent ideology, it has been referred to by analysts as a "political religion." After the formation of the MPR, Mobutu moved swiftly to create a cult of personality, resurrecting precolonial concepts of patriarchal authority to portray himself as the "Father" of the nation and Zairians as his "children." Drawing on the notion of the supreme role of the African chief, Mobutuism designates the Zairian leader as the one chosen by God and the ancestors to lead the state. As such, he has unlimited power and, being above the law, has no accountability.

Mobutuism, like authenticity before it, "exalts the authoritarian state and the president as the agencies of national renovation, national independence and peace."[6] Over the years it has therefore served to legitimize Mobutu's form of personal rule. The power of the Zairian state is centralized in the office of the president. Every decision relating to domestic affairs or foreign policy issues is made by Mobutu himself. All individuals involved in the state-party apparatus are totally dependent on Mobutu for selection and maintenance in power. Mobutu perpetuates uncertainty and vulnerability among officials by frequently rotating government and party posts. Ironically, in the past some observers have attributed Zaire's relative stability since the Congo Crisis to Mobutu's ability to control the bureaucracy in this way.[7] Since the beginning of the Second Republic, frequent cabinet reshuffles during every year have been the norm. It is this uncertainty coupled with the relative scarcity of economic resources, particularly foreign exchange, that results in corruption and "grabbing."

In Mobutu's state, political office is the primary avenue for upward mobility and the accumulation of wealth. This condition is not unlike that of other countries in Africa where the state is all pervasive. In the case of Zaire, the trend began shortly after independence when educated Congolese holding lower-level government posts rushed to fill the void in upper management left by the hasty departure of the Belgians. At that time political office guaranteed upward mobility, and it soon became the means to appropriate the resources of the state. This process has been perfected under the Mobutu regime. Government service is also seen as the primary vehicle for entering business. Political influence allows one to negotiate bureaucratic red tape, obtain seed money, and gain access to contracts—often through bribes.[8] The system has spawned the development of a "political aristocracy," an elite that contributes nothing to the productive process of the state but exists to maximize its own wealth. Systematic corruption originates with Mobutu and his clique, but it permeates the entire society through patron-client networks. Since the 1970s this situation has been aggravated by economic crisis. Economic scarcity and uncertainty have encouraged personal enrichment by those in positions of power at the expense of the majority.

Kleptocracy in Zaire is viewed by some as a pyramidal system based on patrimonial redistribution.[9] The process begins with the relatively small presidential clan linked to Mobutu through familial or personal ties.

This group also includes certain expatriates who act as "personal advisers" to the president. The second tier is composed of a larger group of
government officials, administrators, and businessmen, some of whom
originate from the president's region, Équateur. Corruption at this level is
condoned and even encouraged by the president. In turn, it can serve as a
useful tool for dismissing officials who are "robbing the nation." Finally,
the base of the pyramid consists of a large group of individuals aspiring
to positions of power, who have some access to state resources, and their
own less-extensive patron-client networks. Although the process of corruption is by no means unique to Zaire, it has been "institutionalized"
there over time until it has become part of the very fabric of the state, the
way of conducting business. It is a deliberate strategy that facilitates
control of the state apparatus by the ruling elite and allows this group to
stay in power and consolidate its own economic position at the same
time.[10]

Over the years there have been many reports in the international
press detailing the extent of "le mal zairois" (the Zairian sickness), the
term used by Mobutu himself to describe the system he has fostered. For
the political elite the state's resources, particularly foreign exchange, are
viewed as fair game for personal use. This group's strategic connections
at the center of the political system not only facilitate access to funds but
are often used to illegally extract resources from the many foreign corporations, donor agencies, and other external actors who interact with
the state. Throughout the 1970s, for example, as much as 20 percent of the
government's operating budget went directly to the office of the president without any financial control. A 1988 study of Zaire's 1986 budget
still revealed amounts going to the office of the president representing six
times the budgetary appropriations allotted for that purpose, while the
funding of crucial areas such as education and health was virtually
ignored. Copper, cobalt, and diamonds from Zairian mines and lucrative
agricultural products such as coffee have consistently been sold abroad
illegally in secret deals, costing Zaire millions of dollars in foreign
exchange earnings. In one such interesting development leaked to the
press in 1989, $300 million to $400 million in foreign exchange receipts
largely from the state mining company GECAMINES could not be
accounted for by International Monetary Fund (IMF) and World Bank
officials. Even development aid funds, including the agricultural products under the U.S. PL 480 program, channeled through government
institutions have been stolen by prominent government officials.[11]

The extent of Mobutu's personal fortune is well known, having
been estimated at over $5 billion in the early 1980s. He has acknowledged
owning properties in Belgium, France, Italy, and Switzerland. In addition,
there have been press reports of his real estate holdings in Portugal,

Spain, Senegal, Chad, and the Ivory Coast as well as interests in many major Zairian companies. The president himself has decried all estimates of his wealth in the Western press. He puts the figure at less than $50 million—an estimate he considers quite in keeping with his position as leader of "such a big country" for over two decades. Further, he claims that this so-called wealth has given valuable military assistance and disaster relief to neighboring countries such as Rwanda, Burundi, and Chad.[12]

Rather reminiscent of the "big chief," the president bestows favors on his subjects based on personal discretion, frequently pardoning officials who have "fallen from grace" and bringing them once again into the party or state apparatus. The fate of the former prime minister, Nguza Karl-i-Bond, is instructive in this regard. Despite links to Moise Tshombe, he became a trusted member of Mobutu's cabinet, serving as foreign minister and political director of the MPR in the early years of the Second Republic. He soon became widely respected in the West as a capable Zairian official. In 1977 he was accused of treason and sentenced to death. After strong international protest, he was released and "rehabilitated" by being appointed prime minister in 1979. By 1981, allegedly disgusted with the corruption and excesses of the Mobutu regime, Nguza was in exile in Brussels outlining explicit details of the regime's dealings in a widely publicized book, *Mobutu ou L'incarnation du Mal Zairois.* During this time he attempted to organize the opposition "movement" in Brussels, becoming head of a new alliance of several opposition groups— the Front Congolais pour la Restauration de la Démocratie (FCD; Congolese Front for the Restoration of Democracy). He suddenly returned to Zaire in 1985 on the occasion of the country's twenty-fifth anniversary of independence. He was then formally "pardoned" and brought back into the "inner circle," being appointed ambassador to the United States in 1986 and subsequently foreign minister and prime minister. Commenting on his decision to pardon Nguza, Mobutu remarked that his actions were in keeping with the benevolent style of an African chief.[13]

In Mobutu's Zaire glorification of the president by the party and the press has been the order of the day. Known as Le Guide (the Guide) and Le Maréchal (the Marshal), his portrait hangs in all important buildings. At the height of Mobutuism, he was constantly praised at the various mass meetings and marches organized by the party. Although the MPR ideology has largely lost its appeal, the government-owned media still attempt to perpetuate the false image of Mobutu's benevolence toward his "family," the nation. Policy moves, both in the political and economic spheres, are presented by the official press agency, Agence Zaire-Presse (AZAP; Zaire Press Agency), and the Kinshasa daily Mobutuist newspaper *Salongo* as initiatives taken out of concern for the socioeconomic needs of the population.

The importance and influence of the notion of the chief, or father figure, which has important roots in precolonial Zaire, were further underscored by Belgian paternalism during the colonial period. Having been carried over into the postcolonial state, the notion highlights an important element of continuity with Zaire's past.

AZAP often gives the impression that every development project and all expenditures, no matter how routine, are the result of presidential generosity. Over the years, this impression has been deliberately reinforced by Mobutu himself with gifts from his "personal" funds that he bestows on the population in his trips around the country. The practice has several consequences. First, the notion of "gift" underscores the centralized nature of the state and reinforces the reality of Mobutu's total control as, in effect, all resources pass through his hands. Second, gifts and other such favors buy political support, contributing to Mobutu's ability to remain in power. Third, they inherently imply a moral obligation to reciprocate this fatherly generosity, a condition that in turn serves to legitimize Mobutu's system of corruption.[14] Commenting in 1987 on the president's appropriation of state resources as his own, Zaire's minister of information at the time gave the following justification: "Without this man, we would be in a mess. . . . We are an underdeveloped country. The role of the chief is quite different than in America. When he comes to a village, people expect him to solve their problems on the spot. They sing to him, 'The Father has come. We are not going to be hungry.'"[15]

TERRITORIAL ADMINISTRATION AND LOCAL POLITICS

As the Belgians did in the Colonie Belge, Mobutu has sought to extend authority and control through an extensive territorial administration.[16] It is at the local level—the point of interaction between traditional authority structures and the administrative state apparatus—that the effects of Mobutu's policies are most felt.

After Mobutu assumed power, the basic units of the Belgian territorial administration were resurrected and renamed. Provinces, districts, and territories became regions, subregions, and zones. The twenty-one regions were reduced to eight, with the capital of Kinshasa having the status of a separate region. Furthermore, as in the colonial period, territorial units were conceived as purely administrative subdivisions, accountable to the central government in Kinshasa. Although the regional commissioners (formerly provincial governors) were political appointees, subregion and zone commissioners were prefectorial representatives. With the formal institutionalization of the MPR in 1970, all territorial personnel posts were converted into politico-administrative positions. Commissioners therefore assumed party as well as administrative functions. During the 1970s and 1980s, in an effort to maintain control, all matters relating to recruitment, assignment, and promotion of territorial administrators were directed from Kinshasa. Commissioners were assigned outside their regions of origin to facilitate control over the local population and subordinate staff.

In the final analysis, territorial officials are the regime's instruments of political control and extraction. The central authorities in Kinshasa attempt to keep a tight rein on these activities throughout the country by requiring an elaborate system of reporting that has to move up the hierarchical chain of command—zone, subregion, region, and finally to Kinshasa. All activities in an official's jurisdiction must be reported, and at each administrative level officials are in charge of the staff below. Control also emanates from Kinshasa through constant requests and requirements that have to be addressed. Nevertheless, territorial officials do have some flexibility and scope for exercising discretion in carrying out their duties. Poor communications between Kinshasa and the regions, the brief and general nature of instructions from the capital, and limited supervision by superiors create many opportunities for independent action or, indeed, no action at all.

In spite of rather sweeping powers in some cases, territorial officials have found control most difficult in the zones and their subunits, known as the local collectivities. It is at this level that the rural majority in Zaire comes in contact with the regime and that traditional institutions of authority compete with the state. The regime superimposed its territorial administrative framework on a myriad of existing traditional structures controlled by chiefs, using a cover-over strategy. In many cases, these structures were weakened but not destroyed.[17] Mobutu initially sought accommodation with the local chiefs, viewing them as an indispensable part of the Zairian political mosaic. But by 1973 the autonomy of the collectivities was abolished, as was the distinction between chieftaincies, sectors, and centers. All chiefs, traditional as well as elected, were to be integrated into the territorial administration, and in 1974 the regime decided to transfer chiefs outside their regions of origin. Storms of protest, unclear instructions to territorial officials about how these changes were to be implemented, and open defiance by chiefs quickly led to the regime's tacit retreat from these reform measures.

Over the years the regime has sought to control the collectivities effectively, and like the Belgians, it has met with limited success. In areas such as eastern Zaire, with a history of rebellion and resistance to the central government, traditional authorities are more autonomous than elsewhere in Zaire. Order and control have been difficult. In Nord Kivu, for example, powerful chiefdoms exist that are organized on the basis of custom and that trace their roots to the precolonial period. Territorial officials can often reach people only by using the chiefs as intermediaries. In this kind of situation, directives from the central authorities are often brushed aside and ignored by the local population, and traditional practices are the order of the day. Physical distance from Kinshasa further reinforces the problem. Centralized control has been easier in Bas Zaire, however, with its proximity to the capital and a history of fragmented traditional structures.

Tax collection, another key function of the territorial administration, is also a formidable task. Although initially only collectivities had fiscal autonomy, an ongoing Zairian economic crisis has prompted the central government to decentralize its financial operations with respect to other larger territorial units. Except for payment of salaries, territorial commissioners must now generate their own income. In this new system the onus of revenue collection falls on the collectivity. Accordingly, administrators resort to what is commonly known in local circles as "Article 15"—they improvise.[18]

Main sources of revenue are the *contribution personnelle minimum* (CPM; head tax), a relic from the colonial period, fines and fees for legal infractions, special taxes that can be levied with the permission of the subregional commissioner, and up to 1990, a yearly tax contribution to the MPR. The CPM applies to all nonsalaried employees, and thus rural farmers bear the burden of payment. Taxes are often collected by force with the help of the local army and secret police.[19] In the situation of uncertainty and economic hardship that characterizes Zaire, in which local officials are themselves poorly and irregularly paid, the tax collection system has broken down. Where tax revenues are collected, more often than not most of the proceeds are expropriated for personal use. Article 15 is often considered a license to steal, and bribery and extortion (illegal taxes) are common in an effort to get by. Obviously villagers are the victims in such a scenario, and protests on some level are not uncommon.

A women's tax revolt in eastern Zaire in 1982 illustrates the point.[20] At that time about 100 women staged a peaceful demonstration in front of the administrative offices of Buloho collectivity. Opposed to the taxes and tolls being levied on produce they transported to market (cassava and peanuts), the women presented the matter to the collectivity chief. Apparently the women were subject to three separate tolls. The first was a tax decreed by the collectivity. According to the women, the tax was not being used for the public good. The road on which they had to travel had fallen into disrepair and nothing was being done to maintain it. The second toll was collected at a vine bridge just outside the market and was levied by a local official without the knowledge of the collectivity chief. The official purpose of the tax was the upkeep of the bridge, but the women knew that the maintenance was in fact being done by *salongo* (compulsory communal labor) and that the local official was appropriating the toll for his own use. The third tax was collected at the entrance to the market, technically outside the Buloho collectivity. When the chief proved unresponsive to their demands, the women presented their case to his superiors. When this effort failed, they elected new local officials sympathetic to their case.

The successful action by the women was supported by their involvement in the local electoral process. More generally, however, Zairians are apathetic in local elections and abstention rates of 50 percent are not uncommon. In many instances, voters cannot register because of inadequate communications and the poor state of the roads. Lack of interest is also frequently due to the ineffectiveness of local legislatures. There is often conflict between local councils and local representatives of the central government.[21]

INSTRUMENTS OF CONTROL

Political control has been central to Mobutu's strategy of state consolidation. The nature of the political process fosters uncertainty, but ironically in this scenario the survival of the regime is never assured. Hence, over the years, the Mobutu regime has sought to avert popular

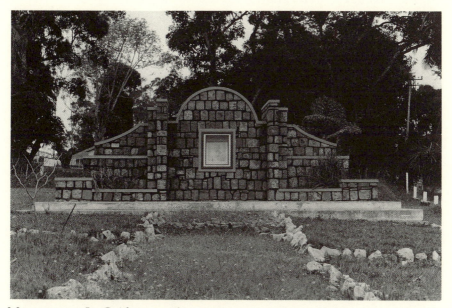

Monument to Le Guide, erected in every town square throughout the country.

dissent on several levels. Strategies range from political mobilization to overt uses of force demonstrated by the military, gendarmes, secret police, and, to a lesser extent, the youth arm of the MPR.

Political Mobilization

As the propaganda arm of the Zairian state, mobilization of the masses to support and legitimize the policies and actions of Le Guide has been a major goal of the MPR.[22] In the heyday of Mobutuism, mobilization was achieved by means of *rassemblements populaires* (mass meetings) held at all levels of the territorial administration (regions, subregions, and zones), *marches de soutien* (marches of support), and the perpetuation of symbols and erection of monuments glorifying the state and the president. Local administrators convened meetings regularly to inform the population about regime policies and expectations. Such gatherings were often preceded by *animation* in which supposedly devout MPR followers—dressed in "uniforms" made of special fabric printed with pictures of Le Président and party slogans—sang songs, cheered, and danced specially choreographed routines to stir up political fervor. Meetings generally focused on major themes and drew limited participation from the crowd. In these early Mobutu years, certain ideas were consistent—national unity, support for authenticity and *salongo,* vigilance against threats to the regime, and citizens' duties.

Marches de soutien were held at all administrative levels and

MPR party headquarters for the Lukaya subregion of Bas Zaire.

were carefully organized to include the participation of various societal groups—schools, church, the military, state and private workers. The *marches* were organized to show general support for Mobutu or to thank him for specific "gifts." In addition to these mobilization strategies, administrative officials were also responsible for ensuring that Mobutu's picture appeared in all public buildings and that party monuments (with a picture of Mobutu, the party torch, and the inscription "Long live President Mobutu") were found in all urban and rural administrative units.

In all these efforts the Zairians were continually viewed by officials as "subjects" rather than "citizens," a perspective reminiscent of the Belgian approach. Communication occurred from state to citizen; there were no channels for similar interaction between citizen and state. As a result, the popular response to these attempts at mobilization quickly became increasing indifference. According to a study conducted between 1972 and 1973 in Kamalondo (an urban zone in Lubumbashi), of a diverse subject population of 250 people, only 25 percent were politically active participants, 38 percent were occasionally active, and 24 percent were inactive.[23] Assuming this distribution was representative of the population at large, mass mobilization even at the height of Mobutuism in the mid-1970s was limited. With growing skepticism and cynicism toward the state and the Mobutu regime since the mid-1980s, demonstrations of support have become meaningless and are all but nonexistent.[24] Furthermore, most citizens get their information about political and economic issues from the *radio trottoir*—the astonishingly accurate informal gossip network that permeates the streets.

The Security Forces

Although political mobilization efforts have weakened, the coercive apparatus of the state has remained intact. In terms of terror and intimidation, it is one of the few branches of the state that operates with amazing efficiency. Paradoxically, it is a crucial source of security and reassurance for the Mobutu regime, but it creates insecurity for the Zairian people.[25]

Forces Armées Zairois. The Forces Armées Zairois (FAZ; Zairian Armed Forces), formerly the *Armée Nationale Congolaise,* is one of the visible control mechanisms in the Mobutuist state. Although it continues to be the recipient of foreign assistance (training and equipment), the FAZ has been unable to adequately protect the regime in times of crisis. Two consecutive invasions of Shaba province (formerly Katanga), in 1977 and 1978, clearly highlighted the army's incompetence in battle.

In the first Shaba invasion members of the Front pour la Liberation Nationale du Congo (FLNC; Front for the National Liberation of the Congo) invaded the Shaba province from bases in neighboring Angola on

March 8, 1977.[26] Meeting virtually no resistance from the Zairian military, the invaders were approaching the key mining center of Kolwezi by mid-April. They were turned back only with the help of Moroccan troops with logistical support from France.

A second invasion, this time from Zambia, occurred approximately a year later. FLNC forces seized Kolwezi and were driven back by French and Belgian paratroops with American logistical support. Given the ineptitude of the FAZ, the expatriate population attached to the mining area refused to work unless they were protected by non-Zairian forces. Consequently an inter-African peacekeeping force, composed of 1,000 Moroccan troops and a few detachments from French-speaking Africa, returned to Shaba, where they remained until 1979.

The two invasions triggered a major reorganization of the army to improve its fighting capability. Recruitment from the president's native region of Équateur was accelerated, and there was an accompanying deemphasis on the other regions. The Belgians agreed to staff the officer training school and to train the special forces known as the Kamanyola Division; the French undertook the command of a paratroop brigade; the Chinese began training a counterinsurgency brigade; and after Zaire's resumption of ties with Israel in 1982, the Israeli military undertook the training of the elite Presidential Guard. Finally, the United States continued to provide equipment and spare parts.[27]

In stark contrast to the FAZ's general lack of combat capability is its skill at intimidating the Zairian population. Poor morale and resentment stemming from pay irregularities, poor living conditions, and lack of equipment are taken out on civilians, who have no recourse or protection. Harassment can take the form of roadblocks allegedly to check for papers but that in reality are a shakedown for money. It is common practice among the expatriates in Kinshasa who "know the FAZ system" to out-smart these officers by avoiding those routes where they are known to be or simply by driving quickly through the roadblocks. In the latter case the unarmed soldiers on foot are powerless. Aside from specialized units such as the Presidential Guard, Mobutu fears the consequences of arming the FAZ rank and file. A visitor to Zaire in the early 1980s describes the shakedown situation succinctly:

> Better not to be grabbed at all, which is the strategy the American Embassy recommends to its staff. It issues a manual to arriving Americans that . . . tells them never to roll down the windows of their cars when they are stopped by police officials and never to hand over their driver's licenses or travel documents. They are to show their papers through a rolled up window and from behind a locked door. . . . The gendarmes are known for

robbing with impunity not only on the city streets but also at fraudulent roadblocks, where passage is granted for money or for an impromptu gift, like a pack of cigarettes or a wristwatch.[28]

Stories abound of atrocities committed by the army against the civilian population. A report presented to the Belgian Parliament by two Belgian politicians in 1988 highlighted several abuses over a period of months during that year. The Zairian Green Berets arbitrarily killed several peasants and merchants in Nord Kivu. The army also went on a plundering and looting rampage in this area, as well as in the Kibali-Ituri region. Commenting on the incidents, the Belgian weekly magazine *Knack* claimed that the locals in the area were sufficiently intimidated to offer to feed the soldiers free of charge. In 1989 there were also intermittent reports of rape involving schoolgirls in various regions, as well as assaults against women who participated in a demonstration protesting economic conditions in Kinshasa.[29]

Persistent abuses by the FAZ erupted into anarchy in 1991. On September 22 elements from the Airborne Troops Training Center and the 31st Parachutist Brigade seized N'Djili Airport in Kinshasa and began looting airport warehouses stacked with merchandise. Soldiers were protesting abysmally low wages and the government's failure to grant a promised salary increase. Word soon spread to Camp Kokolo—Kinshasa's largest army barracks—whose soldiers began to systematically plunder commercial areas in the capital and residences in the affluent suburbs of Binza and Ma Campagne. Very little was spared. Particular targets were homes and businesses of wealthy Zairians, as well as companies and small shops owned by Lebanese, Greeks, and Portuguese—groups long resented by Zairians for their treatment of locals. Expatriate observers described scenes of drunken soldiers driving around in cars stolen from dealerships, firing their weapons in the air indiscriminately. Senior officers led their troops in looting the same businesses they had previously obtained protection money from illegally. Ordinary citizens suffering economic hardship soon followed the soldiers, taking whatever they had left behind.

Wholesale markets in stolen goods soon opened in Kinshasa and operated for weeks after the looting. Soldiers charged admission to Camp Kokolo, where everything could be purchased—cars, food, appliances. Army deserters occupied an unfinished hospital across from the camp (one of the government's prestige projects), named Kuwait City, and ran another thriving market until they were cleared out by Mobutu's Presidential Guard. Goods also found their way to Brazzaville, where they were sold at bargain prices—refrigerators for as little as $90. The widespread lawlessness and instability resulted in over 100 people dead and 1,500 wounded and led to foreign intervention by French and Belgian troops to evacuate the expatriate population.

In almost predictable fashion, abysmally low wages again resulted in violence in January 1993. At that time, soldiers in Camp Kokolo began looting shops and opened fire in the capital, protesting payment in the new Z5 million banknotes commissioned by Mobutu, which they claimed were worthless (equivalent to $2 at January 1993 exchange rates). In the confusion, the newly appointed French ambassador, Phillipe Bernard, was killed, allegedly by a stray bullet. Fighting soon spread to Lubumbashi, Kisangani, and other Zairian cities, becoming a confrontation between soldiers loyal to Mobutu (his Presidential Guard) and the opposition. The riots resulted in at least three hundred deaths, according to overseas estimates.[30]

More often than not, Mobutu has paid lip service to curbing his troops. However, since the late 1980s he has acted more decisively because of an increased concern with his human rights image. In 1989, for example, the FAZ army officer who allowed his troops to open fire on students during a February demonstration in Lubumbashi was sentenced, with Mobutu's blessing, to five years in prison by the Lubumbashi Higher War Council. Soldiers have been periodically confined to their barracks, denied provisions, or dismissed for criminal records. In response to the 1991 riots, Mobutu imposed a curfew, fired his army chief of staff, and ordered a complete restructuring of the army.[31] In spite of these types of measures, the fact remains that Mobutu cannot control persistent citizen harassment by the army.

FAZ security activities are supplemented by the Guarde Civile (Civil Guard), created in 1984 to be responsible for guaranteeing public security, ensuring public order, and assisting the Gendarmerie Nationale (National Police Force) in controlling mineral smuggling out of Zaire. The Civil Guard operates at all territorial levels and carries out the primary duties of the gendarmerie. Over the years it has been involved in political repression against opponents of the regime and has inflicted gross human rights abuses against the population.

The Secret Police. The Agence National de Documentation (AND; National Documentation Agency) is the most important coercive arm of the state.[32] The AND is the direct descendant of the Belgian colonial secret police, the Sûreté, whose principal tasks were providing political intelligence and keeping track of citizen movements. When Mobutu assumed power in 1965, he kept the Sûreté as part of his plan for centralized control. Furthermore, it was brought under the authority of the president's office and granted political autonomy. When the Sûreté became the Centre National de Documentation (CND; National Documentation

Center) and subsequently the AND, its basic structure remained, and it continued to be accountable only to the president.

Like other government units attached directly to the presidency, the AND enjoys an unusual degree of financial, judicial, and political autonomy. Its agents are free to arrest, interrogate, and detain anyone who is considered a threat to the state. This brings the AND into direct conflict with territorial administrators at all levels, who want to exert control in their respective areas without what they view as outside interference.

The AND operates through a vast countrywide network of informers. In the past this made Zairians hesitant to publicly discuss political issues owing to fears of being overheard and imprisoned for criticizing the Mobutu regime. In the face of prolonged oppression, frustration, and abysmal living standards, citizens have become bolder and more willing to attack so-called informers. Throughout the years Amnesty International reports on Zaire have consistently documented instances of physical abuse in jails and harassment of the population by AND officials. Many of these incidents have been verified by investigations by the New York–based Lawyers Committee for Human Rights. Torture and mistreatment of detainees is routine in Zairian prisons. Prominent Zairian Nguza Karl-i-Bond describes his experience with what was then the CND in his book detailing the excesses of the Mobutu government.[33] Indeed, the AND's mandate also includes surveillance on any government official whose loyalty to Mobutu appears questionable. It is common knowledge among Zairians that the agency intercepts mail from the national postal service on an ongoing basis. Arbitrary arrest and imprisonment are also used to exert control. Political prisoners are often tortured in ways ranging from beatings to electric shock. Countless Zairians have died as a result of ill treatment in custody. As a result of these types of activities, the AND is one of the state's major instruments of fear and contributes to the atmosphere of personal insecurity that pervades the country.

The AND has traditionally provided the Mobutu regime with crucial information on social, political, and economic affairs such as local reaction to presidential decrees and reports on party rallies and acts of protest. Reports from the rural areas note prices of staples, shortages of basic items, and other signs of hardship. In a somewhat ironic situation, AND agents have reported consistently on the coercive, oppressive acts being conducted by officials at the local level—another source of conflict with the territorial administration.

Finally, the AND provides symbolic reassurance to the Zairian leadership that all is well in various parts of the country and that everything is under control. It is said that Mobutu receives reports several times daily in which the familiar phrase "the situation is calm" appears repeatedly, regardless of the obvious contradiction with the disturbing events being reported. Such an unrealistic picture is often supported by claims that citizens in a particular area are responding positively to presidential decisions and are enthusiastic supporters of the regime when things are quite the contrary.

To the average citizen the AND is an instrument of intimidation. AND officials often use their positions to extract resources from citizens who want to avoid arrest and harassment. Nevertheless, the AND's control is incomplete. Zairians are still able to frustrate its efforts by remaining ambivalent to government policies, voicing discontent openly, or frustrating the AND's efforts more generally. In recent years the AND has become somewhat weakened, as rank and file agents are poorly paid.

In many respects the AND's work is being performed more efficiently by the Division Spéciale Presidentielle (DSP; Special Presidential Brigade), the security arm of the army organized to protect Mobutu and his family. The DSP is an elite, Israeli-trained force with sophisticated technology at its disposal. It is quite adept at spreading terror. Members are recruited from the Ngbandi (the president's tribe) in Équateur province, and allegiance to Le Maréchal is all the more assured as DSP commandos are well compensated, in contrast to other security forces. As a result, the DSP has been used extensively since 1989 to quell growing civil unrest demanding political and economic change. A June 1990 *Africa Confidential* report highlighted additional security arrangements for the president—namely, the recruitment of South African mercenaries—to supplement the DSP.[34]

Another significant component of the secret security forces is the Service d'Action et de Renseignements (SARM; Military Action and Intelligence Service). Officially, this unit is responsible for military intelligence and ensuring the army's loyalty to Mobutu. Established in 1985, it is in fact another instrument of repression, with its own network of informers and, like the AND, its prisons.[35]

The Jeunesse du Mouvement Populaire de la Révolution. The Jeunesse du Mouvement Populaire de la Révolution (JMPR; the youth arm of the MPR) is the final segment of the state's coercive machinery. Created in 1967, it became a specialized branch of the party three years later, with responsibility for political matters relating to Zairian youth.[36] Accordingly, the JMPR progressively replaced all religious youth movements in the country, and JMPR sections were created in all primary and secondary schools. JMPR leaders were given a mandate to supervise schools in addition to their other duties, which included vigilance and information gathering for government security forces. In addition, a Disciplinary Brigade was created to carry out the security functions of the JMPR.

During the 1970s, despite their official status as keepers of law and order, the JMPR Brigade became simply another source of oppression. Like FAZ members, JMPR youths were usually incompetent and undisciplined. It was not uncommon to hear reports of theft, arbitrary arrest, and extortion taking place on nightly patrols. The brigade was treated with suspicion by the population and territorial administrators. The attitude of the latter was compounded by the fact that the brigade often uncovered and reported financial irregularities in the territories to higher administrative officials.

Following persistent reports of flagrant abuses, the brigade was abolished, but it was immediately reinstated under a new name—the Corps des Activistes pour la défense de la Révolution. Although it was intended that this new group would not repeat earlier abuses, it simply reinforced the status quo. In the wake of the dismantling of the one-party state in 1990, the corps has been formally disbanded, although elements still roam the streets.

OPPOSITION

Needless to say, in spite of all efforts to impose control in the highly centralized state, the regime is by no means secure. Regardless of the fact that opposition can be met with force, over time internal and external groups have been reacting to and retaliating against Mobutu's oppressive rule. Prior to 1989 such protests had been ad hoc, isolated, and largely ineffective. This situation changed radically in 1989 in response to the fall of the Berlin Wall in November and the subsequent prodemocracy movement in Eastern Europe and elsewhere. Resistance to the regime has become more sustained, open, confrontational, and violent. The MPR has lost its legitimacy. To the man in the street, the party's acronym means *mourir pour rien* (to die for nothing), an indication of the blame placed on the regime for the socioeconomic deprivation.[37]

In the wake of the democracy movement in Eastern Europe, Mobutu declared initially that *perestroika* did not concern the MPR, given that Zaire had its own brand of democracy based on authenticity. Nevertheless, in the face of increasing popular dissatisfaction and unrest, he initiated a two-month tour of Zaire in January 1990 to engage in what he termed a "direct dialogue with the people." As part of this process, Zairians at large were invited to submit thoughts and ideas with respect to the running of state institutions and the nation as a whole. A Bureau National de la Consultation Populaire (National Board of Popular Consultation) was appointed to compile a comprehensive list of recommendations based on memoranda submitted. Government authorities in Kinshasa were completely overwhelmed by the response. In anticipation of·what the local press was calling a "Zairian *perestroika*," individuals submitted over 6,000 memoranda, including a detailed commentary from civil servants in the Foreign Ministry on the abysmal state of affairs in the country and a rather scathing letter from Zairian Catholic bishops. Pamphlets began to circulate in Kinshasa openly criticizing the president, calling for his resignation, and urging mass demonstrations. As the unrest mounted, security forces—the Special Presidential Brigade; the paramilitary Civil Guard; and a newly created antiterrorist corps, the Special Intervention Regiment—began sweeps in the capital. It was in this atmosphere that Mobutu announced the abolition of the single-party state and the creation of a multiparty system on April 24, 1990.

Although protests against the regime have been pervasive, sustained internal opposition has come from key societal groups—the church, students, and to a lesser extent the labor force represented by the trade union movement.

Internal Responses

The Churches. In addition to their missionary activities in Zaire, churches (Catholic as well as Protestant) have traditionally been deeply involved in the provision of social services and education. Having pursued these activities since colonial times, the churches have periodically come in conflict with the state. This pattern has been particularly true of the Catholic church, which worked alongside the Belgian colonial administration and therefore had the most widespread influence on the Zairian population. During the initial period of the Second Republic (1965–1970), the Catholic church was left to pursue its activities unhampered by the government. The regime's noninterference came to an end in August 1971, when after major student demonstrations the Catholic-run Lovanium University in Kinshasa was nationalized and became part of the newly created Université Nationale du Zaire (UNAZA; National University of Zaire).

Even before this move, Cardinal Joseph Malula, the Zairian head of the Catholic church at the time, had chosen to be highly critical of the Mobutu regime at a mass celebrating the tenth anniversary of independence. The sudden nationalization of Lovanium was seen as an infringement on the church's jurisdiction. When Mobutu announced a few months later that JMPR branches had to be established in the seminaries, it was taken as yet another indication of the government's intention to control the church. Several seminaries refused to comply, and after several months of threats on both sides the government agreed that the church would retain ultimate control over JMPR student activities in these institutions.

Another source of conflict was the concept of the "authenticity" program, which required the rejection of Christian names. Although the church acquiesced on this issue, the Catholic weekly *Afrique Chrétienne* questioned the ideology of authenticity, which allegedly supported a return to the values of traditional Zairian culture as the basis for Zairian modernization. The article in question was condemned by the regime as subversive; and publication of the magazine, which at the time had a circulation of 40,000, was suspended for six months. The government cracked down further by announcing that religious services would no longer be a part of state functions. Mobutu attacked Cardinal Malula as a "renegade of the revolution" in response to his objection to adapting hymns and prayers to praise the president. Malula was evicted from his official residence (which was taken over by the JMPR) and forced to leave the country for a few months. Only the pope's intervention saved him from arrest and trial.[38]

By late 1972 the regime had banned all religious radio and television broadcasts and prohibited the activities of all religious youth movements in order to further strengthen the impact of the MPR ideology. A ban on the printing, sale, and distribution of thirty-one religious publications followed. Further, all religious groups were required to publish detailed information on their membership. Things came to a climax at the end of 1974 when all religious school networks were nationalized and the government declared that Christmas would no longer be a public holiday. The schools were returned to the churches eighteen months later when it became clear that the state could not operate them effectively.

Aside from occasional criticisms of the government, the church had become rather reticent by the early 1980s. Some felt that the church had succumbed to the system of corruption, paying necessary bribes to conduct its business and obtain foreign exchange rather than be frustrated by bureaucratic red tape. In addition, critics charged that some local bishops had allowed themselves to be co-opted into Mobutu's system by accepting presidential largesse, albeit for conducting the church's social work.[39]

However, in Zaire change can come quickly; and as economic conditions deteriorated, church protests soon escalated. Even after Cardinal Malula's death in 1989, individual clergy continued to criticize the regime. This effort culminated in the famous pastoral letter to the president leaked to the international press in April 1990. The nation's twelve Catholic bishops, presenting a united front, launched a candid appraisal of the Mobutuist system, describing at length the crisis of the Zairian state and calling for extensive reform including the separation of party and state as well as the effective de facto and de jure separation of legislative, judicial, and executive institutions. Not surprisingly, Mobutu refused to consider the letter as part of the other memoranda received.

Because of its ongoing budgetary difficulties, the government has tended to leave the religious community to its own devices. In the contemporary Mobutuist state, the government has quietly acknowledged its limited capacity by virtually relinquishing social welfare activities to the churches. In the rural areas the Catholic church and its Protestant equivalent, L'église du Christ au Zaire (Church of Christ in Zaire), are the most extensive and effective providers of education and health care, areas in which the government has limited capabilities.

Schools. Zairian students have been one of the most consistent internal opposition groups. They have focused their protests on economic issues (increased stipends) and, in recent years, on regime change. Students became organized at a national level shortly before independence, when the Union National des Étudiants du Congo et du Ruanda-Urundi (UNECRU; National Union of Students of the Congo and Ruanda-Urundi) was formed in March 1960. This organization played no role in the drive for independence. In May 1961 students meeting at Lovanium University formed the Union Générale des Étudiants Congolais (UGEC; General Union of Congolese Students) to fight tribalism and to defend the nationalist ideals for which Lumumba stood.[40] Initial demands of the organization were rather moderate and focused largely on educational reform. The UGEC's first congress in 1961 insisted that education be adapted to African conditions and advocated the expansion of adult education and the defense of the universities' autonomy against ideological pressure.

By 1963 the UGEC had become more overtly political in the midst of growing opposition to the Adoula government. At its second congress members passed a series of resolutions that echoed the views of the Lumumbist faction of the MNC. Delegates demanded the release of Gizenga (former leader of the rival government in Stanleyville), Lumumba was proclaimed a national hero, and the students called for an end to "imperialist" intervention in the Congo. By the following year, however, divisions had developed within the organization over the return of Tshombe to the Congo as the new prime minister. There was a serious rift between students who opposed Tshombe and those who saw the need for national unity. On his part, Tshombe sought to mute student resistance at home and abroad through surveillance and attempts at co-optation. This action undermined the UGEC as a political force, although it continued to call for a socialist single-party state and other "radical" changes in the Congo. After Mobutu's coup there appeared to be a meeting of the minds between the UGEC and the new government, with the latter seeking to reduce Belgian influence over the economy and to improve relations with so-called radical African states. Further, Mobutu sought to bring the university-educated elite into his administration by including several members of the former Collège des Commissaires, which had been established in 1960.[41]

Ultimately, however, Mobutu decided to control student dissent by replacing the UGEC with the JMPR. Regime attempts to suppress opposition through JMPR informers served only to further politicize students at all levels. Demonstrations, although technically illegal, have been an ongoing feature of Zairian student life.

A serious student strike in 1969 led to a clash between Lovanium University students and the army. Dissatisfied with low living allowances provided by the state, high prices, and extravagant expenditures by the government, the students marched from the campus into Kinshasa to present their grievances. After the students defied army attempts to stop them, the FAZ opened fire and many students were killed. Five hundred students were arrested, and many more were confined to campus. Of those arrested, thirty-four were charged with subversion. Some escaped to Bulgaria, and the rest were sentenced for up to twenty years. In true Mobutu style the president pardoned the students on October 14, 1969, the occasion of his thirty-ninth birthday. Further major demonstrations in 1971, 1979, and 1980 had to be put down with force.

Students protested in 1971 in memory of the victims who died in the 1969 incident. Again the army intervened, and Lovanium University was closed. This incident led directly to the nationalization of all the universities under the umbrella of the National University of Zaire. In 1979 there were widespread strikes on all the university campuses related primarily to the abysmal conditions of student life but also characterized by distinctly political overtones. Both teachers and students began calling for political liberalization, demanding the creation of two additional political parties. In early 1989 students were again demonstrating over stipends, grants, and transport and insisting on Mobutu's resignation. According to government reports, one student was killed and thirty-seven injured in Kinshasa and Lubumbashi. As a result, about twenty-five students were jailed, and the universities were closed. The Lubumbashi demonstration was prompted by the discovery of a student's body near the town's military camp. The chief of staff ordered the arrest of ten soldiers involved in the affair in view of strong evidence that they fired at demonstrators in violation of instructions.[42]

Perhaps the most serious instance of government retaliation against students came on May 9, 1990, two weeks after Mobutu's liberalization initiative. The trouble began when students at the Lubumbashi campus of the university attacked fellow student "informers" who they believed were responsible for student disappearances. After weeks of student demonstrations urging democracy and general student unrest, the regime moved swiftly on the campus. Acting in conjunction with local authorities, the Special Presidential Brigade cut electricity to the campus and moved quickly through the dormitories, cutting the throats of students they believed to be the perpetrators. Apparently students from the president's region (Équateur) were spared, having been removed from the campus prior to the incident. According to an interview with a Belgian professor at the campus, many students fled the campus in a daze, carrying their mattresses on their heads.[43]

The Lubumbashi incident provoked countrywide sympathy demonstrations at the high school and university levels, as well as international criticism. To deflect calls by foreign governments (Belgium and France) for an international commission of inquiry, the government launched its own investigation. The inquiry revealed that the incident had been planned by senior administration and security officials, including the governor of Shaba province, who was subsequently arrested, as well as individuals from the AND and the Civil Guard. Nevertheless, no precise figure was acknowledged with respect to the number of students killed, although Amnesty International and the Belgian press stated estimates of 100 to 150 individuals. Furthermore, it could not be established whether the attack was initiated under orders from the office of the president—another aspect of the investigation that was not surprising from the point of view of the regime's foreign critics. Ultimately, under continued international pressure, a formal trial of all those implicated in the affair was held in Kinshasa in 1991, and the former governor of Shaba, Koyagialo Ngbabe Te Gerengbo, was given a fifteen-year sentence.[44]

In view of the Lubumbashi massacre and subsequent acts of repression, students have formed a new political organization to represent their interests—the Progressive Union of Zairian Students and Pupils (UPEZA)—even as the door to democracy has in theory been opened.

Trade Unions. Zairian workers have only recently formally joined the ranks of the regime's opponents. When Mobutu assumed power in 1965, he merged the three existing labor unions into one association, the Union National des Travailleurs Congolais (National Union of Congolese Workers), now known as the Union National des Travailleurs Zairois (UNTZA; National Union of Zairian Workers). It soon became a semi-autonomous unit of the MPR. The secretary-general of the union became a member of the party's central committee, and as a result, the organization could not effectively promote worker interests that diverged from those of the government and party. When IMF austerity measures began to be felt in the 1980s, the Union organized several strikes, focusing on wage issues, that came to the attention of the international press.

Early in 1990, civil servants at the Ministry of Foreign Affairs went on strike and returned to work only in October that year. Aside from wage issues, the strike visibly demonstrated grievances outlined in a letter to the president. In the letter the group attacked the policies of regionalism and tribalism favoring the president's region in high level government appointments. Doctors also struck during the same period because of low salaries. Following negotiations with UNTZA, the government was forced to grant 55 percent salary increases to government employees across the board in defiance of IMF restrictions on the government budget. In the aftermath of Mobutu's April 24 announcement of the end of the one-party rule, UNTZA declared itself independent of the MPR, and by late 1990 UNTZA had become more assertive vis-à-vis the government. The union issued a detailed statement in October calling on the regime to take serious steps to reduce inflation and stabilize the currency, establish a new minimum wage, and institute a new labor code. Many workers—civil servants, teachers, and medical personnel—have organized into unions, and several unions have been legalized in keeping with the government's new policy of pluralism.

External Groups

External opposition to the regime has traditionally been fragmented and uncoordinated. Prior to 1990 there were several opposition groups but no overall leader and no coherent ideology. Periodic efforts were made to organize parties with similar ideological views under a common umbrella, but by and large these efforts were undermined by rivalries, infighting, and Mobutu's consummate skill at neutralizing his opponents.[45]

During the 1970s and 1980s two opposition groups launched attacks against the regime from bases outside the country. The first, the Front pour la Liberation Nationale du Congo, launched the two Shaba invasions from Angola and Zambia in 1977 and 1978 and has undertaken sporadic incursions since then. The second group, the Parti Révolutionnaire du Peuple (PRP; Revolutionary People's Party), has conducted sporadic guerrilla activity in the Sud Kivu–Shaba area near Lake Tanganyika.[46] In November 1984 and June 1985 the PRP launched attacks on Moba, a town on the shores of Lake Tanganyika. To date, Zairian army units have failed to dislodge PRP militants from their guerrilla base.

Perhaps the most serious challenge to the regime has been the Union pour la Démocratie et le Progrès Social (UDPS; Union for Democracy and Social Progress) with its group of internal and external supporters. UDPS was originally formed as a de facto second party by thirteen members of the Zairian Legislative Council arrested in 1981 for issuing a highly critical document calling for a multiparty system, free elections, and Mobutu's resignation. The group quickly became the major

opposition force. Over time, however, it was somewhat weakened by de-
fections, internal divisions, and the detention of its key leaders, particularly Etienne Tshisekedi, the symbol of the party in Zaire.

In June 1984, after previously having been arrested and banished to
their home villages, five members of the Group of 13, as they came to be
known, announced their reintegration into the MPR. A few months
before, in August 1983, seven members of the Group had been severely
beaten by the security forces after a meeting with several members of
the U.S. Congress led by Congressman Howard Wolpe, chairman of the
House Subcommittee on Africa. The members of Congress were on a fact-
finding tour of Zaire and requested discussions with the "opposition."
Sending a clear message to Mobutu, the Zairians appeared attired in suits
and ties instead of the customary *abacost*.[47] By 1987 the president announced at an MPR rally that the seven would be readmitted to the fold,
as they had written to him admitting their "mistakes." In fact, four leading UDPS members were subsequently appointed to the MPR Central
Committee in October 1987.[48] Tshisekedi himself has been under house
arrest and exiled several times throughout the years for illegally organizing and holding mass rallies condemning the regime. Refusing to be co-
opted, he soon came to represent democracy for Zairian citizens.

Originally the UDPS was moderate in terms of its aims, seeking to
effect change as a parliamentary opposition group in the context of the
existing political system. Its main goal was the establishment of a plur-
alist political system to replace the existing one-party state. With the
increasing oppression and economic deprivation characteristic of the late
1980s, the UDPS rode the tide of popular dissatisfaction, becoming more
"radical" in its demands and ultimately calling for the complete dismantling of the Mobutuist system. With political liberalization in 1990 and the
prospect of a genuine Third Republic, the UDPS began to enjoy widespread popularity and massive support. Indeed, throughout 1990 and
1991 several major UDPS political rallies were held in open defiance of
political authorities and in spite of attacks and harassment by the security
forces.

In response to the ongoing challenge of the opposition, Mobutu has
largely been successful at co-opting members of the various groups by
offering attractive opportunities for them to join the ranks of the political
establishment in Kinshasa. Throughout the years he has made repeated
offers of amnesty, although frequently these offers have been pretexts to
eliminate prominent members of the opposition. As early as 1968, he
made such an offer to Pierre Mulele, Lumumba's education minister in
1960 and leader of the 1964 Kwilu rebellion. Despite signed assurances of
his safety, he was murdered at a reception in his honor, allegedly by mili-

tary officers who had been fighting his rebel forces four years earlier. Mulele was tried and sentenced to death posthumously.[49]

On the occasion of the MPR's sixteenth anniversary in 1983, Mobutu announced yet another amnesty for those sentenced for endangering state security or banned for violating party discipline. Amnesty also applied to individuals guilty of such crimes but living abroad, as long as they returned to Zaire by June 30 of that year. Opposition groups condemned this move as a trap designed to convince the Western aid donors of the regime's good faith in order to secure additional financing. In their view, this announcement was merely a smoke screen, hiding the fact that Mobutu refused to tolerate any internal opposition from those exiles who did return. Evidently individuals who had returned in 1978 under a similar amnesty had been forced to recognize the supreme authority of the MPR. Some were later appointed to the government, such as Kamitatu Massamba, who was made minister of agriculture despite having written books critical of the regime while in exile. Aimé Betou, of the Parti Socialiste Zairois (PSZ; Zairian Socialist Party) and briefly head of a government in exile in 1980, claimed that he and some of his colleagues returned to Zaire at Mobutu's urging, believing that they would be allowed to function as a legitimate opposition. However, they were jailed and then given various government posts on their release.[50] Similar moves toward the UDPS were designed to destroy the group as a viable opposition force.

Opponents of the regime became more united in 1991 than at any other point in the Mobutu era. The president's speech in April 1990 called for dramatic changes in the political landscape—a triparty system, constitutional reform, dissolution of MPR institutions such as the Central Committee, depoliticization of the army and security forces, and "free" elections in 1991. By early October 1990 Mobutu had decided to lift the three-party limit on political liberalization in response to growing pressure from societal groups. With the existing constitution modified to permit this new political arrangement, over 100 parties emerged within a few months, each vying for recognition and competing for support. The regime quickly took steps to exert control over the process by requiring prohibitive registration fees from all aspiring political groups. In order to be recognized and to be eligible for the proposed elections, each party had to register with the Supreme Court after depositing a fee of Z5 million.[51] All these funds had to be collected locally, effectively preventing the smaller groups from participating. Once registered, groups were to be barred from holding public meetings or demonstrations without prior permission from municipal authorities.

In 1992, irrespective of registration requirements, several groups in addition to the UDPS appeared to be enjoying popular support. Joseph Ileo, an elder statesman appointed prime minister for a brief period in 1960, heads the Parti Démocrat et Social Chrétien (Democratic and Social Christian Front). Two established groups that claim Lumumba's legacy remain: the Mouvement National Congolais–Lumumba (MNC-L; National Congolese Movement) and the Parti Lumumbiste Unifié (PALU; United Lumumbist Party) led by Antoine Gizenga, a prominent figure in the Congo Crisis who established a rival government in Kisangani (Stanleyville) in 1960. Until he was appointed prime minister in November 1991, Nguza Karl-i-Bond led the PRI-Fenadec, a merger of his own Union des Fédéralistes Républicains Indépendants (UFERI; Party of Independent Republican Federalists) and the Fédération Nationale des Démocrates Convaincus (Fenadec; National Federation of Conservative Democrats). Meanwhile the MPR has been resuscitated under a new name, the Mouvement Populaire pour le Renouveau (Popular Movement for Renewal), obviously in an effort to regain its former preeminence. Mobutu reassumed leadership of the party in April 1991, one year after he relinquished the post. About 130 parties have formed a united front known as the Union Sacrée (Holy Alliance) in order to take a common position against the regime. Mobutu himself has funded the creation of several "opposition" groups in an attempt to shape the political landscape. These Mobutu "loyalists" compose the Forces Démocrates Unies (United Democratic Forces) that stand opposed to the Union Sacrée. There has been talk of the formation of a third political force, separate from both the Union Sacrée and the Forces Démocrates, to regroup all the liberal parties that back neither the formal opposition nor the president.

Although the various parties opposed to Mobutu and the MPR have different solutions for a future Zaire, they are united on one central issue: Mobutu's unconditional departure from the political scene. In the view of the Union Sacrée, political and economic reform are not possible with the president's continued presence and influence over local developments. Mobutu's system of kleptocracy has been condemned, and there have been clear statements made by the various party leaders that Zaire must be put on a new path. In 1990 there was opposition consensus on the convening of a Sovereign National Conference to formulate a new constitution and to decide on a framework for political liberalization. This arrangement was belatedly endorsed by Mobutu in April 1991. The Sovereign National Conference finally convened in August after several delays and the refusal of the Union Sacrée to participate following widespread accusations that many of the proposed delegates were representing the Forces Démocrates Unies. On a positive note, the conference managed to reject pro-Mobutu candidates and elect Monsignor Laurent

Monsengwo Pasinya, the Catholic archbishop of Kisangani, as chairman of its Interim Bureau. Nevertheless, as of 1992 a true transition government has yet to materialize.

Following the September 1991 riots Etienne Tshisekedi of the UDPS was appointed prime minister after Mobutu was pressured by Western governments to come to terms with the opposition. However, the president initially refused to relinquish control over four vital areas—defense, finance, foreign affairs, and mining. In an apparent settlement, party representatives from the Forces Démocrates Unies were finally appointed to head the Ministries of Defense, Foreign Affairs, and Mining. The opposition's euphoria was short-lived. Tshisekedi was dismissed by presidential decree after less than a week in office when he refused to swear allegiance to Mobutu and the constitution. Unofficially, foreign and local observers have noted that the dismissal took place because of Tshisekedi's refusal to release foreign exchange funds from the Bank of Zaire so that the president could pay his troops.

While Tshisekedi established a rival government, refusing to recognize his dismissal, Bernardin Mungul-Diaka, the leader of a small, lesser-known opposition party in the Union Sacrée, was appointed to the post. Mungul-Diaka, head of the Rassemblement des Démocrates pour la République (RDR), had no legitimacy, being widely perceived as pro-Mobutu. This attempt by Mobutu to stall the democratic process sparked new rounds of violence in Kinshasa and more importantly in Lubumbashi, where clashes occurred between pro-Mobutu and opposition forces and, for the first time, between rival opposition groups. Many sections of the mining town were looted and in flames. By late November 1991 there was a third transition government, led by new Prime Minister Nguza Karl-i-Bond. Nguza held several key posts including foreign minister and prime minister in the heyday of the MPR, and at the time of the latter appointment, headed the opposition party PRI-Fenadec. Nguza and UFERI were subsequently expelled from the Union Sacrée for participating in a Mobutu-orchestrated government. In a further blow to the liberalization process, Nguza suspended the Sovereign National Conference indefinitely in January 1992, allegedly because of problems with regional representation. In addition, the conference expenses were described as prohibitive, resulting in an impasse after the government refused to pay for meals and lodging for delegates. In turn, representatives objected to the government's alternative plan to house them free at Nsele at the president's expense.[52]

In this chapter, I have described the key features of the Zairian state in some detail. It is clear that although the country is in transition, in principle, and the modern Zairian polity has attributes of patrimonialism and personal rule, the key authoritarian features of the colonial state have persisted. The Zairian state in 1992 is centralized and coercive, yet weak and insecure. These coexisting dynamics are as much a result of the legacies of colonialism and the Congo Crisis as of deliberate policy choices taken by Mobutu himself. I will now turn to an examination of society and culture to discern how factors such as ethnicity and class relations have affected and have been impacted by state structures.

NOTES

1. For the full text of Mobutu's speech see *La Semaine*, April 25, 1990.

2. Thomas Callaghy has succinctly outlined the stages in Mobutu's strategy of state formation, culminating in what he refers to as an absolutist state, reminiscent of the early modern French absolutist state in seventeenth century France. See his excellent analysis in *The State-Society Struggle: Zaire in Comparative Perspective* (New York: Columbia University Press, 1984), pp. 165–194.

3. "An Interview with Mobutu Sese Seko," in *Voices of Zaire: Rhetoric or Reality*, ed. Jeffrey M. Elliot and Mervyn M. Dymally (Washington, D.C.: Washington Institute Press, 1990), p. 43.

4. Callaghy highlights two powerful translations of Mobutu's "authentic" name. The first, the Ngbendu translation, is: "The warrior who knows no defeat because of his endurance and inflexible will and is all powerful, leaving fire in his wake as he goes from conquest to conquest." The second is the Luba translation: "Invincible warrior, cock who leaves no chick intact." Callaghy, *State-Society*, p. 181. For pro-Mobutu analyses of authenticity see Victor D. DuBois, "Zaire Under President Sese Seko Mobutu," pt. 1, "The Return to Authenticity," American Universities Field Staff, Central and Southern Africa Series, vol. 27, no. 1 (Zaire), January 1973; Mobutu Sese Seko, *Dignity for Africa: Interviews with Jean-Louis Remilleux* (Paris: Éditions Albin Michel, 1989), pp. 106–109. For a critique of the concept, see Nzongola-Ntalaja, "The Authenticity of Neo-Colonialism: Ideology and Class Struggles in Zaire," paper presented at Annual Meeting of African Studies Association, Boston, November 3–6, 1976.

5. Callaghy, *State-Society*, p. 173.

6. Edward Kannyo, "Postcolonial Politics in Zaire, 1960–79," in *Zaire: The Political Economy of Underdevelopment*, ed. Guy Gran (New York: Praeger, 1979), pp. 61–62.

7. William Gutteridge, "Africa's Military Rulers: An Assessment," *Conflict Studies*, no. 62 (October 1975), p. 17.

8. "Zaire Without Mobutu," an interview with Nzongola-Ntalaja in Elliot and Dymally, *Voices of Zaire*, p. 151.

9. Jean-Claude Willame, "Zaire: Système de Survie et Fiction d'Etat," *Canadian Journal of African Studies* 18, no. 1 (1984), p. 83. See also David Gould, "The Administration of Underdevelopment," in Gran, *Zaire: Political Economy*, p. 102.

10. For an excellent analysis of corruption and the Zairian administration, see David Gould, *Bureaucratic Corruption and Underdevelopment in the Third World: The Case of Zaire* (Elmsford: Pergamon, 1980).

11. Crawford Young, "Zaire: The Unending Crisis," *Foreign Affairs* 57, no. 1

(Fall 1978), p. 172; Howard Wolpe, Chairman, Subcommittee on Africa, House Foreign Affairs Committee, "Testimony on Zaire Before the Foreign Operations Subcommittee," April 1990, p. 3.

For details on the abuse of economic aid funds, see Winsome J. Leslie, *The World Bank and Structural Transformation in Developing Countries: The Case of Zaire* (Boulder: Lynne Rienner, 1987), chap. 6, pp. 135–138.

12. "An Interview with Mobutu Sese Seko," in Elliot and Dymally, *Voices of Zaire*, pp. 25–26.

13. Nguza Karl-i-Bond, *Mobutu ou L'incarnation du Mal Zairois* (London: Rex Collings, 1982). *Foreign Broadcast Information Service (FBIS) Daily Report: Sub-Saharan Africa,* March 2, 1989, p. 4.

14. For the complete argument see Michael Schatzberg, *The Dialectics of Oppression in Zaire* (Bloomington: Indiana University Press, 1988), especially pp. 79–81.

15. Blaine Harden, "Mobutu Is Unchallenged 'Messiah' of Zaire," *New York Times*, November 10, 1989.

16. This section draws on the following sources: Richard Vengroff, *Development Administration at the Local Level: The Case of Zaire* (Syracuse: Maxwell School of Citizenship and Public Affairs, Syracuse University, 1983); Michael Schatzberg, *Politics and Class in Zaire: Bureaucracy, Business and Beer in Lisala* (New York: Africana, 1980), chap. 4; Crawford Young and Thomas Turner, *The Rise and Decline of the Zairian State* (Madison: University of Wisconsin Press, 1985), chap. 8; Callaghy, *State-Society*, chaps. 5–7.

17. Note that during the colonial period, three types of traditional structures existed: (1) the *chefferie,* a traditional unit headed by a chief chosen according to custom; (2) the sector, an artificial unit created by the Belgians composed of groupings too small to stand alone; (3) the *centre extra-coutumier,* consisting of Africans living in the larger towns or outside a traditional unit. The sectors and *centres extra-coutumiers* were run by "chiefs" elected by the state.

18. Article 15 is a nonexistent clause in the 1960 South Kasai constitution that instructed state officials to *débrouillez-vous* (improvise). Young and Turner, *Rise and Decline,* p. 228.

19. A common method is via the *ratissage,* where troops supervised by local officials stage a house-to-house "raid," demanding that everyone show their state-mandated identity cards and checking to see if taxes have been paid.

20. M. Catherine Newbury, "Ebutumwa Bw'Emiogo: The Tyranny of Cassava—A Women's Tax Revolt in Eastern Zaire," *Canadian Journal of African Studies* 18, no. 1 (1984), pp. 35–54.

21. *FBIS Daily Report: Sub-Saharan Africa,* June 1, 1989, p. 6.

22. For this section, see Callaghy, *State-Society,* pp. 318–330. Callaghy discusses mobilization in terms of the regime's effort to achieve a "normative domain consensus."

23. Ibid., p. 328.

24. Conversation with Zairian scholar, New York, August 14, 1990.

25. Young and Turner, *Rise and Decline,* p. 248. The security forces include the army, numbering 22,000; the navy, 1,200; the air force, 2,500; the gendarmerie,

25,000; and the Civil Guard, 10,000. *The Military Balance, 1991–1992* (London: International Institute for Strategic Studies, 1991), p. 146.

26. The origins of the FLNC can apparently be traced to Moise Tshombe's Katanga gendarmes. After the Katanga secession, many were incorporated into the Zairian army. After they mutinied in 1966 and 1967, they found a haven in Angola, initially fighting for the Portuguese against liberation movements there, then allying themselves with the MPLA. By the early 1970s the FLNC's ranks had expanded with deserters from the defeated Zairian army in Angola and Zairians who had fled Shaba because of oppression. Michael Schatzberg, *Mobutu or Chaos? The United States and Zaire, 1960–1990* (New York: University Press of America, 1991), p. 51.

27. Callaghy, *State-Society*, pp. 208–209; *New York Times*, February 8, 1987.

28. Helen Winternitz, *East Along the Equator* (New York: Atlantic Monthly Press, 1987), p. 19.

29. *New African*, September 1989, p. 22.

30. The average monthly salary of a soldier was Z 100,000 ($5.75 at September 1991 exchange rates). Soldiers were demanding that their salaries be brought in line with junior civil servants who earned twice that amount. *FBIS Daily Report: Sub-Saharan Africa*, September 23, 1991, p. 2.

For information on the looting and subsequent intervention, see *Africa Confidential* 32, no. 20 (October 11, 1991), p. 3; *FBIS Daily Report: Sub-Saharan Africa*, September 25, 1991, pp. 2–9; ibid., September 26, 1991, pp. 6–11; ibid., September 30, 1991, pp. 5–11; "Brazzaville Views Zaire's Strife with Mixed Emotions," *Africa Business*, December 1991, p. 29; "Une opération plus lourde qu'à Kolwezi," *Liberation*, September 25, 1991; "Mobutu à la Dérive," *L'Humanité*, September 27, 1991, p. 14; "Belges Fondent sur Kinshasa," *Liberation*, September 25, 1991, p. 3.

For details of the 1993 riots, see "French Troops Amid Mutiny in Zaire," *Washington Post*, January 30, 1993, p. A17; "Mobutu Troops Attack Homes of Opponents," *New York Times*, February 1, 1993, p. A9; "1,000 Dead Reported in Zaire Fighting," *Washington Post*, February 2, 1993, p. A17.

31. *FBIS Daily Report: Sub-Saharan Africa*, May 2, 1989, p. 4; ibid., September 30, 1991, p. 12.

32. The Agence National de Documentation was created in 1983 out of two previously separate organizations—the Centre National de Recherche et d'Investigation (CNRI; National Center for Research and Investigation) and the Service National d'Intelligence (SNI; National Intelligence Service). The CNRI was larger and more visible, with responsibility for internal investigation and surveillance. The SNI dealt with external affairs. These two units were established after the previous security agency, the Centre National de Documentation, came under serious international criticism for human rights abuses.

The section on the AND draws on Michael Schatzberg's excellent analysis. See Schatzberg, *Dialectics of Oppression*, pp. 38–51. See also Lawyers Committee for Human Rights, *Zaire: Repression as Policy—A Human Rights Report*, New York, August 1990, pp. 42–43.

33. See *Political Imprisonment in Zaire*, Amnesty International, 1983; Nguza Karl-i-Bond, *Mobutu ou L'incarnation du Mal Zairois* (London: Rex Collings, 1982).

34. *FBIS Daily Report: Sub-Saharan Africa,* June 27, 1990, p. 6.

35. Lawyers Committee for Human Rights, *Zaire: Repression as Policy,* p. 45; *FBIS Daily Report: Sub-Saharan Africa,* June 27, 1990, p. 6.

36. For information on the JMPR, refer to: Michael Schatzberg, "Fidelité au Guide: The J.M.P.R. in Zairian Schools," *Journal of Modern African Studies* 16, no. 3 (1978), pp. 417–431; Schatzberg, *Dialectics of Oppression,* pp. 64–65.

37. Schatzberg, *Mobutu or Chaos?* p. 50.

38. For an analysis of the church-state conflict in Zaire up to 1974, see Kenneth Lee Adelman, "The Church-State Conflict in Zaire: 1969–74," *African Studies Review* 28, no. 1 (April 1975), pp. 102–116.

39. *National Catholic Reporter,* July 29, 1988, p. 14.

40. Nzongola-Ntalaja, "Authenticity of Neo-Colonialism," p. 4.

41. Jean-Claude Willame, "The Congo," in *Students and Politics in Developing Nations,* ed. Donald K. Emmerson (New York: Praeger, 1968), pp. 44–49.

42. *FBIS Daily Report: Sub-Saharan Africa,* April 13, 1989, pp. 1–2; ibid., March 7, 1989, p. 3.

43. Ibid., May 22, 1990, p. 5; ibid., May 30, 1990, p. 13; ibid., January 2, 1991, p. 8.

44. Ibid., January 8, 1991, pp. 1–2; Economist Intelligence Unit (EIU), *Country Report: Zaire,* no. 2, 1991, p. 15; Makau wa Mutua, "Decline of the Despot," *Africa Report,* November-December 1991, p. 15.

45. On October 1, 1982, former prime minister Nguza Karl-i-Bond announced in Brussels the formation of a new umbrella opposition movement, the Front Congolais pour la Restauration de la Démocratie, with himself as leader. Previously, shortly after his defection from the Mobutu government in 1980, he had formed the Comité pour la Liberation du Congo-Kinshasa (CLC). However, internal divisions and resentment at Nguza's perceived long association with Mobutu precluded the CLC from gaining much credibility. The Front hoped to provide the West with an alternative to the Mobutu regime and was a rather unusual alliance—the pro-Western Nguza, the Marxist-oriented PRP, and the more moderate UDPS. According to its manifesto, a key goal of the Front was the dismantling of the Tel Aviv–Kinshasa–Pretoria axis and the ending of Zaire's complete dependence on foreign powers that provided the regime with its legitimacy. *Guard,* April 22, 1983. For historical information on the external opposition, see Ghislain Kabwit, "The Growth of Internal and External Opposition to the Mobutu Regime," in Gran, *Zaire: Political Economy,* pp. 287–290; Nzongola-Ntalaja, "The Continuing Struggle for National Liberation in Zaire," *Journal of Modern African Studies* 17, no. 4 (1979), pp. 595–614.

46. The PRP was founded in 1967 by Laurent Kabila, one of the few survivors of the 1964 rebel regime in Stanleyville. The group has Lumumbaist roots and has been dedicated to the violent overthrow of the Mobutu regime.

47. Colin Legum, ed., *Africa Contemporary Record: Annual Survey 1983–1984* (New York: Africana, 1984), p. B394. The *abacost* is the Zairian version of the bush-jacket suit. As part of his rejection of the European tradition, Mobutu had made this style of dress mandatory, in the spirit of *authenticité.*

48. EIU, *Country Profile: Zaire, 1988–89,* p. 7.

49. *Africa,* no. 47 (July 1975), p. 15.

50. *Africa Now,* July 1983.

51. The zaire (Z) is the official unit of currency. The zaire replaced the Congolese franc in 1967 after the economic and financial disorder created by the Congo Crisis necessitated an IMF stabilization program (see Chapter 4). Z5 million is approximately $6,900, using an average exchange rate for 1990 of Z718 = US$1.

52. *FBIS Daily Report: Sub-Saharan Africa,* January 21, 1992, p. 3.

3

Society and Culture

Zairian society is itself a mirror of the changes taking place in the political arena. As is the case in the political realm, Zairian society is in transition, reflecting the instability that often accompanies any process of change. Ethnic and class pressures are building as the country moves tentatively toward democracy. Growing ethnic and class competition is reinforced by unequal access to education and other social welfare services for most Zairians. At the same time, with political liberalization, disenchanted societal groups have become more vocal about politics as well as the economy, and this behavior is reflected in a newly independent press. Finally, religion and culture are important sources of support for citizens as they attempt to cope with the economic hardship and political uncertainty in their daily lives.

POPULATION AND DEMOGRAPHY

Like many countries in Sub-Saharan Africa, Zaire has a rapidly increasing population, with an average annual growth rate of 3 percent since the early 1970s. Population growth has exceeded the rate of economic growth by an average of 1 percent per annum in the postindependence period. Between 1955 and 1986 the population more than doubled, increasing from 12.5 million to 31.3 million. At these rates, the World Bank projects that the population will reach 49 million by the year 2000. A high birthrate (45 per 1,000) coupled with a notable decrease in infant mortality (from 160 per 1,000 in 1960 to 94.4 per 1,000 in 1989) has contributed to high population growth. Life expectancy at birth is 52.5 years—above average for Sub-Saharan Africa. Population is unevenly distributed, with the lowest population density in the equatorial forest of the Central Zaire Basin. Nord Kivu, Sud Kivu, Haut Zaire, Shaba, Bandundu, and Équateur are the most populated regions. According to the national census conducted in 1984, Kivu alone had over 5 million inhabitants, representing 17.5 percent of a total population of 30.7 million (see Table 3.1).[1]

Rapid urbanization—due to significant migration of people from the rural areas in search of a better life in the cities—began in the postwar boom of the 1950s and continued into the First Republic. Urbanization rates remain high, with 39 percent of the population living in urban centers as of 1990. The growing urban population has caused a strain on social welfare services. However, with Zaire's ongoing economic difficulties and consequently a narrowing of options in the formal sector, urban migration has been decreasing in many areas; levels nevertheless remain significant. According to World Bank data, population growth in Kinshasa declined from 10.4 percent per annum in the period from 1958 to 1970 to approximately 5.1 percent in 1986.[2] In recent years population movements have corresponded to perceptions of increased economic opportunity outside the formal economy. The liberalization of diamond mining and the subsequent growth of trading opportunities have resulted in high levels of population growth in Kasai Oriental in rural as well as urban areas. A similar phenomenon can be observed in northern Kivu

TABLE 3.1
Zaire: Population by Province
(census data)

Province	1970	1984
Kinshasa	1,308,361	2,664,309
Shaba	2,753,714	3,979,354
Kivu	3,361,883	5,391,938
Haut Zaire	3,356,419	4,314,672
Bandundu	2,600,556	3,769,741
Equateur	2,431,812	3,574,385
Kasai Oriental	1,872,231	2,645,225
Kasai Occidental	2,433,861	2,395,246
Bas Zaire	1,519,039	1,994,573
Total	21,637,876	30,729,443

Sources: Irving Kaplan, H. Mark Roth, and Gordon C. McDonald (eds.), Zaire--A Country Study (Washington, D.C.: American University, 1979), table 2, pp. 281-282; Republic du Zaire, Institut National de la Statistique, Zaire: Recensement Scientifique de la Population, July 1984, p. 12.

and the eastern part of Haut Zaire owing to expanded formal and illicit border trading opportunities in gold and coffee.

At the same time, some regions have been experiencing reverse migration—from urban to rural areas—within the last decade. One such case is Shaba province, where a combination of factors—rebel attacks, the closing of the Lobito railway, as well as a production slowdown at GECAMINES, the largest single employer in the province—has left many towns depressed. The entire province of Kasai Occidental is stagnant, with below-average levels of population growth except for the few areas that benefit from diamond mining.[3] In some rural areas, such as parts of Kivu, population pressure on land has begun to cause soil erosion and depletion, with resulting consequences for crop yields.

Population pressures in some areas have been exacerbated by the presence of refugees from neighboring countries. Coming mainly from Angola, these individuals have settled in the regions of Bas Zaire, Kinshasa, Bandundu, Shaba, and Kivu. Although precise figures are difficult to ascertain, the UN High Commission for Refugees estimates that as of December 1990 at least 310,000 Angolans, 13,000 Burundese, and 12,000 Rwandese were in Zaire. Conversely, growing numbers of Zairians have been migrating to Angola, Zambia, Rwanda, and Burundi in the face of economic stagnation at home.

The government of Zaire has taken tentative steps to deal with the growing population problem. A Population Planning Unit was established within the Department of Planning in 1986 to serve as the institutional support for a National Population Committee. The Planning Unit has a mandate to coordinate and monitor all population-related activities in both the public and private sectors, including close collaboration with the National Institute of Statistics to conduct demographic research and surveys. The work of the unit is being funded by the UN Development Program, the UN Fund for Population Activities, and the International Labor Organization.

Measures have also been implemented in the area of family planning. Fertility rates for the country as a whole among women of childbearing age have remained largely constant on average since 1955 (refer to Table 3.3). Factors such as marriage at a young age, the low prevalence of contraceptives, and low levels of education account for continued high levels of fertility. Family planning activities began officially in 1973 when the National Committee for Wanted Births was established to provide family planning services. Five years later the committee became a nongovernmental organization (NGO)—the Zairian Association for Family Planning—and it received some assistance from the International Planned Parenthood Federation. Small numbers of medical personnel were trained in family planning techniques, and education activities took

place on a limited scale. However, an official commitment to family planning efforts was assumed by the Department of Health only in 1982. At
that time a family planning project financed by the U.S. Agency for International Development (USAID) and affiliated with the department was
launched to establish a network of seventy-five family planning units in
fourteen urban areas. The project aimed to increase contraceptive prevalence from 1 percent to 12 percent by 1986 but by January 1985 had
achieved only a 1.6 percent rate of prevalence. Indeed, overall acceptance
of family planning services by the population at large remains extremely
low.[4]

ETHNIC PLURALISM
AND LINGUISTIC DIVERSITY

Zaire is a multiethnic mosaic of at least 200 ethnic groups in the
various regions of the country. Historically, through migration and resettlement, certain groups came to be known and identified with particular
areas. In Équateur groups such as the Ngbandi, the Zande, and the
Ngombe are found. Haut Zaire is inhabited by the Mongo, the Lokele,
and the Kumu; the Shi and the Kusu are based in the Kivu region. The
Lunda, the Chokwe, and the Luba are found in Shaba, and the two Kasais
are home for groups such as the Tio, the Lulua, the Tetela, and the Luba.
The Pende can be found in Bandundu; the Kinshasa and Bas Zaire
regions include the Chokwe, the Kongo, and the Lunda (see Map 3.1).

Although each ethnic group has traditionally had its own language,
over time certain dialects came to be spoken over a wider area beyond
the boundaries of a given community. This phenomenon can be attributed to the fluid nature of traditional Zairian society, coupled with the
tendency for missionaries, explorers, and ultimately the Belgians to give
preeminence to certain ethnic groups based on their reactions to "modernization" or their power and influence in a given region. The Kongo are
a case in point. With their long history as traders with Europeans and
their fairly advanced agricultural techniques, they were soon marketing
agricultural crops in the major urban centers in the Bas Zaire region
during the colonial period. As a result, their language, kikongo, began to
be spoken beyond the confines of the original kingdom.

Early Europeans also had limited understanding of the nature of
ethnicity. Heterogenous communities surrounding foreign outposts were
often erroneously categorized as being in the same ethnic group. Groups
were sometimes artificially created, as in the case of the Ngala, the name
the explorer Stanley ascribed to trading people living along the bank of
the Zaire River in Équateur. Although the Ngala in fact comprised several
different tribes, their language, lingala, soon came to be the language of
choice in areas all along the river. Further, the Ngala formed an important

MAP 3.1   Ethnographic map of the Republic of the Congo, 1960. *Source:* Crawford Young, *Politics in the Congo* (Princeton: Princeton University Press, 1965).
Copyright © 1965 by Princeton University Press. Map 4, p. 233, reprinted by permission of Princeton University Press.

part of the Force Publique under the Belgians, and as a result, lingala also
became the language of the army.

Ironically, this selectiveness and lack of understanding on the
part of the Europeans often created mistrust and antagonisms between
groups. Missionaries first fanned the flames of ethnic differences when
religious materials were translated into various tribal languages. These
efforts often resulted in the creation of an "official" language among
different tribes of a particular province. The Belgians unconsciously
entrenched ethnic stratification through the creation of territorial subdivisions (provinces); an accompanying strategy promoting inequality
with respect to social mobility for different cultural groups; and
the system of identity cards, which the Congolese were required to
carry, listing the individual's ethnic group. Even so, ethnicity was often

situational in the Congo. In confrontation with the Bula Matari state, Congolese were simply "African," and ethnic roles tended to be less important. In interethnic conflict, however, group affiliation became crucial.

Ethnicity was not encouraged by the Belgians because of the imperatives of political control. Nonetheless, with increasing urbanization during the colonial period, ethnically based organizations developed as support mechanisms vis-à-vis other ethnic groups. These institutions were tolerated as long as they presented no threat to public order. Ethnic polarization and mutual suspicion occurred with urbanization and the resulting competition for social, economic, and political status. Belgian positive and negative stereotypes of various cultural groups became embedded in the popular consciousness and further fostered divisions.[5] The Luba in Kasai, for example, had been viewed by the early European explorers as superior to other groups based on their willingness to adapt to new ideas. This positive image gave the Luba a high status in the colonial framework relative to other ethnic groups, as they soon occupied lower level administrative posts in many of the Congo's largest cities. Other groups viewed them with hostility, condemning what was viewed as aggressiveness and opportunism. It is therefore not surprising that both preindependence political mobilization and the Congo Crisis had important ethnic dimensions. Rivalries long held in check by the colonial administration were unleashed with the departure of the Belgians, and ethnicity became highly politicized.

Ethnic stereotypes still persist in Zaire. Mobutu's early efforts at unification were clearly in response to the ethnic fragmentation of the 1960–1965 period and were aimed at muting ethnic differentiation in favor of a national identity. In addition to promoting nationalism through a common ideology, initially termed "authenticity" and then "Mobutuism," the regime attempted to create common linguistic identification. French was made the official administrative language of the state, which chose to formally recognize only four of Zaire's many languages: kikongo, lingala, swahili, and tshiluba. Political parties and ethnic associations were made illegal. Finally, Mobutu attempted to remove regionalism and tribalism from the political arena through the transformation of provinces into purely administrative units and the assigning of territorial officials away from their regions of origin.

Although overt ethnic competition has been suppressed by the state, ethnicity is still a salient issue and has in fact been heightened. The majority of the population resides in rural areas where tradition and custom are still strong, though altered in varying degrees by colonialism, and primary allegiance is to the family and the group rather than the larger society. Given the fact that the state's control is weak in many areas, ethnic differences have gone unchecked. In the urban setting competition for socioeconomic status coupled with unequal access to economic opportunity has increased ethnic awareness, particularly for those groups who feel deprived.[6] In this sense, colonial ethnic antagonisms remain.

Mobutu initially made feeble attempts to maintain an ethnic balance within the state institutions, but this in itself further promoted ethnicity by reinforcing ethnic consciousness. This effort quickly gave way to ethnic "favoritism" with respect to his own region for state appointments. It is widely perceived with much resentment on the part of Zairians that the political elite under the Mobutu regime is composed almost exclusively of individuals from Équateur. In turn, these government officials discriminate with respect to their subordinates on the basis of ethnicity. Furthermore, army recruitment, particularly for the elite Presidential Guard, has focused on Équateur and excluded areas such as Bandundu and the Kasais. A March 1990 memorandum condemning the regime, sent to Mobutu from civil servants in the Ministry of Foreign Affairs, was highly critical of the high percentage of senior government and MPR officials who were either directly related to the president or from his region. It was noted that individuals from Équateur made up 19 percent of the Central Committee, 27 percent of the Executive Council, 46 percent of the officer corps in the army, and 34 percent of Zaire's diplomatic representatives.[7]

Often the regime's repressive measures against popular protest have an ethnic dimension. The massacre of students in Lubumbashi in June 1990 brought this home when individuals from Équateur were removed from the campus prior to the incident. Such policies have increased apathy toward the regime, particularly among certain groups in the south and east—Shaba and Kivu—interestingly enough, areas of rebellion in the 1960–1965 period.

Moves toward political liberalization, which began in April 1990, have fueled the desire for participation in government among ethnic groups that have traditionally been excluded from the political process. Within weeks after Mobutu's announcement of a multiparty system, a myriad of political parties sprang up, many formed on the basis of ethnic ties, rather reminiscent of the immediate preindependence period when parties grew out of existing ethnic associations. Furthermore, ethnic representation was a sensitive issue in the debate over the National Conference, whose mandate was to draft a new constitution and guide the transition to democracy.

THE POLITICS AND ECONOMICS OF CLASS FORMATION

Ethnic affiliations are also impacted by issues of class and social stratification. The seeds of class distinction in contemporary Zaire can be found in the social hierarchy of the Colonie Belge, in which the Congolese were denied social mobility as well as access to economic resources and political and administrative offices. A dual system existed—one was African, based on European interpretations of custom, and the other was European and Western. At the height of the colonial period, those who had been exposed to Western education and who qualified for low-level white-collar employment acquired a privileged status. Although these *évolués* were not permitted to accumulate wealth and power, their positions in society were subsequently passed on to their children.

Independence produced a different picture. Positions of power in the state were open to Africans, and *évolués* rushed to fill the higher-level government positions vacated by the departing Belgians. In the turbulent years of the First Republic, education was seen at first as the means to social mobility and wealth. But soon access to political office was viewed as the means to socioeconomic advancement. Once installed in the system, politicians sought to consolidate their position by gaining effective control of the state apparatus. The process has been heightened under the Mobutu regime, and a political elite with substantial privilege and wealth has become firmly entrenched in the authoritarian state. Political office gives license to appropriate the resources of the state and is the means to acquire business and commercial interests. Policies such as Zairianization, in which many foreign-owned businesses were appropriated by the state, helped to consolidate the position of this group.

In Mobutu's Zaire class formation is shaped by power relations, not by production relations.[8] Power is used by those at the top of the social hierarchy to deny opportunity to those below. The political elite itself is dependent on the state for privilege and wealth, and the focus is on extraction for personal profit rather than on investment in the productive resources of the state. Membership in this "class" is dependent on obeying the rules of the political game with respect to Mobutu's authority. Patron-client networks expand outward from the elite to the rest of society, and corruption feeds into this system. Outside this small group of individuals, access to education and economic opportunity are denied to most Zairians because of lack of resources for either fees or bribes. The dual societal structure of the colonial period is being perpetuated, except that the new political elite is African, unproductive, and primarily from Équateur. Zairians are fully aware of this irony, referring to Mobutu's clique as *les gros légumes* or *les barons du regime* (the big shots, in popular jargon). They are distinguished by their sumptuous lifestyle, including expensive houses and foreign cars (driven without license plates to indicate that they are above the law). Since the 1980s, as life has become increasingly difficult for the majority of Zairians, the *gros légumes* have been the focus of hostility. Such feelings peaked during the September 1991 riots that began in Kinshasa and quickly spread to other parts of the country. Zairian army officers and civilians alike systematically targeted and looted the businesses and houses belonging to the Zairian elite. More recently a small entrepreneurial class has been developing independently of the state—a by-product of a thriving second economy, itself a result of economic hard times. Individuals and businessmen have established commercial and productive ventures—often with the help of resources misappropriated from the state—that are outside state control.

As is the case in many parts of Africa, class in Zaire is a dynamic, fluid concept in which an individual has different class allegiances at the same time—oppressor in one context, oppressed in another.

RELIGION

Religion, both Western and indigenous, occupies pride of place in today's Zaire. The Catholic church and the various Protestant groups that make up L'église du Christ au Zaire together claim well over half of Zaire's population as active members.[9] About 40 percent of the population is Catholic, indicating the strength of the Catholic missionary presence in the colonial period.

Catholics and Protestants

Christian missionaries first came to the Congo as early as 1484, when Catholics accompanied Diogo Cão, the Portuguese explorer, on his expedition to the mouth of the Congo River. Subsequently, additional groups of missionaries traveled to the Congo where they successfully converted the Bakongo in the kingdom of the Kongo. After a period of decline, the late nineteenth century saw a resurgence of missionary activity when Protestants in the United States and Britain began to make incursions into the Congo. In January 1878 the Baptist Missionary Society landed at Banana at the mouth of the Congo River and soon established a mission at San Salvador (in present-day Angola). King Leopold encouraged the spread of both Protestant and Catholic missions in an effort to strengthen his claims to the area. By the end of the nineteenth century, in the face of Protestant protests against his atrocities in the Congo, he retaliated against this group, denying them land concessions and raising their taxes. At the same time, Catholic activities were encouraged, and by 1906 the Congo Free State had signed an agreement to subsidize Catholic mission schools and provide subsistence for missionaries. Besides religious teachings, the schools were to provide academic training on behalf of the state, which in turn would grant each mission generous land concessions for commercial activities.

After annexation the close relationship between the Catholic missions and the state continued. The Catholic missions were strong defenders of Belgian colonialism, and in a real sense, continued state support made them an integral part of the system. By contrast, the Protestant missionaries were seen as troublemakers and viewed with mistrust. As a result, Protestant missions were unable to make major inroads with respect to mass conversions and the education of the Congolese.

Missionary efforts in the Congo were quite extensive. By the late 1950s Catholics had 699 mission posts throughout the Congo supported by approximately 6,000 European missionaries and about 500 African priests, with over 26,000 catechists offering basic religious instruction in villages.[10] Indeed, prior to the 1950s and the start of serious attempts at higher education, involvement in the church and training for the priesthood were the primary avenue for Congolese advancement in colonial society. The creation of an African clergy sprang from these fledgling beginnings. In 1917 there was only one Congolese ordained priest, but by 1959 there were more than 600, as well as about 500 Protestant pastors. Efforts to Africanize the church continue. Until his death in 1989, Cardinal Malula, Zaire's first black cardinal, championed these measures, introducing African music and other elements of Zairian culture into Catholic mass.

With state encouragement in the colonial period, the Catholics were soon operating an extensive network of schools and health clinics in the rural areas and providing basic social services to the population. This state of affairs still existed at the beginning of the Second Republic in 1965. Even though Mobutu is himself Catholic, the pervasiveness of the Catholic church was soon seen as a threat to government mobilization efforts. From the perspective of the regime, Mobutuism would have to compete with Catholicism for the population's allegiance—hence the previously described restrictions imposed on the church.

With respect to foreign religion, most Zairians operate in two worlds. Although many have been baptized as Christian, precolonial traditional concepts of god and the world, as well as an individual's spiritual connection to the ancestors, are deeply held beliefs. The practice of witchcraft is still prevalent and actively practiced throughout society. It is thought to be the cause of misfortune and unexplained success or wealth. Often those who advance too quickly economically are taken to anti-sorcerers by force, arrested, or even killed. In times of trouble individuals resort to diviners, fetishers, or magicians even while they are practicing Christian rituals.[11]

Kimbanguism and Indigenous Religious Movements

Indigenous religious movements arose in Zaire during the colonial period as a response to the Congolese population's inability to change the course of events under Belgian rule. Such movements continue to flourish and multiply in Mobutu's Zaire, reinforcing the fact that they are a means of coping with the realities of an oppressive state. There are an estimated 700 syncretic movements operating locally that have not been officially sanctioned by the government.[12]

In contrast to religion brought to the Congo by missionaries, Kimbanguism is an indigenous movement created by self-proclaimed prophet and healer Simon Kimbangu in 1921. Kimbangu, a native of the Bas Zaire region, was originally a member of the British Baptist Mission Church in the village of Nkamba. After a vision called him to the ministry and he healed a child, he was quickly welcomed in the Bas Zaire region as a black prophet. Kimbanguism found many willing adherents among the Congolese because of the perceived failings of conventional Christianity, particularly in the areas of healing and warding off witchcraft.[13] The colonial authorities saw Kimbanguism as a threat to public order and stability in the area and thus moved quickly to suppress the movement, arresting Kimbangu and many of his followers and sentencing Kimbangu himself to death. The judgment was subsequently changed to life imprisonment after Protestant missionary appeals to Belgian King Albert. Simon Kimbangu remained in jail until his death in 1950. His sons subsequently founded the Église de Jésus-Christ sur Terre par le Prophète Simon Kimbangu (EJCSK) in the late 1950s based in the town of Nkamba, which they renamed "the New Jerusalem." The movement claims no less than 300,000 followers, largely in Bas Zaire, although estimates run as high as 3 million to 5 million. The leader of the church as of 1992 is Kimbangu's youngest son, Diangienda ku Ntima.

Kimbanguists have always consciously sought good relations with the Mobutu regime. Their efforts bore fruit when Mobutu announced in 1972 that the EJCSK would be one of the major religious movements recognized by the government of Zaire (GOZ) as part of its strategy to control the church in Zaire. Certainly in the political arena, the EJCSK stands in stark contrast to the Catholic church, which enjoyed the support of the state during the colonial period but has had strained relations with the Mobutu regime. Kimbanguism, forced to operate underground under Belgian rule, is viewed rather positively by the state.[14] Like the Protestant and Catholic churches, the EJCSK has become intimately involved in the socioeconomic development of Zaire, specifically in the areas of health and education.

Although there is a myriad of other indigenous religious groups operating in Zaire, the Kitawalists are an interesting case.[15] The group is an outgrowth of the Watch Tower Bible and Tract Society (Jehovah's Witnesses), whose teachings spread to the Shaba region in the early 1920s via migrant mine workers. There the movement gradually became known as Kitawala, a linguistic variant of the words "Watch Tower."

Watch Tower missionaries preached racial equality and an end to a colonial order in which blacks were oppressed. Not surprisingly, the movement quickly spread throughout the province, and colonial authorities attempted to repress the movement by confining converts to centers in remote rural areas. When such efforts were unsuccessful, the Watch Tower was banned throughout the Congo in 1949.

Kitawala became progressively decentralized and more radical with respect to the original Watch Tower teachings, denouncing all symbols of colonial authority such as forced labor. Nevertheless, Kitawala still maintained Watch Tower's fundamental belief in the existence of a black God, as well as its condemnation of witchcraft. In response to Kitawala's "radical" views, Watch Tower soon distanced itself from the movement. Kitawala survived Belgian colonialism and the First Republic, although its opposition to authority has brought it into conflict with the centralizing efforts of the Mobutu regime. In contrast to Watch Tower adherents, Kitawalists have largely resisted participation in the mainstream of Zairian life (not paying taxes or voting), although this behavior has been tempered by their particular circumstances. Nonetheless, both groups are still considered illegal by the Mobutu regime and have been victims of the GOZ's intermittent attempts to control religious organizations.[16]

EDUCATION

The education system in Zaire is in crisis, although it is still viewed by many as one of the avenues for social mobility. The Belgian colonial structure remains as the basis of the system: six years of primary school beginning at age six; three to six years of secondary education, including vocational and training programs; and four to six years of university training. Although the Belgians left a legacy of an extensive primary school system with high enrollment in 1960 (70 percent of the population of primary school age), dropout rates were high, and the majority of schools provided only the first two grade levels. There were significant variations in enrollment rates between regions, and many teachers were nationals with no teaching qualifications. As of 1980 enrollment ratios at the primary and secondary level compared favorably with Sub-Saharan Africa as a whole (see Table 3.2), but these figures mask persistent interregional differences, dropout rates at all levels, and administrative and financial problems. World Bank data from 1988 put primary enrollment at 76 percent, one of the highest rates in francophone Africa, but only 55 percent of the student population actually completes primary education. Of the school age population, 22 percent actually go on to secondary school, and only 13 percent complete the six-year cycle. Literacy rates

TABLE 3.2
School Enrollment Ratios, Zaire and Sub-Saharan
Africa, 1965-1988
(percentage of age group enrolled)

Category	Zaire			Sub-Saharan Africa		
	1965	1980	1988	1965	1980	1988
Primary school						
Male	95	114	84	52	87	n.a.
Female	45	82	65	30	67	n.a.
Total % enrollment	70	98	76	41	79	n.a.
Secondary school						
Male	8	51	32	6	21	n.a.
Female	2	19	14	2	10	n.a.
Total % enrollment	5	35	22	4	16	n.a.

Sources: World Bank, Sub-Saharan Africa: From Crisis to Sustainable Growth (Washington, D.C.: IBRD, 1989), table 32, pp. 274-275; UNDP, Human Development Report, 1990 (New York: Oxford University Press, 1990); World Bank, World Development Report, 1991, table 29, p. 260.

have increased since 1970, although there is still a considerable gap between males and females.[17]

The Belgian colonial administration's late commitment to education beyond the primary level, coupled with the monopoly that the Catholics and Protestants had over the Congolese education system until the 1950s, meant that seminaries and technical schools were the only avenues for higher education. Indeed, at independence in 1960 there were only 30 university graduates, compared with 1,000 priests and pastors and 400 specialists in medicine and agriculture.[18] The absence of a large competent technocratic cadre who could contribute to nation-building efforts was a structural weakness that would plague the Zairian state well into the Second Republic.

The advent of the Mobutu regime brought symbolic rhetoric about the need to bring education under government control, making it more accessible and responsive to the needs of Zairians. As is often true in developing countries, education was viewed by many in Zairian society as the primary means to social advancement, and there was optimism, at least in some circles, that meaningful changes would be made. As part of its reform efforts, the government introduced local language instruction at the primary level in the early 1970s in order to make education more relevant to rural life, although the colonial emphasis on literacy skills in the curriculum was maintained. Innovations did not occur at the university level, and student protests about the Belgian orientation of higher education in Zaire brought a swift response from the government. In 1971, when the authenticity campaign was under way, higher education was brought under state control with the nationalization of all three universities—Kinshasa, Kisangani, and Lubumbashi—to create one entity, the Université Nationale du Zaire.

As subsequent years would indicate, unification failed to facilitate reform of the system but served to increase political control over the student population and further politicize it. University administration, staff recruitment, and student admissions mirrored the weaknesses in postcolonial Zaire. A regional bias in favor of Équateur was soon reflected in hiring and admissions practices. Top university personnel formed part of the privileged elite loyal to the MPR and exploited their positions for private gain. Under these circumstances, there was no effort to modify the curriculum to cater to the critical need for graduates with professional and technical skills.[19] Throughout the years sporadic student protests against the regime and against economic conditions have resulted in frequent closings of the university campuses and the drafting of students into the army, which in turn have negatively impacted the process of learning. Education has thus been used by the regime as an instrument of political control.

The extensive involvement of the church in primary and secondary education continued well into the 1970s. Indeed, by 1973 85 percent of enrollment at the primary level and 60 percent at the secondary level were in schools controlled by religious organizations. As part of its effort to control the church, the government also nationalized primary and secondary education in 1974.[20] But by 1979 financial constraints and administrative inefficiency caused the GOZ to invite the churches to once again take charge of their former schools. Approximately 10 percent of all schools are public, and 5 percent are privately funded and controlled by major companies such as GECAMINES, the state mining conglomerate. The remaining schools are managed by religious entities subsidized by the government.

Problems in the education system abound. Although primary education is compulsory from ages six to twelve, many children cannot attend owing to lack of school facilities, the cost of education, and lack of transportation. Where schools exist, they are ill equipped and short staffed—a situation that permeates the secondary and higher education system as well. In increasingly difficult economic times, many parents, particularly in the rural areas, take their children from school to assist with mining, agricultural, and informal sector activities such as petty trading. The situation is particularly acute with respect to girls, who are taken from school at a very young age, if they are sent at all, because of the low priority given to the education of females and the expectation that they will be married and taken care of by husbands. The lack of attention to female education is a legacy from the colonial period. In 1960 fewer than 1,000 females were enrolled in secondary school, and none had graduated.[21]

Government expenditure on education at all levels has declined, particularly since the onset of the economic crisis in 1974. According to UN data, expenditure as a percentage of GNP declined from 2.4 percent in 1960 to 0.4 percent in 1986.[22] Salaries represent the bulk of expenditures; with government constraints, teachers are poorly and irregularly paid, often going without wages for five months or more. Strikes have therefore become common. In 1987 teachers' salaries averaged Z3,000 per month, equivalent to $50 at 1987 exchange rates. Protests over low salaries in 1989 and 1990 resulted in significant increases, bringing annual earnings of primary and secondary school teachers to $700 and $1,000, respectively. Nevertheless, salaries are unable to keep up with inflation, and as a result, many teachers seek employment elsewhere, take part-time jobs, or extort money from students to supplement their income. Lack of effective government control over the salary payment process (decentralized in 1981) has resulted in wastage and corrupt practices. At the same time, austerity measures have caused cutbacks, particularly in the rural areas, that have exacerbated classroom overcrowding. As many as 50 percent of primary schools have inadequate facilities, and there are critical shortages of books and other education materials even at the university level. Finally, the Ministry of Education has neither the financial resources nor the proper institutional framework to operate effectively. As a result, schools are unsupervised and have to fend for themselves.

Ironically, in the midst of all these problems, Zaire has a surplus of secondary and university graduates who are not able to find jobs. According to UN Educational, Scientific, and Cultural Organization (UNESCO) data, in 1985 there were approximately 2.1 million students registered at the secondary level, about 41,000 students in technical and vocational schools, and 16,239 enrolled at the university level.[23] The fact that students are ill equipped for the workplace is largely due to the high concentration of students in less difficult courses in the humanities as opposed to the sciences and the more technical fields. A solid education has increasingly become closed to the masses, who cannot afford the modest fees or the bribes to gain entrance into the better schools. And there is no true incentive for the elite to improve the quality of education, as their children are either sent to local private schools or educated in Europe or the United States.[24] Although external aid for the education sector has tended to favor university and technical training, attempts by external donors such as the World Bank and UNESCO to fund successful projects have floundered, largely because of a lack of government commitment to meaningful reform and the inability of the government to provide counterpart funds.

HEALTH CARE

Inequity and lack of quality in social welfare are also reflected in the area of nutrition and health. During the early 1970s, for example, 50 percent of the government's health allocation went to two facilities in Kinshasa, including the Mama Yemo hospital (named after Mobutu's first wife). In 1972 303 of 304 Zairian doctors and 40 percent of all doctors worked in Kinshasa.[25] A decade later, according to a 1983 USAID report, the Bas Zaire region around Kinshasa had the lowest doctor to population ratio in the entire country—1 doctor for every 35,000 people. This stands in stark contrast to the ratio for Kasai Occidental, for example, where there is 1 doctor for every 72,000 people.

The Belgians developed a fairly comprehensive health care system, although the best medical facilities were reserved for Europeans. The health system was heavily dependent on Belgian support and subsequently suffered from Belgian withdrawal and the upheavals following independence. By the early 1970s most health care was being provided by missionary groups, private voluntary organizations, and major multinationals operating in Zaire. Nevertheless, large segments of the population remained outside the system. In 1973 the GOZ issued a "Health Rights Manifesto" and established a National Health Council. But by 1975 Zaire had begun to experience serious economic problems, and the steady deterioration of the health sector continued. The shortage of foreign exchange, complicated by mismanagement, has closed down clinics because of lack of medicines and the absence of personnel. At the beginning of his new seven-year term in 1984, Mobutu announced that this period would be one of social progress (Septennat du Social), with particular emphasis on nutrition and health.

Despite this apparent interest, government initiatives have been negligible, and health issues still remain low on the government's agenda. The Ministry of Public Health has always been institutionally weak and underfunded. As a result, it cannot monitor public health effectively. In 1973–1974 the ministry accounted for a miniscule 0.12 percent of the government budget; by 1989 this figure had increased only to 1.6 percent.[26] According to estimates by foreign experts, government health spending in 1989 was less than $.15 annually per person.[27] Needless to say, this amount is totally inadequate to maintain existing facilities. As a result, more often than not hospital patients even in large city hospitals such as

Mama Yemo have to be provided with food, linens, and other essentials by their relatives.

Because of the lack of medical care, many people, particularly in the rural areas, have come to rely increasingly on unlicensed practitioners—traditional healers as well as individuals with some medical training practicing privately—although most people tend to seek treatment first from Western facilities. In 1977, as part of its return to "tradition," the government legitimized traditional medicine as a complement to Western techniques.[28]

A visit to Zaire in the early 1980s revealed that many health facilities in the rural areas had fallen into disrepair and were often closed. Most pharmaceutical products shipped to clinics in the interior never arrived at their destinations, having been diverted and sold on the black market. By 1990 shortage of medicine remained a serious problem. Indeed, in the aftermath of widespread urban looting in September 1991, pharmacists were appealing to the public to return drugs that had been stolen.

Diseases such as tuberculosis, malaria, sleeping sickness, and leprosy are common. Intestinal parasites affect as much as 70 percent of the population. The effects of poor health care seem to fall disproportionately on children under five years old. Representing almost 20 percent of the population, they account for about 80 percent of all deaths. Although infant mortality has been falling since the 1950s, it is still very high by Western standards (see Table 3.3). According to USAID data, the infant mortality rate in 1988 alone stood at 109.[29] Malnutrition is increasingly rampant in urban as well as rural areas and is a major cause of death among young children. In 1983 it was estimated that a third of the children in Kinshasa's main hospital, Mama Yemo, were suffering from acute protein malnutrition (kwashiorkor).[30] With high infant mortality rates, women tend to have more children, thereby perpetuating the cycle.

In addition to the list of curable diseases affecting the Zairian population, the health system has to cope with a far more serious threat—AIDS. Like many countries in Sub-Saharan Africa, Zaire is fighting a difficult battle against the disease. One of the highest concentrations of AIDS in Africa is found in a region encompassing southern Uganda, northwestern Tanzania, eastern Zaire, Rwanda, and Burundi.[31] The first cases of the disease were recognized in 1983; to its credit, Zaire was one of the first countries in Africa to report cases of AIDS and to appeal for international assistance. Since that time, Zaire has been a center for AIDS research, with local researchers working with Egyptian, French, and American colleagues. In contrast to prevailing patterns in industrialized countries, AIDS in Zaire is transmitted through heterosexual intercourse and infected blood transfusions. High levels of prostitution put not only

TABLE 3.3
Infant Mortality Rates, 1950-1990

Year	Average Infant Mortality Rate (under 1 year)	Number of Live Births per Woman (total fertility rate)[a]
1950-55	157	6.0
1955-60	151	6.0
1960-65	146	5.9
1965-70	137	6.0
1970-75	127	6.1
1975-80	117	6.1
1980-85	107	6.1
1985-90	98	6.1

[a] Average number of children that would be born alive to a woman during her lifetime if she passed through her child-bearing years conforming to the age-specific fertility rates of a given year.

Source: Center for International Health Information, Zaire: USAID Population and Health Profile, June 1990, p. 6.

this group of women at high risk but also their male clients, who carry the virus to their wives and girlfriends.

A particularly disturbing trend is the spread of the virus to off-spring of infected mothers. According to 1987 data on AIDS rates in Kinshasa, between 4 percent and 8 percent of the general population were HIV positive (that is, tested positive for the AIDS virus); 6–10 percent of pregnant women and as many as 30 percent of prostitutes tested positive. Females aged 15–29 are a major high-risk group. Although studies suggest that infection rates in Kinshasa appear to be leveling off, this trend does not diminish the economic and demographic impact of AIDS on the society as a whole. At the Fifth International AIDS Conference held in Kinshasa in October 1990, the direct cost of the disease was estimated at $200 to $300 per individual per year. If loss of production is also taken into account, these estimates are ten to fifteen times higher.[32] There are also genuine concerns that AIDS could in effect eliminate the cadre of educated, technically competent Zairians who should form the next generation of leadership. Obviously the implications for future economic development are serious.

The general health situation is all the more bleak in view of the steady decline in salaries vis-à-vis increasing consumer prices since the early 1970s. In this scenario, nonwage benefits such as medical care have become increasingly important to Zairian workers and are often the major justification for keeping a job. Access to health services is an even more appealing benefit in private sector employment. A survey of 43 firms in 1981 revealed that the base salary of unskilled workers accounted for only 40 percent of total compensation, with nonwage benefits such as health care, transportation, food, family allowance, and so forth, accounting for 60 percent.

Low salary levels also directly impact the medical profession itself. Young doctors are reluctant to take positions in government hospitals, particularly in the rural areas, where the pay is equivalent to $18 per month (at 1985 exchange rates). In the face of a steady decline in the value of the zaire throughout the 1980s, any nominal salary increases granted by the government have not resulted in pay increases in real terms. Furthermore, abysmal working conditions and a lack of equipment and supplies add to frustrations. In May 1990 doctors went on strike demanding higher salaries and improved working conditions, particularly the rehabilitation of hospitals that they called "death traps" due to lack of equipment, drugs, and qualified personnel. At that time the Mama Yemo hospital had been without a usable operating room for several months. Within four weeks the strike had resulted in over fifty recorded deaths in Kinshasa alone.[33] The situation remained bleak in 1992, when Mama Yemo and other state hospitals had to be closed and patients sent home in the face of a nonfunctioning local economy near collapse. Not surprisingly, doctors vie for the limited opportunities available in donor-supported health facilities, where salaries are about ten times those in government-owned centers and equipment as well as drugs are available. In addition, the quality of medical training has been declining steadily for the past decade. With the lack of government financial support, teaching conditions are poor due to a lack of equipment and a deterioration in training facilities. There are few prospects for change in the immediate future, as foreign aid targeted specifically to Zaire's three medical schools is minimal.

The donor community (Belgium, USAID, Italy, the UN Children's Fund [UNICEF], and the UN Fund for Population Activities) has attempted to make a positive impact on the Zairian health situation by supporting primary care. Donor support for primary health care began in 1970, often in close collaboration with private voluntary organizations (PVOs) and nongovernmental organizations working at a local level. Based on these pilot projects, the formulation of a government health care policy focusing on decentralization of primary care was begun. By 1981 the Department of Health had prepared the first five-year plan (1982–

1986) based on a national health zone network. The decentralization effort initiated in 1982 sought to establish a national network of 300 health zones, including 6,000 health centers by 1991. The idea was to attempt to standardize and coordinate health services in a given geographic area, ensuring the entire population in question access to primary care. Each health zone was to cover a population of 100,000–150,000 based on geographic and ethnic criteria and to consist of a reference hospital and fifteen to twenty-five health centers. Centers were to be staffed with at least one certified nurse and several nurses' aides responsible for basic medical care and preventative medicine. Medical officers were to be in charge of referral hospitals.

Financing for the health zone system has involved donor and GOZ assistance as well as user fees charged to target populations. External aid provided most of the start-up costs for individual centers as well as initial operating costs, and the government retained responsibility for personnel salaries. By 1986 about 150 health zones were operating in both rural and urban areas with the help of donors and NGOs (Catholic, Protestant, and Kimbanguist missions and the Red Cross). As part of the GOZ's proposed five-year Health Investment Plan (1987–1991), UNICEF agreed to assist with the establishment of primary health care in 184 additional health zones serving 18 million people, and USAID indicated that

Abandoned Red Cross headquarters building for the Lukaya subregion of Bas Zaire.

it would fund 100 zones covering 7 million people.[34] Although the health zone scheme is a good one, in reality the government has not been able to meet its financial obligations to health centers and government hospitals. Therefore, its role in the health area is shrinking and appears to be confined to administration and regulation through the Department of Health. But even here, there are major managerial and financial problems. Low salaries of civil servants in the department, shortage of operating funds, and lack of equipment compromise the government's ability to supervise health activities.

WOMEN AND SOCIAL CHANGE

As with many things in Zaire, there is a considerable gap between theory and practice in the status of women in Zairian society. Theoretically the regime is committed to improving the status of women and guaranteeing them equal rights. An Office for Women's Affairs was created in 1980 as part of the Political Bureau to monitor and enforce women's rights. Furthermore, at that time the only recognized trade union (the National Union of Zairian Workers) already had a Women's Bureau in place to protect women's rights and ensure better working conditions on the job. Yet in spite of all this, women are second-class citizens with generally poor access to proper health care and social welfare services. They are underrepresented in the state apparatus, and the legal system guarantees male control over their activities. Although a few token women have been appointed to civil service and political posts, the regime has clearly stated that women must "know their place" and that the man is head of the household. The apparent contradiction in the attitude toward women was evident in a speech given by Mobutu before the MPR Third Party Congress in 1982:

> This inclusion of women, we wish to achieve it at all levels. . . . We wish to ensure for the Zairian mother recognition of the rights that are conferred on her by her role as an equal partner to men. But it remains understood, of course, that there will always be one head in each household. And until proof to the contrary, the head, in our country, is he who wears the pants. Our women citizens also ought to understand this, to accept it with a smile and revolutionary submission.[35]

Generally fewer educational opportunities prevent women from being gainfully employed, but there is a small cadre of professional women in urban Zairian society—those fortunate to have received more than a postsecondary education. Most hold typically "feminine jobs" such as clerk and secretary. Indeed, only 4 percent of employees in the formal sector are women. For the most part, the notion of a woman holding a position of authority in the work force is still considered unacceptable and the disapproval is supported by law. According to the Civil Code, a married woman cannot run a business or accept employment without her husband's permission. The notion of woman as housewife and mother is deeply rooted in Zairian culture. A 1975 study of professional women in Lubumbashi found that most respondents felt that their most meaningful activity was having children and raising them. This attitude is encouraged by the regime that proclaimed 1975 the Year of the Mama rather than the Year of the Woman.[36] As a result, women are often caught in the conflict between traditional roles and any professional aspirations they might have. Other urban-based women either engage in petty trade or are *femmes libres* (prostitutes or mistresses). *Femmes libres* are independent with respect to men and manage their own resources; use of their sexuality can result in the accumulation of capital for informal trading or small-scale commercial ventures.

The bulk of Zairian women, however, are tied to the land. This condition dates back to the precolonial period, when the primary food producers were women, freeing the men to enter the colonial work force. Prior to that time, land ownership was vested in the chief, and the community as a whole had farming rights. With the advent of colonialism, the concept of private property and male ownership of land superseded this sense of community. In addition, the large-scale recruitment of men for work in the mines, coupled with male cultivation of export crops, shifted the responsibility for food crop cultivation to women. But although women continued to produce food crops for family consumption and trade in the local market, they came to occupy an inferior status in the family unit.

Little has changed. Women are the main food producers of subsistence agriculture, dominating the cultivation of cassava, the main Zairian staple. They can also be found on the plantations but in the lowest-paying jobs. For rural folk in general, plantations are the only source of wage employment to supplement meager incomes from market sales. Women also play a crucial role in food distribution, particularly in the urban areas where over 70 percent of the traders in the marketplace are female.

A contemporary study of eastern Kivu illustrates that peasant export crop production has reduced the land available to women for food crop production and as a result has increased male-female conflict. Although women make decisions about food crop production, decisions on land allocation are made by men, who have rights to land either through inheritance or various contractual arrangements.[37] Some rural women have a greater access to resources; however, many female peasants feel powerless to effect change and remain subordinate to the men of

Women carrying firewood into the town of Matadi.

their households. Men often claim rights to the income from food crops sold at the market. As a result, women often sell produce without their husbands' knowledge, using the proceeds to purchase essential consumer items. Rural women are becoming more vocal. Like their counterparts in the urban areas, women are being politicized, and they are no longer hesitant to protest and condemn the injustices and oppression of the socioeconomic system.

In another area, many women have benefited from the decline in the administrative capacity of the state and the phenomenal growth in informal economic activities that evade state control. Women are very active in this area, engaging in either petty trade, the importing of goods from neighboring countries, the smuggling of products from the interior, or the transporting of foodstuffs from the rural areas to the cities. Women are also directly involved in the parallel market in foreign currency (U.S. dollars, francs de la Coopération Financière en Afrique [CFA], and Belgian francs). Most informal money changers are women. These enterprises are frequently pursued quite independently of husbands or male relatives and are a crucial source of family income, frequently ensuring economic survival. As a result, household disputes over control of women's independent income are not uncommon. In some instances where more lucrative types of trade require political connections, state

Woman selling soap and other staples at a small stall in front of her house in Kinshasa.

bureaucrats facilitate their wives' business activities by arranging free transportation aboard military or civilian aircraft. For women without such contacts in the political system, protection money and bribes have to be paid to the security forces.

Women are denied access to financing for business ventures without their husbands' permission, so they rely on informal credit clubs—*likelemba* or *musiki*—organized among the women themselves. A number of women have accumulated significant wealth, which is often invested in productive ventures in the formal sector. They form part of an emerging capitalist class that is independent of the Zairian state and the political process. They can be distinguished from many wives of the political elite who merely own businesses on behalf of husbands to conceal the extent of their holdings.[38]

Women's accumulation of wealth in their own right through informal activities has the potential to transform male-female relationships and marriage. Some successful women traders refuse marriage or provoke divorce so that a husband or his relatives will have no access to their resources. In a few cases, women are becoming as important as men in supporting dependents. Female business activities take time away from child-rearing and other traditionally female activities, and this newfound female economic independence poses problems for the traditional male role in the context of marriage.[39]

LAW AS SOCIAL AND POLITICAL BATTLEGROUND

The Zairian legal system has its roots in the colonial experience, particularly in the period of indirect rule that essentially created a plural society regulated by two separate legal systems. The European population was governed according to Western statutory principles, whereas the Congolese population was guided by customary law. Customary law was allegedly based on tradition and precolonial experience but was in reality an artificial creation that represented the adaptation of custom to the political realities of colonialism. It also included new rules imposed by the administration in the name of custom.[40]

In the preindependence negotiations a constitutional system—the Loi Fondamentale—was drawn up for the new Congolese state. It was a blueprint for a parliamentary regime on the Belgian model, with both a prime minister and a president. This structure was duplicated at the provincial level with an assembly headed by a president and a *commissaire d'état* (state commissioner) appointed by the Congolese head of state. The constitution of the First Republic drawn up in 1964 was designed in a similar fashion. Both proved unworkable with their federalist orientation and separation of powers. When Mobutu seized power in 1965, he suspended existing legislative arrangements and ruled by decree until the new constitution of the Second Republic became law in 1967.[41]

This constitution, like many of its Western counterparts, outlined the broad principles for a liberal democracy, but it also gave sweeping powers to the president, which were further reinforced and enhanced by modifications made before it officially took effect. Although the constitution had provisions for a multiparty system, the N'Sele Manifesto issued by the MPR in 1967 firmly established the reality of a one-party state. Constitutional revisions in 1974 effectively merged the party and state structures. Subsequent amendments up to 1990 left the supreme power of the Central Committee and the president unchanged, except for a brief two-year period between 1978 and 1980 when the government undertook political liberalization as a prerequisite to continued external economic assistance in the debt crisis. Mobutu's control over the legislative process in Zaire has been pervasive, as he appoints all officials to public office, including the judiciary. The announcement outlining political democratization measures—the introduction of a multiparty system, with the accompanying loss of the MPR's privileged status, and the reintroduction of the post of prime minister—was made independently of the MPR's Central Committee. Although constitutional changes are being made to reflect the new republic, there are no indications that Mobutu has relinquished control over the legal process.

The upper reaches of the Zairian legal system are governed by Western principles of Roman law, whereas at the local level (zone and collectivity) many variations of customary law operate in addition to this European overlay. So far, these variations have defied attempts at central government control.[42] On the whole, local magistrates have been only partially integrated into the state's hierarchy, and as a result, they feel they can operate relatively independently of the system. This practice causes friction with territorial officials and, at higher levels, with the government itself.[43] In the early 1970s the commitment of the president of the Supreme Court, Lihau Ebua, to an independent judiciary brought him on a collision course with the regime. He was dismissed by Mobutu from the court as well as from the faculty of the National University law school in Kinshasa. Lihau is an important figure in the UDPS, the most popular political opposition group in Zaire.

The constitution guarantees personal liberty and freedom, but ironically the average Zairian's first encounter with the legal system begins with a violent arrest.[44] It is here that basic human rights are violated contrary to legal principles. Amnesty International and, more recently, the Lawyers Committee for Human Rights have detailed records of countless cases of arbitrary arrest and detention allegedly for political "crimes" against the Mobutu regime. Detainees are routinely denied access to legal counsel or a magistrate and frequently released without charge after a period of imprisonment ranging from one day to several months. It is here that corruption finds its way into the judicial process. As a result of low pay and economic scarcity, bribery manifests itself in the judicial system at all levels—prison guard, lawyer, prosecutor, judge—undermining the rule of law. More often than not, detentions are not acknowledged by authorities, and relatives often have to travel to several facilities, bribing prison guards for information. Individuals have no recourse in incidents involving the political elite. They are above the law.

In response to his critics and in an effort to enhance Zaire's human rights record in the international arena, Mobutu announced the creation of a Department of Citizens' Rights and Liberties (DCRL) in 1986. The DCRL has two distinctly separate mandates: to protect citizens' rights and to defend the government's human rights record in the international arena. To date, however, its record has been poor. Although it has the authority to reverse judicial decisions, it has been unable to resolve cases involving arbitrary arrest, detention, and physical mistreatment. The DCRL has no authority to prosecute offenders or even to investigate incidents without the cooperation of other government departments. Its status as a government department reduces its credibility and effectiveness in the eyes of Zairian citizens.

Although Zairians clearly have no recourse within the government with respect to legal rights, there are two human rights organizations in Zaire that focus on raising public awareness about human rights violations. The Voix des Sans Voix (Voice of the Voiceless), founded in 1983, and the Ligne des droits de l'homme (Zaire) (Zairian Human Rights League) systematically report incidents of human rights abuses by the security forces in their monthly bulletins. The ultimate goal is to educate Zairians about their rights.

In the final analysis, the oppressive, authoritarian aspects of the Mobutu regime and the preeminence of the political elite are supported by the legal system. Equality before the law on every level falls away before the capriciousness of court officials, who make arbitrary decisions based on their own economic imperatives. In this state of affairs, many individuals look to religion and culture for support in their efforts to cope.

MEDIA AND THE ARTS

The official media in Zaire are the primary link between the government and its citizens. Agence Zaire-Presse, the government news agency, and Voix de Zaire (Voice of Zaire), the government-supervised radio and television complex, defend and justify the actions of the regime, and therefore the distinction between information and propaganda is more fictional than real. From the perspective of these organizations, "Mobutu is the news,"[45] and his domestic and international maneuvers are defended and lauded. If issues such as corruption are addressed, the blame is attributed to the system rather than the regime.[46] The four major daily newspapers—*Elima* and *Salongo* in Kinshasa, *Mjumbe* in Lubumbashi, and *Boyoma* in Kisangani—have been equally "conservative." Things, however, are changing. With increasing economic hardship and pressures on the president for political reform, an independent press emerged in 1990, led by two prominent new newspapers—*La Semaine* and *UMOJA*— that are highly critical of the government and the quality of life in Zaire. As of 1991 Zaire had 104 newspapers officially recognized by the Ministry of Information and Press, 67 of which were being published in Kinshasa.

In addition to its propaganda function, the official press has always lauded Zaire's cultural achievements. The country has a rich heritage in the arts that is recognized worldwide. Regrettably, most traditional Zairian art is found in Europe and the United States rather than in Zaire itself. Western museums began building collections as early as the first decade of the twentieth century with the help of missionaries, explorers, trading companies, and agents of the Congo Free State. At that time, it was discovered that the various regions of Zaire each had unique art forms. The Mangbetu from northeastern Zaire, for example, became known for their ivory and wooden carvings, ceramics, and musical instruments featuring human figures with a distinctive elongated head and a fanlike coiffure.[47] By the 1940s artistic traditions of many ethnic groups were being virtually eliminated, and actual production either was on the decline or had ceased. This situation was due partly to plunder but also to colonial and missionary policies operating at the local level within the Belgian administrative framework. Colonial territorial reorganization and the ensuing manipulation of social customs by both state officials and missionaries had a negative impact on the arts. Many artworks were intimately linked with certain societal rituals—circumcision, harvesting, burial practices—that were discouraged or outlawed as subversive by state agents. Although traditional art declined, new forms emerged that incorporated the native's experience with the Bula Matari state by using colonial and Christian themes.[48]

Contemporary art is the most developed aspect of Zairian culture, with the exception of contemporary Zairian music (*soukous*). There is an art institute in Kinshasa, the Institute des Beaux Arts, with art students in residence. Paintings are usually in oil on flour sacks as the canvas, but art pieces are also done in copper and wood, ivory and malachite. Artists are supported in principle by stipends from the government that supplement sales made to the public. There is also a makeshift market in the capital where young artists sell their work. However, they are often harassed by the security forces there.

Tshibumba Kanda-Matula, one of the most well-known urban artists, portrays many themes common in popular painting: traditional life (village chief, hunting), the Congo's past (the slave trade, the Colonie Belge, rebellion, independence), and Zaire today (market scenes, scenery, portraits). On the whole, responsibility for art and culture has shifted between various government departments. A new Ministry of Information, Arts and Culture was created in the transitional government announced in May 1990. In the previous government reshuffle in January of that year, responsibility for culture had been assigned to the deputy prime minister in charge of the Department of Citizens' Rights and Liberties, probably indicating the low priority accorded this vital area.

Zaire's National Dance Theatre is also well known worldwide, having toured the Soviet Union and France in 1980 and the United States in 1981 and 1990. The Dance Theatre's objective is to promote Zaire's musical and dance heritage and to expose Zairians to their own tradi-

Pende dancer at the annual Gunga Festival (a celebration of Pende culture) held in Bandundu every spring. Photo courtesy of Learned Dees.

tions in a new format. The troupe's various productions set Zairian folktales and legends to music, dance, and drama, often utilizing mime and songs in various local languages. The themes highlighted in each production draw on traditional religion and cosmology, which still have much relevance in Zaire. A well-known major work of the company is *Nkenge*, which was performed in the United States in 1981. Nkenge, the central character of a folktale known in much of Zaire, is a *belle de village* (village beauty) who wants to marry a wealthy suitor. Rejecting the poor, simple men in her village, she marries a prosperous outsider despite the warnings of her younger brother, known as the village idiot. As Nkenge and her husband are returning to his village, he is met by friends who retrieve the clothing they have lent him. His identity is revealed, and Nkenge finds herself in the devil's cemetery, her husband's true home, and other demons join in to terrorize her in a strange, frightening ceremony. After narrowly escaping death, she is rescued by her brother, who has followed them, and returned to her village. Nkenge is rejected by everyone; finally the village elders intervene to purify her of the evil spirit, and she prays for forgiveness and acceptance once again as part of their world.

Zaire has no tradition in film, but in the late 1980s a production made entirely in Zaire, *La Vie Est Belle* (Life Is Great), had a limited distribution in New York. The film succinctly captures contemporary Zairian life using the common theme of a love triangle. Papa Wemba, a renowned Zairian singer, plays an aspiring young singer who falls in love with a young woman who has been taken as the *deuxième bureau* (second "wife") of a prominent Zairian businessman. In the film Papa Wemba composes and sings the title song, "La Vie Est Belle."

Soukous (from *"secouer,"* to shake)—Zairian music—is rich and vibrant and is thriving even as economic hardship prevails. It is largely an outgrowth of the urban centers, with most lyrics in lingala. This "good-time" music has its roots in the 1940s and 1950s, when increasing migration to the urban centers resulted in the intertwining of traditional and modern music forms. Traveling musicians created these new Zairian rhythms using acoustic guitars, which were gaining popularity in Africa at that time. Zaire and the Republic of the Congo (Congo-Brazzaville) came to share common musical forms. As Kinshasa and Brazzaville are separated by a mere fifteen-minute boat ride across the Zaire River, musicians moved freely between the two capitals; and as records were cheaper in Brazzaville, they were smuggled constantly into Zaire. Influenced by rhythms from Europe, the United States, and most importantly, Cuba (the rhumba), Zairian music came into its own in the late 1950s and early 1960s when major bands were formed and several recording studios were established by foreign businessmen. Franco (François Luambo Makiadi), known as the king of Zairian music and *le grand sorcier* (grand sorcerer) of the guitar before his death in 1989, formed his first band, O.K. Jazz (Orchestre Kinois de Jazz), in 1956. Within a few years the band had grown from nine members to thirty-seven and had gained the title of T.P.O.K. Jazz (Tout Puissant [All Powerful] O.K. Jazz), indicating its widespread popularity. By 1970 three groups dominated the local music scene—O.K. Jazz, Docteur Nico (Nicolas Kasanda) and his l'Orchestre African Fiesta, and l'Orchestre African Fiesta National of Tabu Ley Rochereau, known among Zairians as "Le Seigneur" (the Lord).

Soukous became popular internationally when many musicians were forced to move abroad in the late 1970s because of economic decline in Zaire. Many of the leading artists such as Wemba and Abeti Masiniki, the first female *soukous* star, were drawn to Paris because of recording opportunities and continue to reside there. Zairian artists such as Rochereau and his former protegée, M'bilia Bel, relative newcomer Kanda Bongo Man, and several youth bands founded in the 1970s such as Zaiko Langa Langa have loyal fans in the United States, Europe, and the rest of Africa. Their musical themes focus on love and individual misfortune, but many are overtly more political. In the heyday of Mobutuism, the glorification of Le Guide was a recurring subject, but lyrics now focus on exploitation by agents of the state, the decadence and moral decline of the political elite, and overt criticism of the regime.[49]

This overview illustrates how Zairian society interacts and copes with the state. Over time, state-society relations are most poignant in the economic arena, particularly in times of economic crisis, when declining state capacity results in the development of various coping mechanisms by individuals to provide life's necessities. Zaire brings such a state of affairs sharply into view.

NOTES

1. World Bank, *Population Report, 1989,* pp. 80–81. Data on the birth rate and infant mortality rates are estimates for 1986–1990 from the National Institute of Statistics, Kinshasa, Zaire. Ibid.

2. World Bank, *World Tables, 1991* (Baltimore: Johns Hopkins University Press, 1991), p. 631; World Bank, *Poverty Report, 1990,* pp. iii, 9.

3. World Bank, *Poverty Report,* p. 9.

4. World Bank, *Population Report, 1989,* pp. 32–33, 52–53.

5. On this point see Crawford Young, "Patterns of Social Conflict: State, Class and Ethnicity," *Daedalus* 3, no. 2 (Spring 1982), pp. 79–80. Such perceptions persist to the present day. By way of example, the Luba are still said to be aggressive and opportunistic, based on their positive relationship with Belgian officials of the Belgian colonial state.

6. Michael Schatzberg, *Politics and Class in Zaire: Bureaucracy, Business and Beer in Lisala* (New York: Africana, 1980), pp. 175–209.

7. Lawyers Committee for Human Rights, *Zaire: Repression as Policy—A Human Rights Report,* New York, August 1990, p. 25.

8. For the argument see Richard Sklar, "The Nature of Class Domination in Africa," *Journal of Modern African Studies* 17, no. 4 (December 1979), pp. 531–552.

9. At the turn of the century, attempts were made to stimulate cooperation and contact between the various Protestant churches operating in the Congo. This effort culminated in the formation in 1934 of the Église du Christ au Congo (Church of Christ in the Congo), which became the Église du Christ au Zaire at the time of Mobutu's authenticity campaign in 1971. By 1982 ECZ had eighty-two member churches. See F. Scott Bobb, *Historical Dictionary of Zaire,* African Histor-

ical Dictionaries, no. 43 (Metuchen, N.J.: Scarecrow Press, 1988), p. 77. The head of the ECZ in Zaire in 1991, Bishop Itofo Bokeleale, is said to be a staunch supporter of Mobutu, although Protestant churches as a whole have been rather apolitical with respect to the actions of the regime.

10. Crawford Young, *Politics in the Congo: Decolonization and Independence* (Princeton: Princeton University Press, 1965), pp. 12–13.

11. Thomas Callaghy, *Politics and Culture in Zaire*, monograph in Politics and Culture series (Ann Arbor: University of Michigan, Center for Political Studies, Institute for Social Research, 1987), pp. 16–20; Wyatt MacGaffey, *Religion and Society in Central Africa* (Chicago: University of Chicago Press, 1986), p. 248; Mukohya Vwakyanakazi, "Small Urban Centers and Social Change in South-Eastern Zaire," *African Studies Review* 31, no. 3 (December 1988), p. 91.

12. Kuzumba K. Tshiteya, "Le discours savant et le développement du sous-développement au Zaire," *Canadian Journal of African Studies* 18 (1984), p. 59.

13. MacGaffey, *Religion and Society*, p. 215.

14. Michael Schatzberg, *The Dialectics of Oppression in Zaire* (Bloomington: Indiana University Press, 1988), p. 124.

15. Schatzberg, *Dialectics of Oppression*, pp. 125–130.

16. After the government's initial announcement in 1972 recognizing only the Catholic, Protestant, and Kimbanguist churches, a 1979 ordinance required other religious groups to register with the state as nonprofit organizations. Registration was permitted only in cases in which a group's teachings differed substantially from the officially recognized churches. In 1986 the GOZ officially dissolved the Jehovah's Witnesses in Zaire and in July 1989 ordered the 400 sects not recognized by the government to end their activities. District heads, assisted by court inspectors, specialized branches of the MPR, and officials of the Metropolitan Division of the Judicial Council were responsible for enforcing the measure. It is fair to assume that this new policy will have minimal impact, as a similar pronouncement in 1988 failed. *FBIS Daily Report: Sub-Saharan Africa*, June 27, 1989, p. 22.

17. According to 1985 data, male literacy rates registered 79 percent as compared to 45 percent for females. In 1970 61 percent of males compared to 22 percent of females were literate. World Bank, *Poverty Report, 1990*, p. 30.

18. Eyamba G. Bokamba, "Education and Development in Zaire," in *The Crisis in Zaire: Myths and Realities*, ed. Nzongola-Ntalaja (Trenton: Africa World Press, 1986), pp. 193–194.

19. Galen Hull, "Education in Zaire: Instrument of Underdevelopment," in *Zaire: The Political Economy of Underdevelopment*, ed. Guy Gran (New York: Praeger, 1979), pp. 149–154.

20. Ibid., p. 142.

21. World Bank, *Zaire Report*, 1982, p. 87; United Nations, Economic Commission for Africa, "Le Droit et la Condition de la Femme au Zaire," Addis Ababa, 1985, pp. 29–30; Hull, "Education in Zaire," p. 142.

22. UN Development Programme, *Human Development Report, 1990*, table 14, p. 154.

23. UNESCO, *Statistical Yearbook, 1987*, p. 237.

24. According to one source, the Collège du Leman, an exclusive boarding school on the outskirts of Geneva, Switzerland, has educated the children of many

wealthy Zairians. It is said that Mobutu has spent as much as $3 million on tuition and fees for his own children. *Africa Confidential,* October 11, 1991, p. 4.

25. Crawford Young and Thomas Turner, *The Rise and Decline of the Zairian State* (Madison: University of Wisconsin Press, 1985), p. 82.

26. World Bank, *Zaire: Current Economic Situation and Constraints* (Washington, D.C.: World Bank, 1979), p. 24; *Banque du Zaire Report, 1989,* table 58, Kinshasa, 1990.

27. *FBIS Daily Report: Sub-Saharan Africa,* June 13, 1990, p. 8.

28. Brooke Grundfest Schoepf, "Primary Health Care in Zaire," briefing in *Africa: The Health Issue,* Review of African Political Economy, no. 36, p. 56; Rashim Ahluwalia and Bernard Mechlin, eds., *Traditional Medicine in Zaire: Present and Potential Contributions to the Health Services* (Ottawa, Ont.: International Development Research Centre, 1980), p. 9.

29. USAID, *Congressional Presentation, Fiscal Year 1990,* Annex 1, Africa, p. 413.

30. Winsome J. Leslie, *The World Bank and Structural Transformation in Developing Countries: The Case of Zaire* (Boulder: Lynne Rienner, 1987), p. 68.

31. *New York Times,* September 16, 1990, p. 15.

32. World Bank, *Health Report,* p. 24; EIU, *Country Report: Zaire,* no. 4, 1990, p. 18.

33. *FBIS Daily Report: Sub-Saharan Africa,* May 28, 1990, p. 2; ibid., June 13, 1990, p. 8.

34. United Nations Children's Fund, Staff Working Paper no. 2, "Community Financing Experience for Local Health Services in Africa," ed. Pierre-E. Mandl and Samuel Ofoso-Amaah (New York: UNICEF, November 1988), p. 11.

35. R. Beeckmans, "Afrique-Actualités: Décembre 1982," *Zaire-Afrique* 172, pp. 117–120. Quoted and translated in M. Catherine Newbury, "Ebutumwa Bw'Emiogo: The Tyranny of Cassava—A Women's Tax Revolt in Eastern Zaire," *Canadian Journal of African Studies* 18, no. 1 (1984), p. 53.

36. Terri F. Gould, "Value Conflict and Development: The Struggle of the Professional Zairian Woman," *Journal of Modern African Studies* 16, no. 1 (March 1978); Brooke Grundfest Schoepf and Walu Engundu, "Women's Trade and Contributions to Household Budgets in Kinshasa," in *The Real Economy of Zaire: The Contribution of Smuggling and Other Unofficial Activities to National Wealth,* ed. Janet MacGaffey et al. (Philadelphia: University of Pennsylvania Press, 1991), p. 149.

37. Brooke Grundfest Schoepf and Claude Schoepf, "Land, Gender and Food Security in Eastern Kivu, Zaire," in *Agriculture, Women and Land: The African Experience,* ed. Jean Davison (Boulder: Westview Press, 1988), p. 118.

38. MacGaffey, "Evading Male Control: Women in the Second Economy in Zaire," in *Patriarchy and Class: African Women in the Home and Workforce,* ed. Jane Parpart and Sharon Strichter (Boulder: Westview Press, 1987), pp. 9–11; Schoepf and Engundu, "Women's Trade," pp. 131–132, 134, 137, 145–148.

39. MacGaffey, "Evading Male Control," pp. 13–15; Schoepf and Engundu, "Women's Trade," p. 148.

40. Wyatt MacGaffey, *Modern Kongo Prophets: Religion in a Plural Society* (Bloomington: Indiana University Press, 1983), p. 85.

41. Lawyers Committee for Human Rights, "Zaire: Repression as Policy," pp. 31–32.

42. See Callaghy, *The State-Society Struggle: Zaire in Comparative Perspective* (New York: Columbia University Press, 1984), pp. 362–368, for details about the local courts.

43. Schatzberg, *Dialectics of Oppression*, p. 102.

44. Presentation by Father Michael Perry, O.F.M.—Catholic priest working in Zaire—at conference on Prospects for Democracy in Zaire, Howard University, Washington, D.C., November 16, 1990.

45. V. S. Naipaul, "A New King for the Congo," in *The Return of Eva Peron* (New York: Vintage Books, 1981), p. 218.

46. David Ettinger, "Media-Government Relations in Zaire: A Case Study in Comparative Perspective," Ph.D. diss., Columbia University, 1986.

47. Notes from "African Reflections: Art from Northeastern Zaire," exhibit at the American Museum of Natural History, New York, June 8, 1990–January 6, 1991.

48. Daniel Biebuyck, *The Arts of Zaire*, vol. 1, *Southwestern Zaire* (Berkeley: University of California Press, 1985), p. 12.

49. This section draws on the following sources: Gary Steward, "Soukous—Birth of the Beat," *Beat* 8, no. 6 (1989), p. 18; Billy Bergman, *Goodtime Kings—Emerging African Pop* (New York: Quill, 1985), chap. 3; Gary Stewart, *Breakout—Profiles in African Rhythm* (Chicago: University of Chicago Press, 1992), chaps. 1, 2.

4

Economics, Politics, and Interdependence

Like many countries in Sub-Saharan Africa, Zaire has yet to resolve its economic problems. The country's overdependence on mineral exports for foreign exchange and the predominance of plantation agriculture, which were established with the arrival of the Belgians, are structural weaknesses that remain unchanged. This vulnerability to world market prices has been complicated by rapidly escalating debt, corruption, and generally poor economic decisionmaking.

THE COLONIAL ECONOMY: EXPLOITATION AND THE ESTABLISHMENT OF EXTERNAL LINKAGES

In economic terms the Belgian colonial state was highly extractive. By the beginning of the twentieth century, Belgian financial groups were receiving overly generous incentives to develop Zaire's mineral resources. Moreover, the development of infrastructure went hand in hand with this process. In 1902 the Groupe Empain agreed to establish a railway—the Chemin de Fer du Congo Supérieur aux Grands Lacs (CFL)—in the eastern part of the country. In return, the company secured 4 million hectares of land and extensive mineral rights. Four years later the financial conglomerate Société Générale de Belgique launched three major undertakings: the Union Minière du Haut-Katanga (UMHK), the Société Internationale Forestière et Minière (Forminière), and the Compagnie du Chemin de Fer du Bas-Congo au Katanga (BCK). UMHK was granted mineral rights in south Katanga, the site of extensive copper deposits, and Forminière received a ninety-nine-year monopoly on any mineral deposits it could identify within a six-year period in an area of 140 million hectares, equivalent to half the size of the colony. BCK obtained mineral rights to 21 million hectares in the area in the Kasai Basin crossed by its prospective rail line. The Belgian state agreed to provide all the capital for the construction of the railway, and BCK was responsible for its actual construction and operation.[1]

Copper exports from Katanga began as soon as the BCK railway reached Elisabethville, and by 1923 the Congo had become the world's third largest producer of copper. Indeed, copper exports from Katanga alone represented half of the total exports from the Congo. At the same time, agricultural production of oil palm, cotton, and coffee for the export market had also become well established. Growth was enhanced by the rapidly expanding road and rail network and the use of forced peasant cultivation introduced during World War I to serve the war effort.[2] During this period the large Belgian financial groups became firmly established in the Congo. By 1928, for example, Société Générale controlled 70 percent of the local economy, a level of involvement comparable to that of the Oppenheimer Group in South Africa.[3]

A rail-river link—the Voie Nationale—between the port of Matadi, Leopoldville, and Katanga was completed by the 1920s, constituting the first major step in the integration of Katanga with the rest of the country. The province had considerable autonomy because of a particularly strong provincial government, and it had established close links with Rhodesia and South Africa because of Union Minière's recruitment of workers in these areas for the copper mines. Railways brought new settlers and economic development to their sites. At the same time, the spread of a transportation network went hand in hand with the government's program of social services throughout the country. Besides education and health, towns were given basic amenities—water and electricity— and communications between the Congo and the outside world became fairly sophisticated, including a telephone link with Brussels. All in all, the Congo could well have been the best-equipped colony in Africa.[4] During this early period all the prerequisites were put in place for extensive exploitation of local resources and indigenous labor.

The precipitous fall in the prices of primary products on the world market during the Great Depression drastically reduced the colony's foreign exchange. Furthermore, copper production fell dramatically from 139,000 tons in 1930 to 54,000 tons in 1932.[5] With decreased levels of investment coming in from Belgium, forced cultivation was extended to food crops to support the mining and industrial sectors. Congolese were legally restricted to production of raw materials, whereas processing and marketing could be undertaken only by the foreign companies.The native population was confined by the state to shifting cultivation (working a plot of land until the soil was depleted, then moving to another plot) and temporary wage labor. Such policies were not implemented without local resistance. A serious revolt by the Pende in the western Congo, for example, resulted in over 500 deaths and the imprisonment of local chiefs following the repressive intervention of the Force Publique.

By the early 1950s the Congo was second only to South Africa in terms of industrial development. In 1953 it was Africa's leading producer of cobalt, diamonds, tin, zinc, and silver, as well as the second largest producer of copper after Northern Rhodesia (now Zambia). Nevertheless, economic development masked the ill effects of the colony's incorporation as a producer of primary products for the global market. The economy had a dual nature—an industrial sector heavily dependent on imported capital equipment and foreign expertise and a rural sector based on subsistence and plantation agriculture. The native Congolese had been marginalized economically, while the small European population (1 percent of the total) held 95 percent of the capital assets and accounted for 50 percent of the national income. Finally, the economic resources of the state, including land, were overwhelmingly in the hands of the giant corporations operating locally. The financial fortunes of the colonial government were tied to the mining sector. Union Minière alone provided the government with 70 percent of its foreign exchange needs and 50 percent of its budget revenue.[6] The cumulative effect of these trends was a system that soon began to show signs of strain. The consequences of the massive expansion in social welfare services began to be felt as public debt quickly accelerated, investments from Belgium slowed dramatically, and capital flight began in anticipation of Congolese independence.

INDEPENDENCE AND ECONOMIC DISRUPTION: 1960–1966

The chaos and uncertainty of the immediate postindependence period had a serious effect on the economy, even though disintegration was not a general phenomenon. Local governments continued to operate in Leopoldville, Équateur, and Oriental, but secessions and political instability destroyed the infrastructure in many areas, such as Katanga and Sud Kasai. As a result, plantation agriculture in some instances was interrupted, making it impossible to transport products from the interior to the urban centers. Further, many Europeans in the agricultural sector hastily left the Congo at this time, and their departure—together with the dismantling of forced cultivation—also had a negative impact on production. Overall production of major export crops fell between 10 percent and 40 percent a year between 1960 and 1965. Cotton, the only export crop produced solely by peasant farmers, registered a dramatic 89 percent fall during those years (see Table 4.1).

More specifically, the Katanga secession adversely affected the eco-

TABLE 4.1
Mineral and Agricultural Production, 1960-1990
(per 1,000 metric tons unless indicated)

Category	1960	1961	1962	1963	1965	1970	1975	1980	1985	1989	1990[a]
Copper	302.3	295.2	296.9	270.0	287.6	387.1	495.9	459.4	502.1	460.0	320.0
Cobalt	8.2	8.3	9.7	7.3	8.4	13.9	13.6	14.5	10.7	9.3	4.5
Diamonds (mil. carats)	13.4	18.0	14.7	15.2	--	14.0	12.8	10.2	19.9	17.6	16.0
Gold (1,00 kg.)	11.0	1.5	7.3	7.0	--	5.6	3.2	1.3	3.2	1.4[b]	--
Zinc	190.0	185.0	167.0	170.0	180.9	185.1	141.5	122.8	64.0	54.0	38.2
Crude oil (mil. barrels)	--	--	--	--	--	--	25.5	6.8	12.2	9.9	10.9
Coffee	58.6	34.2	30.5	34.4	19.0	67.5	59.4	80.2	86.0	101[c]	--
Oil palm	168.9	153.8	153.6	138.5	--	170.5	145.0	93.1	87.3	95[c]	--
Cotton	42.4	10.8	10.9	8.5	4.5	17.1	16.3	9.7	7.4	4[c]	--
Contribution to GDP[d]											
Commercial Agriculture	--	--	--	--	--	79.0	84.1	82.9	93.5	106[c]	--
Mining	--	--	--	--	--	211.2	242.0	220.4	260.9	250[c]	--

[a] Provisional
[b] January-June
[c] 1988 figures
[d] Value added in zaires mil. constant 1970 prices.

Sources: Robert Cornevin, Histoire du Congo: Leopoldville-Kinshasa (Paris: Editions Berger-Levrault, 1966), pp. 303-304; Banque du Zaire, Rapport Annuel, 1975, 1980, 1986 (tables 5, 25, 26); Economist Intelligence Unit (EIU) Country Report Zaire, no. 4 (1990), p. 22; EIU Country Profile, 1991-1992, pp. 20, 23; Crawford Young, Politics in the Congo (Princeton: Princeton University Press, 1965), pp. 356-357.

nomic fortunes of the central government in Leopoldville. During the two and one-half years of Katanga's independence, the central government was cut off from its principal source of revenue in the mining area. Government revenues fell from 5,542 million congolese francs in 1958 to 2,730 million congolese francs in 1961. Expenditures grew from 6,726 million congolese francs to 13,266 million in the same period.[7] Government revenues also fell as a result of the decline in agricultural production and difficulties in collecting taxes because of regional instability. Declining revenues without a corresponding reduction in government expenditures resulted in high prices and inflation, a thriving black market, and illegal exports. Most of the diamond production of Kasai was illegally exported. Forminière, the diamond mining company, had to terminate operations at Tshikapa in Kasai owing to ethnic conflict and difficulties in monitoring the mines. By 1961 diamond smuggling had become so profitable that Congo-Brazzaville established a diamond-purchasing office, and Belgium became its largest client. Smuggling also flourished in the eastern part of the country, especially in areas under the control of the Stanleyville regime, which had established a rival central government in 1960. Agricultural products, particularly coffee, were sold illegally in the face of favorable black market exchange rates for the congolese franc.[8]

The mining facilities themselves in Katanga were virtually untouched by the disturbances. In 1960 Union Minière's copper output was a record total of 302,300 metric tons, and in subsequent years output fell only slightly to a low of 270,000 tons in 1963 (refer to Table 4.1). Mineral production remained intact as expatriate personnel in the mining sector remained in place, in contrast to other areas of the economy. In addition, companies such as Union Minière continued to receive technical assistance and financing from abroad to maintain operations. Moreover, political instability and a weak central government led to an increase in the relative power and autonomy of these large companies, which were protected by the Belgian government.

STABILITY AND GROWTH: 1967–1974

In an attempt to reestablish economic stability, the government of Zaire reluctantly concluded an agreement with the IMF in 1967. The program was supported by a one-year standby arrangement for $27 million; the primary goal was the establishment of monetary stability and resumption of economic growth. At the IMF's insistence a new monetary unit, the zaire, was introduced at a new exchange rate that masked an effective 300 percent devaluation of the currency. At the same time, the government agreed to stringent fiscal, wage, and credit policies.[9] With a favorable world market for copper, no drawings had to be made under the standby arrangement. Nevertheless, as later years revealed, this early involvement with the IMF initiated a worrisome trend that continued into the 1990s.

Almost a decade after independence, the economic resources of the state remained exclusively in foreign hands. As part of Mobutu's policy of authentic Zairian nationalism, the government embarked on what it claimed was a quest for economic sovereignty and economic development. Consequently, the GOZ began to reevaluate the status of the large conglomerates such as Union Minière with a view to transferring their resources to local and state control. With respect to economic development, the government had visions of a powerful Zairian state that would be a leading regional economic force in Africa. Achievement of this goal would necessitate centralized government control in directing a major industrialization thrust as well as in further development of the mining sector, all with the assistance of foreign capital.

Accordingly, the GOZ undertook several ambitious and ultimately disastrous development projects during the early 1970s, all financed by external borrowing. German and Italian contractors began construction on a steel mill at Maluku in Bas Zaire to process iron ore from rich deposits in Haut Zaire and Kasai. Because of a very favorable feasibility study conducted by an Italian consulting firm in the late 1960s, President Mobutu had become personally committed to the scheme, even though in strictly economic terms the local market seemed too small to justify the investment. In spite of investor skepticism, the government decided to proceed, bearing the entire cost of the $250 million project. Although the steel plant was proclaimed a major achievement by the regime, it turned out to be a white elephant. Production costs had been seriously underestimated. In addition, the facility could not process Zairian ore because of inappropriate equipment and therefore had to depend exclusively on imported scrap. As a result, it never operated at more than 10 percent capacity, and by 1980 the plant had closed.[10]

Expenditures on other "prestigious" projects were designed to project Zaire's image and stature to the world. All these schemes were funded with external aid, based on optimistic assessments of future foreign exchange earnings. The French provided financing for an elaborate radio and television complex in Kinshasa, as well as $85 million in 1975 for a domestic satellite for the facility. French assistance also helped build an international trade center (Centre Commercial International Zairois [CCIZ; Zairian International Trade Center]) in the capital, designed to mimic the World Trade Center complex in New York. Mobutu's favorable impressions on a visit to China in the early 1970s resulted in the construction, with Chinese funding, of a $34 million Palais du Peuple (People's Palace) for cultural events. Air Zaire ordered new aircraft totaling $125 million, and West Germany provided new cargo vessels for the Zairian shipping line at a cost of DM190 million (approximately $270 million).[11]

Undoubtedly the most far-reaching policy in the government's drive for economic autonomy was Zairianization. In a speech before the National Legislative Council on November 30, 1973, Mobutu announced plans for the seizure of those small and medium-sized enterprises in Zaire that remained in foreign hands—commercial ventures, plantations, transportation companies, and construction firms. This strategy was clearly aimed at the expatriate entrepreneurial class in Zaire, which consisted exclusively of Greeks, Portuguese, Italians, and Jews—many of whom had migrated to Zaire during the colonial period. Measures were announced for adequate compensation, but as it turned out many financial settlements were not made until well over a decade later.

Zairianization was hastily conceived and poorly implemented. State officials were given no indication initially of how the program would be executed, and it was not until weeks later that instructions were issued to local administrators to undertake a census of the foreign-owned enterprises in question, prior to the government's acceptance of applications from aspiring Zairian owners. Although the scheme was presented as a positive step along the road to economic independence, it soon became clear that the government's goals were highly political and self-serving. Distribution of the approximately 2,000 businesses involved was based on political influence. The bulk of the companies therefore went to individuals at the top of the regime's hierarchy—including, incidentally, Mobutu himself and members of his family. Theoretically, civil servants, members of the army, judges, and ambassadors were not eligible to acquire businesses, in order to preserve their professional integrity, but in the prevailing atmosphere of greed, many of these individuals submitted applications through their spouses.

The disastrous effects of Zairianization became visible within a few months. Businesses were being allocated simultaneously at the regional as well as at the central government level, and in the confusion many firms were handed over to more than one prospective *acquéreur* (owner). In opportunistic fashion many new owners quickly liquidated the inventories and financial resources of their enterprises or abandoned them when it became clear that they could not manage them successfully. There were many instances of tax evasion, layoffs of Zairian staff, and failure to pay employee salaries, and as a result, there was a significant shrinkage in the commercial sector. This shrinkage in turn led to many shortages of consumer staples, hoarding, and inflation. In agriculture the integrated facilities of many plantations were separately distributed, virtually paralyzing their operations.

By the end of 1974 the failure of Zairianization was being widely acknowledged, and the press attacked the greed and conspicuous consumption of the *acquéreurs*. The government therefore announced a new Radicalization program, a further expansion of the "Mobutuist revolution." Radicalization was essentially a ten-point program to address major Zairian "scourges" such as unemployment, inflation, social injustice, and individualism. In what he claimed was a war against personal enrichment, Mobutu declared that MPR officials and other top civil servants had to surrender businesses obtained through Zairianization to the state and confine their activities to agriculture. However, it was soon evident that the targets of Radicalization were not businesses that had been acquired by the Zairian elite but the larger, mostly Belgian-owned companies established in the colonial era, which had not been affected by the earlier Zairianization measures. These firms, representing all key sectors of the economy, were to be taken over by the state.

Belgian businessmen in Zaire were seriously affected by the Radicalization measures and retaliated swiftly through their government to this strategy. Parent companies of Belgian firms confiscated under Zairianization and Radicalization cut off credit, and the Belgian office providing export insurance for shipments to Zaire suspended its operations there. At the same time, the GOZ began to experience serious economic difficulties (discussed in the concluding section of this chapter) and rescinded the Zairianization and Radicalization measures under pressures from its foreign creditors for economic reform. Between November 1975 and September 1976 the GOZ effected measures for the large-scale return of businesses to their former expatriate owners.[12]

Although some foreigners did reacquire their businesses, the economic disruption caused by the government's policies was something that Zaire could ill afford. The effects on production were felt well beyond the 1970s. In a sense, Zairianization measures were to have complemented earlier efforts to exert state control over the mineral sector. In principle, the desire for economic autonomy was laudable, and with a less self-serving political elite and a technically competent business class, some level of economic independence might have been achieved.

THE POLITICS OF MINING AND ENERGY

From Union Minière to GECAMINES

Initially independence had little impact on mining, but Union Minière soon became the target of government nationalization measures. After the birth of the Second Republic, relations between the Mobutu regime and Union Minière swiftly deteriorated, triggered by the company raising its prices without consulting the government. The GOZ, convinced that Union Minière was acting too independently of the state, formed the Générale Congolaise des Minérais (GECOMIN) in December 1966, which took over all of the company's assets in the Congo. However, with a lack of local technical and managerial expertise, the government had to sign an agreement with the Société Générale des Minérais (SGM), the former agent for Union Minière, to assume responsibility for mining, processing, marketing, and staffing for twenty-five years. For the first fifteen years SGM would receive 6 percent of the value of GECOMIN's output. For the remaining period the compensation would be 1 percent of GECOMIN's annual gross revenues.[13] In essence, therefore, the foreign presence in the mining sector remained unchanged. GECOMIN was renamed Générale des Carrières et des Mines (GECAMINES) in 1971 at the height of the Mobutu's authenticity program. Three years later the government established its own marketing organization, Société Zairoise de Commercialisation des Minérais (SOZACOM), to handle mineral production—primarily copper, cobalt, and diamonds.

The mining industry remains the focal point of the Zairian economy. Copper production is exclusively controlled by GECAMINES. The company dominates economic activity in Zaire, accounting for 50–60 percent of Zaire's foreign exchange earnings and 20 percent of government revenues (see Table 4.2).[14] GECAMINES produces all of Zaire's copper; it is the world's largest producer of cobalt; and it is the country's leading industrial employer. GECAMINES is also engaged in important agricultural activities in Shaba, mainly livestock and maize production, to supply the mining area with food. For more than a decade, Zaire's adverse economic fortunes have affected GECAMINES at several levels. Falling copper prices on world markets, beginning in 1975 after record levels of production, reduced the company's contribution to government revenues from 50 percent to about 29 percent. Shrinking revenues and a heavy tax burden estimated at about 70 percent further deprived the company of the financial resources necessary to purchase raw materials and spare parts and to maintain production capacity. In 1975 the closure of the most economical and efficient export route for Zaire's mineral products—the Benguela railway in Angola—because of civil war caused further complications. Zaire was forced to rely on a longer, more expensive route through Zambia and Zimbabwe to South African ports, in addition to the Voie Nationale from Shaba to the port of Matadi.

In spite of these difficulties, the GOZ has constantly pressed for expansion of GECAMINES' operations and made unusual financial demands on the company because of its own budgetary imperatives. This situation has been an ongoing concern among Zaire's external creditors, who see the financial health of GECAMINES as vital to long-term economic growth, given its dominant position in the economy.

In the mid-1970s, with growing foreign debt and escalating govern-

TABLE 4.2
Key Economic Indicators, 1970-1989
($ mil. unless noted)

Category	1970	1971	1972	1973	1974	1975	1976	1977	1978	1979	1980	1981	1982	1983	1984	1985	1986	1987	1988	1989
GNP	3,435	3,870	4,285	5,455	6,517	6,879	6,636	8,627	10,769	10,541	10,016	8,875	13,971	10,949	6,790	6,786	7,881	7,352	9,210	9,152
GNP per capita	260	270	280	340	390	430	430	470	510	600	630	590	540	460	340	270	240	240	260	260
Money supply (current zaires bil.)	0.21	0.22	0.27	0.38	0.50	0.55	0.76	1.21	1.86	1.96	3.18	4.84	8.22	13.55	18.78	24.34	38.67	75.74	175.09	293.11
Volume of exports (1985 = 100)																				
Copper	61.3	70.6	76.7	78.9	74.7	94.2	86.1	66.4	71.9	50.0	68.3	76.6	80.8	68.4	66.3	100.0	114.4	70.6	77.1	75.5
Export revenues																				
Copper	519.2	415.6	406.2	618.0	859.2	433.0	400.6	440.3	388.8	421.2	672.0	244.4	231.9	212.0	673.9	636.8	636.0	607.0	1075ᵃ	1,110ᵃ
Cobalt	47.2	46.2	53.6	77.2	71.4	96.8	124.8	108.1	217.7	526.5	328.9	84.3	37.6	7.3	221.0	224.6	148.0	54.0	–	–
Diamonds	40.2	32.0	42.8	57.4	62.2	55.2	60	64.2	124.3	100.7	68.4	42.9	66.8	164.1	176.9	185.6	219.6	169.5	133.5	120.9
Coffee	38.6	49.2	56.0	72.6	60.4	54.2	130.5	192.4	166.5	143.2	163.7	95.5	108.4	141.5	199.6	169.9	324.8	113.6	44.1	62.1
Balance of payments																				
Total exports (FOB)	843	710	704	1,069	1,567	1,051	1,193	1,313	1,924	1,915	2,185	1,632	1,541	1,649	2,153	2,005	2,035	2,007	2,392	2,190
Total imports (CIF)	884	902	1,010	1,300	1,910	1,669	2,095	2,799	1,613	1,757	1,669	2,524	2,300	2,125	2,136	1,858	2,368	2,796	3,213	2,106
Current account balance	-64	-102	-329	-245	-372	-593	-833	-1,451	294	146	-292	-604	-591	-349	-211	218	-399	-648	-694	-641
Foreign exchange reserves	189	154	218	337	212	84	85	177	195	336	380	293	226	269	281	335	451	417	372	218.7
Average exchange rate (z per US$)	0.5	0.5	0.5	0.5	0.5	0.5	0.79	0.86	0.83	1.7	2.8	4.4	5.7	12.8	36.1	49.9	59.3	112.4	187.1	381.4

ᵃ Copper and cobalt revenues.

Sources: World Bank, World Debt Tables, 1988/89 (vol. 2, Country Tables, 1970-79), 1989/90, 1990/91; World Bank, World Tables, 1991; International Monetary Fund, International Financial Statistics Yearbook, 1991.

ment expenditures, the government of Zaire significantly increased its reliance on GECAMINES as a source of foreign exchange, resulting in a shortage of resources for maintenance and rehabilitation. After persistent World Bank and IMF concerns over the foreign exchange issue, the GOZ agreed to an arrangement in 1978 whereby GECAMINES would retain 45 percent of its foreign exchange earnings to meet its own needs. The Bank of Zaire would be allotted 45 percent, crediting GECAMINES with the equivalent in zaires. The remaining 10 percent would be deposited at the Federal Reserve Bank of New York to repay top priority loans.[15] Because of its continued financial difficulties, the government failed to honor the agreement. By the late 1980s GECAMINES was turning over additional foreign exchange to the Bank of Zaire out of its 45 percent allocation, creating a foreign exchange shortage for the company and excess liquidity in zaires.

GECAMINES has been a major topic of discussion at meetings of Zaire's external creditors. Key issues have been the company's fiscal arrangements with the GOZ, excessive government interference in GECAMINES' affairs and government diversion of its funds, SOZACOM's control of GECAMINES' products, and GECAMINES' desperate need for a sustained rehabilitation program. After considerable pressure from the World Bank, the Mobutu regime initiated flexible new fiscal arrangements with the company in the early 1980s, allowing GECAMINES a lighter fiscal burden in times of low copper prices, increased production costs, and overvaluation of the zaire. By 1984 the company was paying only 15–20 percent of export receipts in taxes compared to 70 percent previously.[16]

SOZACOM also became a contentious issue, being viewed by donors as an unnecessary intermediary between GECAMINES and its buyers. It was felt that GECAMINES should have full control over its products. By the late 1970s SOZACOM had become the principal means through which the presidency could intervene in GECAMINES' financial affairs and appropriate the proceeds of metal sales. In late 1978 and 1979, when copper prices were relatively strong, about 10 percent of copper production was diverted directly from GECAMINES' mines and bartered in Europe for military equipment. It is also alleged that some of the proceeds from the sale went to the presidency. At the same time, funds from a 5,000-ton cobalt transaction were credited directly to the presidency instead of to GECAMINES. Finally, in the face of IMF and World Bank prodding, Mobutu suddenly relinquished control over both GECAMINES and SOZACOM in 1983, permitting both companies additional flexibility. By the following year SOZACOM had been formally dissolved, and GECAMINES had been restructured.[17]

A persistent problem has been GECAMINES' inability to undertake successful investment in plant and equipment. Two expansion programs undertaken in the 1970s had to be halted prematurely because of staggering cost overruns and hostilities in the Shaba region. The latest investment plan (1986–1990) has been costed at $750 million, largely funded by GECAMINES, and aims to modernize production and reduce costs. Production improvements include the construction of a copper refinery at Kolwezi capable of processing 100,000 tons of copper a year, representing about half the volume being processed in Belgium. The rehabilitation program has lagged behind schedule because of delays both in funding and in the procurement process. The delays are contributing to GECAMINES' already high production costs. As a result, GECAMINES can no longer compete on a cost basis with more efficient world producers such as Peru. Transport problems are also affecting output and sales. Overall, since 1960 copper output has not averaged more than 500,000 tons (Table 4.1). It was hoped that buoyancy in the copper market, with prices averaging $1.10 per pound in 1990, would allow GECAMINES to be profitable in the short run in spite of the company's high costs of production and Zaire's crucial dependence on mineral exports for foreign exchange. However, by 1991 GECAMINES had experienced several setbacks resulting in declining profits. A major mine collapse at Kamoto near Kolwezi in September 1990 resulted in a 33 percent fall in annual copper production for the year as compared to 1989 (refer to Table 4.1). Frequent strikes by workers protesting economic conditions added to the company's problems; the strikes resulted in a further 32 percent fall in production for the first quarter 1991. As a consequence, GECAMINES announced in May that year that it would be unable to meet 1991 commitments to its customers. Looting and rioting in Shaba in October 1991 destroyed a foundry at Likasi, provoked additional workers' strikes, and resulted in the evacuation of most of the expatriates employed in the mining sector. Annual copper output averaged only 210,000 tons in 1991, and even relatively strong copper prices (averaging $1.04 per pound) did not positively impact the company's cash flow. GECAMINES' officials claim that production losses during the rioting totaled only 3,000 tons of copper and 150 tons of cobalt and that full production was restored well before the end of the year. Nevertheless, output in 1992 is not expected to be more than 200,000 tons of copper and 9,000 tons of cobalt due to continued production problems and lack of needed investment. The long-awaited investment program has stalled. Funding is not forthcoming from donors because of arrears on previous loans, the government's refusal to give GECAMINES control over its own affairs, and justified fears about new rounds of violence.[18]

Inga-Shaba and Oil

Closely tied to Mobutu's quest to effectively control the mining sector was an elaborate hydroelectric scheme at Inga designed to harness the tremendous power of the Zaire River. Plans for developing a series of dams had been conceived as early as the colonial period. However, after much wavering on the part of the colonial government, the scheme was shelved indefinitely because of the Great Depression, World War II, and later the political uncertainties of the preindependence period.[19]

Immediately after independence, the World Bank was approached to provide funding for the preliminary work on the Inga project. The bank was extremely hesitant, however, out of a concern that there were no immediate prospects for utilizing the vast amount of hydroelectric power that would be produced by Inga. Aluminum smelting was a possibility, but major companies had already gone elsewhere in Africa. The Congolese government commissioned a feasibility study from SICAI, the same Italian concern that was linked to the disastrous steel mill project in the early 1970s. Interestingly, the study maintained that the viability of the dams should be linked to "domestically-centered industrialization," focusing on steel production to satisfy local demand, rather than on heavy industry such as aluminum smelting geared exclusively for the export market.[20] The Mobutu regime was totally in favor of the scheme and appeared determined that it should not be controlled by foreign interests. Phase I of the project, Inga I, was intended to supply badly needed electricity to Kinshasa and was completed in 1972; it was financed largely by the government.

Plans were immediately launched for a more ambitious Inga II linked to another major project—a 1,800-kilometer power transmission line from the dam to the Shaba grid at Kolwezi, which would provide an estimated 1,200 megawatts of power to the copper belt. The Inga-Shaba project, as it came to be called, was motivated largely by political considerations. The Mobutu regime, remembering the 1960 secession in Shaba, wanted to make this region crucially dependent economically on Kinshasa. The project was costed at $260 million, financed primarily by the U.S. Export-Import Bank (Ex-Im).

As it turned out, cost overruns on the project were enormous, reaching an estimated $800 million by 1980. In 1979 the U.S. Congress questioned the wisdom of continued Export-Import Bank involvement in the project; by March that year the institution's overall exposure was already $435.8 million. Export-Import Bank funding continued, however, and construction was completed only in 1982, five years behind schedule, because of untold delays attributable to the two Shaba invasions and line losses due to lightning and pilfering by local blacksmiths, who stole the pylons for scrap metal.[21]

Inga-Shaba has yet to pay off in economic terms. The government has not succeeded in locating buyers of Inga-Shaba's cheap power. An international consortium of Swiss origin, ALUZAIRE, initially gave a firm commitment to construct a $1 billion aluminum smelter in a new industrial free zone that the government planned to establish at Banana, near the estuary of the Zaire River. ALUZAIRE was given generous incentives, including veto power over any other aluminum project over a ten-year period, but the consortium abruptly broke its agreement with Zaire when the government could not attract international financing for the free zone. Given existing economic realities, it is unlikely that the industrial zone will ever materialize.

Oil production in Zaire has also been plagued by problems. Two consortia involving U.S. oil companies—Gulf, Shell, Mobil, and Texaco—began exploration as early as 1958 along the Atlantic coast and in the Zaire River estuary. However, it was only in 1970 and 1972 that any major discoveries were made. Initial production off the Atlantic coast began in 1975 through a consortium of Zaire Gulf Oil (now Chevron), Japan Petroleum Zaire, and Société du Litoral Zairois (a Belgian firm), with the Zairian government holding a 15 percent interest. Production was expected to be above 25,000 barrels a day, but actual output has been much lower, falling from 8.83 million barrels in 1985 to 6.65 million barrels in 1988. The second concession, Zairep, owned by Petrofina and Shell, operates in the estuary and has been producing about 3.5 million barrels annually.[22]

As part of its industrialization thrust, Zaire had already had a refinery built by an Italian concern in 1968 near Moanda in Bas Zaire. Operated by the Société Zairo-Italienne de Raffinage (SOZIR), owned jointly by the government of Zaire and Italian interests, the refinery was designed to handle 750,000 tons of crude annually. Like Inga-Shaba, it turned out to be another investment disaster. The plant cannot process the heavy Zairian crude produced by the oil consortium; thus light Iranian crude has to be imported separately for the refinery. As a result, it processes only about 150,000 tons of oil a year. Zairian oil output is exported, and petroleum products are imported separately. A parastatal, Petrozaire, was established in 1978 with an exclusive monopoly over imports of petroleum products. However, this arrangement was dismantled in June 1985 under donor-inspired privatization, giving the local subsidiaries of the oil multinationals the mandate to import. Along with Petrozaire, they share ownership of the distribution company, Zaire SEP. In 1989 Petrozaire and the French company Société Nationale Elf Aquitaine established a new marketing company Société Commerciale Petrozaire

(SCP). The new company controls the purchase, import, export, and distribution of petroleum products.[23]

ECONOMIC CRISIS

Political issues surrounding GECAMINES and Inga-Shaba, as well as the fallout from Zairianization and foreign-financed government overspending on unproductive investments in the early 1970s, have to be viewed in the context of Zaire's ongoing economic "crisis." Zaire has been beset by economic difficulties since the mid-1970s. In the midst of economic reform initiatives prompted by the IMF, World Bank, and bilateral donors, Zaire has been caught in an escalating cycle of debt. As of the end of 1990, the country's total external debt stood at an estimated $10 billion (see Table 4.3). Eighty percent of the debt is owed to bilateral government creditors; commercial banks account for about 6 percent and multilateral institutions the remaining 14 percent.[24] Besides the economic austerity that a debt and economic crisis brings, prolonged decline has had a devastating impact on agriculture and local infrastructure.

The Politics of Debt

Zaire's economic crisis can be viewed in three distinct phases. The first phase (1974–1983) was initially marked by assumptions on the part of both the GOZ and external donors that Zaire's problems were of a short-term nature. Subsequently, from 1978 to 1983 Zaire made piecemeal and halfhearted attempts at reform. The second phase (1983–1986) was viewed by donors as a bold step, perhaps unprecedented in Africa, in which Zaire largely adhered to a rigorous austerity program, with positive effects on the economy. The final phase began with a sharp break with the IMF program in 1986 in the midst of heavy debt service payments that were not tempered by increasing aid. Generally poor economic performance, unsustained efforts with respect to structural reform, and steadily declining standards of living once again became the norm. This phase has continued well into 1992.

The turning point for Zaire's economy came in 1974. After a period of relatively strong growth, Zaire's crucial dependence on copper for foreign exchange proved to be a two-edged sword when the price fell precipitously on the world market from a high of $1.50 per pound to $.53 by 1975. The shortage of foreign exchange proved to be a major obstacle to production in other sectors such as agriculture and industry. Furthermore, the economic dislocations caused by Zairianization and the closing of the Benguela railway during the Angolan civil war, as well as rising prices of oil and other crucial imports, were all factors that plunged the country into an economic crisis.

TABLE 4.3
Zaire: External Debt, 1970-1990
(outstanding and disbursed, $ mil.)

Category	1970	1971	1972	1973	1974	1975	1976	1977	1978	1979	1980	1981	1982	1983	1984	1985	1986	1987	1988	1989	1990
Long-term debt[a]	311	364	503	904	1,343	1,718	2,312	2,900	3,616	4,222	4,161	4,239	3,982	4,260	4,160	4,815	5,786	7,097	7,127	7,571	8,818
Use of IMF credit	--	--	31	34	35	86	210	253	261	251	373	345	423	510	579	807	856	966	786	628	521
Short-term debt	--	--	--	--	--	--	--	277	336	344	326	332	224	210	244	404	411	680	829	643	669
Official creditors	221	111	147	174	311	518	909	1,150	1,552	2,079	2,595	2,862	2,829	3,393	3,392	4,008	4,965	6,289	6,353	6,756	n.a.
Multilateral	6	9	30	49	59	78	116	206	317	384	333	463	512	564	584	608	794	1,188	1,361	1,506	n.a.
IDA	1	3	8	16	26	38	55	87	113	139	159	176	214	255	302	372	471	738	837	962	n.a.
IBRD	5	3	2	1	0	12	32	56	75	70	87	80	73	65	56	46	36	50	37	30	n.a
Bilateral	216	102	117	125	251	440	793	943	1,235	1,696	2,262	2,399	2,318	2,829	2,808	3,401	4,171	5,102	4,992	5,250	n.a.
Private creditors	90	252	426	729	1,032	1,021	1,403	1,750	2,063	2,163	1,567	1,349	1,253	979	844	806	822	808	774	815	n.a.
Banks/financial markets	6	93	203	436	649	794	1,001	1,245	1,484	1,558	1,218	1,091	997	787	691	666	656	636	612	627	n.a.
Other private	84	160	223	293	382	407	402	510	579	585	342	258	256	193	153	437	161	167	158	183	n.a.
Total debt service[b]	37	38	61	97	187	152	88	116	141	169	365	194	135	186	319	515	439	454	373	513	n.a.
External debt/GNP (%)	n.a.	n.a.	26	n.a.	40	25	67	n.a.	56	65	33	47	47	61	96	89	90	119	95	97	n.a.
External debt/exports (%)	n.a.	n.a.	75	n.a.	86	168	195	n.a.	186	212	202	258	265	265	197	300	347	438	369	370	n.a.
TDS[c]/exports (%)	n.a.	n.a.	8	n.a.	12	15	7	n.a.	7	9	23	12	9	11	15	26	22	23	16	21	n.a.

[a] Public and publicly guaranteed with maturities over one year.
[b] Interest and principal repayments.
[c] TDS = Total debt service.

Sources: World Bank, World Debt Tables, 1984-85, 1987-88, 1988-89, 1990-1991; World Bank, Trends in Developing Economies, 1991 (Washington, D.C.: IBRD, 1991), p. 598.

Although levels of foreign investment still remained high, imports virtually doubled in relation to exports, causing the current account deficit to register $650 million, more than twice that of 1973. By the end of 1974 the government budget was showing an overall deficit of approximately Z331 million (see Table 4.4). Aggregate output (GDP) fell from a high of Z1.069 billion in 1974 to Z996.7 million in 1975.[25] Arrears soon accumulated on external payments and debt service totaling approximately $320 million. In mid-1975 Zaire became the first African country to default on its Eurocurrency obligations.

Mobutu was apparently convinced that Zaire's debt problem was short-term and due solely to external factors beyond the government's control. After unsuccessfully exploring other sources of bridge financing, the IMF had to be approached. A one-year stabilization program was adopted in 1976, supported by a $150 million standby arrangement. The program was aimed specifically at economic recovery and included a 42 percent devaluation of the zaire against Special Drawing Rights (SDRs) and cuts in import levels and government spending, as well as priority investment in agriculture. With the IMF seal of approval, a rescheduling agreement was soon concluded with bilateral creditors in the Paris Club, in which $205 million was rescheduled on fairly standard terms: over ten years at an average interest rate of 7.8 percent. Debt relief of some $337 million was provided. At the same time, private banks met in the London Club to discuss the estimated $750 million to $900 million in commercial debt, over half of which was not government guaranteed. The final agreement covered only the $380 million outstanding in syndicated loans. Zaire had to sign a Memorandum of Understanding, agreeing to pay

TABLE 4.4
Zaire: Government Budget, 1970-1977
(zaires mil.)

Category	1970	1974	1975	1977
Consolidated accounts[a]				
Total revenue	345.2	577.4	478.4	810.5
Current expenditure	283.3	513.8	551.9	964.6
Balance	61.4	63.6	-73.5	154.1
Capital expenditure	79.0	338.1	155.0	275.5
Net lending	2.4	56.2	-1.2	0.1
Overall deficiit	-20.0	-330.7	-227.3	-429.7

[a] includes both cash and noncash transactions. The most important noncash transactions are foreign grants and loans to finance technical assistance and investment projects.

Source: World Bank, Zaire: Current Economic Situation and Constraints (Washington, D.C.: IBRD, 1979), p. 56.

immediately $40 million in interest arrears and to regularize payments on the principal, depositing them in a special Bank for International Settlements (BIS) account in Switzerland. In return, the banks—led by Citibank, the key negotiator—agreed to raise a $250 million short-term loan to purchase much-needed equipment for key enterprises. As it turned out, the syndication was never achieved, and Zaire ended payments into the blocked account.[26]

In the midst of deteriorating infrastructure and health and education services, details of pervasive, blatant corruption and government overspending were becoming known (see Table 4.5). A second IMF program and a Paris Club rescheduling in 1977, covering $52 million and $235 million, respectively, occurred in the face of a growing budget deficit, largely due to disproportionate outlays in areas such as the presidency and the army. After two invasions of Shaba province in 1977 and 1978 that aggravated a growing crisis by crippling the mining sector, it was clear to Western donors that the Zaire problem was more fundamental than an externally induced crisis. Far-reaching structural changes were necessary if Zaire were to regain a viable economy.

Consequently, 1978 saw the beginning of unprecedented external creditor involvement in Zaire's economic affairs (see Table 4.6 for levels of official development assistance). As a condition of further aid (new funding and rescheduling), the GOZ had to agree to political liberalization and comprehensive economic reforms. Key measures included the creation of the post of prime minister, a new constitution providing for elections of government officials, reorganization of the Ministry

TABLE 4.5
Current Government Expenses by Department, 1982, 1985, and 1988
(in percentages)

Category	1982		1985		1988	
	Budgeted	Actual[a]	Budgeted	Actual	Budgeted	Actual
Presidency	1.4	11.5	1.6	6.1	6.2	28.6
Defense	7.9	11.0	4.3	5.8	9.4	28.4
Education[b]	22.6	23.6	7.6	0.5	7.6	10.1
Agriculture	2.4	2.3	0.8	0.5	0.4	0.4
Rural development	0.5	0.8	--	--	0.1	0.1
Public health	3.9	4.6	1.8	1.0	0.9	2.7
Women's affairs	--	--	0.04	--	0.05	--
Total Budgeted Expenses (z mil.)	7,391.3		33,940.8		136,664.0	

[a] Actual expenses are percentages of total budgeted expenses.
[b] Includes salaries for school teachers and university staff.

Sources: Banque du Zaire, Report, 1986, tables 58, 59, pp. 143-144. Banque du Zaire, Report, 1989, tables 58, 59, pp. 113-114.

TABLE 4.6
Total Official Development Assistance, 1979-1989
(net disbursements, $ mil.)

Category	1979	1980	1981	1982	1983	1984	1985	1986	1987	1988	1989
Bilateral (all sources)	228.7	316.8	277.1	250.8	197.2	241.4	213.0	322.2	359.7	424.1	461.2
Belgium	153.6	169.7	123.7	103.6	92.7	75.9	80.0	143.1	121.6	136.9	95.9
France	24.9	39.4	25.1	24.7	23.1	27.3	29.9	39.4	42.0	80.1	103.4
United States	44.0	11.0	21.0	16.0	23.0	37.0	39.0	41.0	56.0	53.0	54.0
Japan	3.1	39.4	51.3	42.8	3.0	26.4	9.3	10.5	28.0	23.4	90.8
Multilateral (all sources)	122.9	105.7	102.0	91.8	120.6	107.1	119.1	156.1	292.6	179.8	212.3
IDA (World Bank)	26.3	19.6	17.1	38.0	42.2	50.8	58.5	82.2	213.9	89.0	91.0
EC	19.3	23.0	44.5	18.5	50.7	35.0	21.3	24.0	22.3	38.3	61.0
UNDP	5.7	11.6	10.2	9.2	5.3	0.8	7.6	9.5	7.6	9.7	11.0
Total	411.6	422.5	379.1	342.6	317.8	348.5	332.1	478.3	652.3	603.9	673.5
including grants of	266.4	264.1	247.7	210.0	195.6	188.9	202.5	238.5	272.6	316.5	368.7

Sources: Economist Intelligence Unit Country Profile, Zaire, 1991-1992, p. 39; OECD Development Assistance Committee, Geographic Distribution of Financial Flows to Developing Countries, 1983, 1978-1981.

of Planning, and a Mobutu Plan for economic development—which included a three-year investment program—covering the period 1979–1981. More specifically, with respect to debt reporting, Western donors and the IMF had insisted on the creation of an Office de Gestion de la Dette Publique (OGEDEP; Office of Debt Management) as early as 1976, as the Bank of Zaire had no extensive data on the size of the debt and to whom it was owed. As a final step, the IMF and the World Bank placed technical assistance teams in key positions in the Bank of Zaire as well as the Ministries of Finance and Planning, and Belgium took on the responsibility of reorganizing and managing the Office des Douanes et des Accises (OFIDA; Customs and Excise Office) in order to increase badly needed government revenue.

In the international community hopes ran high that these expatriate teams could stop the many foreign exchange "diversions" from government agencies and companies such as SOZACOM and impose some measure of rationality on the GOZ's economic decisionmaking. On its part Zaire hired a group of consultants known in international circles as the Triumvirate—Lehman Brothers Kuhn Loeb, Lazard Frères, and S. G. Warburg—to assist with London Club, Paris Club, and IMF negotiations. To informed Zairians, it appeared that colonialism had returned and Zaire was once again being run by foreigners. Expatriate experts who had a mandate to regulate government spending appeared to be another version of the Force Publique.

By 1982 Zaire had concluded two additional Paris Club reschedulings (1979 and 1981), an IMF Stabilization Plan (1979) and Extended Fund Facility (EFF; 1981), a London Club rescheduling (1980), and five devaluations of the zaire. Stabilization efforts were supported by World Bank aid coordination between major donors and its own project lending in various sectors. Nevertheless, the country was again on the verge of default, having failed to honor the terms of these agreements. The Extended Fund Facility totaled SDR 912 million (400 percent of Zaire's IMF quota), the largest amount ever extended to a Sub-Saharan African country. By July 1982 this IMF arrangement had to be suspended after only two drawings totaling SDR 175 million. This was allegedly at the GOZ's initiative, after failure to observe performance criteria.

Although Zaire was clearly caught in a debt trap, with no way out except continued reschedulings, persistent appropriation of scarce foreign exchange by the regime helped to worsen the crisis, thereby further increasing dependence on external creditors. Meanwhile the expatriate technocrats were having negligible success in their efforts. Erwin Blumenthal, head of the IMF team at the Bank of Zaire, resigned in disgust after trying in vain to cut off unusual and continuing demands for foreign exchange from companies linked to members of the ruling elite.

Persistently weak prices for copper and cobalt kept Zaire in arrears on both public and commercial debt throughout 1982, and as a further indication of the seriousness of the situation, the Triumvirate severed its contract with Zaire after failing in an effort to raise a $35 million credit for the government using cobalt as collateral. It found itself in the middle of a stalemate between the IMF, on the one hand, and Zaire's public and private creditors, on the other. The IMF sought the full participation of Zaire's creditors in any rescue effort, and the latter were unwilling to grant further loans until existing arrears were settled. Equally important, the Triumvirate realized the futility of trying to work with the uncompromising Mobutu regime.

In what was viewed by donors as an apparent change in strategy, Zaire acceded to the terms of a new IMF standby agreement in summer 1983, after following a year-long "shadow program." This new agreement ushered in the second phase of the crisis. The government agreed to sweeping economic reform including extensive foreign exchange measures. A 77.5 percent currency devaluation of the zaire aimed to narrow the gap between the official rate and the parallel or black market rate. The zaire's link with SDRs was abolished, and an interbank market was established to determine its value on the basis of supply and demand.[27] At the time, this arrangement was unique in Sub-Saharan Africa. Zaire also had to take positive measures toward economic liberalization, including strict controls on public spending, liberalization of the trade system, and revisions of customs duties. Finally, preliminary steps were taken to establish a domestic money market with the public sale of short-term treasury bills.[28] Meanwhile, $1.28 billion, or 85 percent, of the public and publicly guaranteed debt due in 1983 and 1984 was rescheduled— the fifth such arrangement by the Paris Club since 1974.

Throughout 1984 Zaire was being kept on a short leash by the IMF, to the extent that it assigned its first permanent representative to the country. As the IMF program began to take hold and the economy showed the first positive indicators since 1975, Western creditors had nothing but praise for the government's efforts. Zaire was called a "model pupil," and the World Bank targeted Zaire as a prime candidate for structural adjustment lending.

In fact, Zaire was undertaking one of the most comprehensive reform programs ever attempted in Sub-Saharan Africa. Reschedulings continued, with the London Club tying interest payments to fluctuations in copper prices. Nevertheless, despite the positive Western response, the IMF found itself admitting in March 1986 that even though Zaire's image abroad had improved with its acceptance of the IMF formula, economic recovery had been modest. This inability to achieve greater gains was largely attributed to donors' reluctance to increase foreign loans and grants. Mobutu echoed these sentiments at a month-long conference of the country's single party, the MPR, in October 1986. Zaire's austerity plan had not been rewarded with increased aid and foreign investment. The debt burden had increased from 9 percent of total exports in 1982 to 26 percent in 1985 (Table 4.3); and with no new money forthcoming from creditors, there had been a net resource outflow in 1984 and 1985. As a result, the president declared that as of January 1987 Zaire would limit payments on its external debt to 20 percent of its national budget and 10 percent of its export revenue. Furthermore, the IMF was condemned for undue interference in Zaire's economic affairs. To further emphasize this new position, Prime Minister Kengo wa Dondo, a key supporter of the 1983 IMF adjustment program, was demoted to foreign minister and then auditor-general. He had been widely viewed by the IMF as a competent technocrat.

Mobutu's decision was clearly a negotiating tool and an attempt to reassert control over the reform process. Nevertheless, he stood to jeopardize agreements signed with the World Bank and the IMF that year. In reality, the GOZ had already violated IMF criteria by raising public sector salaries by 40 percent in May 1986. Therefore, by the beginning of 1987 it was clear once again that the reform process in Zaire had fallen apart, but interestingly enough the IMF appeared determined to save its program. Within a few months Mobutu had secured a new agreement with the IMF.

Throughout 1987 and 1988 Zaire fell steadily behind in payments to its creditors and failed several IMF performance criteria. Inflation, the money supply, and the current account balance all increased significantly (see Table 4.7 for Zaire's major trading partners). In June 1988 the GOZ unilaterally halted payments to the IMF on the grounds that the existing arrangements were actually resulting in a negative transfer of resources. As a result, the structural adjustment credits negotiated the previous year were blocked by both the IMF and the World Bank. Indeed, in the second half of 1988, Zaire had accumulated arrears of SDR 100 million ($130 million) on its IMF loans alone. Once again the IMF saved the day. Outright failure of economic adjustment in Zaire would have had serious implications for similar programs elsewhere in Africa. Therefore, by June 1989 the IMF had concluded yet another agreement with the GOZ. Mobutu had evidently softened his position and was willing to settle the arrears to the IMF with the help of a short-term bridge loan from the Banque Belgolaise. Kengo wa Dondo was brought back as prime minister and given a mandate to resuscitate the structural reform effort. Zaire's major

TABLE 4.7
Zaire: Principal Trading Partners, 1980-1990 ($ mil.)

Category	1980	1984	1985	1986	1987	1988	1989	1990
Exports to								
Belgium-Luxembourg	1,213.8	659.7	624.5	718.5	646.4	736.8	806.6	694.2
France	30.5	116.7	110.4	127.1	114.3	130.3	99.5	88.3
Germany	16.6	29.3	27.7	31.9	28.7	32.7	126.6	79.1
Italy	1.8	.3	.3	.4	.3	.4	63.5	51.9
Switzerland	106.7	103.6	98.1	112.9	101.6	115.8	67.7	61.1
United States	50.3	34.4	32.6	37.5	33.7	38.5	178.3	159.7
United Kingdom	74.3	18.3	17.4	20.0	18.0	20.5	20.1	14.5
Japan	6.6	10.6	10.1	11.6	10.4	11.9	32.6	21.9
Congo	4.9	16.6	15.7	18.1	16.3	18.6	11.1	18.4
South Africa	.3	.3	.3	.4	.3	.4	.2	.4
Imports from								
Belgium-Luxembourg	277.3	222.5	261.2	286.8	251.6	251.5	323.4	318.2
France	24.4	75.9	89.1	97.8	85.8	85.7	121.3	141.1
Germany	88.1	67.9	79.7	87.5	76.8	76.8	103.0	124.7
Italy	9.8	10.5	12.3	13.6	11.9	11.9	95.4	42.7
Switzerland	96.6	40.3	47.4	52.0	45.6	45.6	36.6	41.0
United States	110.1	86.4	101.4	111.4	97.7	97.6	108.3	122.5
United Kingdom	37.7	41.9	49.2	54.0	47.4	47.4	49.2	54.8
Japan	14.0	10.5	12.3	13.6	11.9	11.9	47.1	33.7
Congo	.6	.1	.2	.2	.2	.2	2.0	.2
South Africa	42.2	42.1	49.4	54.2	47.6	47.5	26.9	58.6

Source: International Monetary Fund, Direction of Trade Statistics Yearbook, 1986, 1990, 1991 (Washington, D.C.: IMF).

bilateral creditors—the United States, Belgium, France, and Germany—made the unusual decision to write off a portion of the credits owed to them.[29]

Mobutu's 1990 New Year's address to the nation emphasized Zaire's improved economic performance. Although the IMF performance criteria for June and September were met during 1989, improved economic performance was largely due to higher than usual export earnings rather than government policies.[30] By midyear the World Bank was claiming that conditions were ripe for sustained growth. But as is often the case in Zaire, the appearance masked a deeper reality. Before the end of the fourth quarter, it was painfully apparent that the structural adjustment process was stillborn yet again. Copper prices had collapsed on world markets, costing Zaire an estimated $450 million in foreign exchange in the first quarter of 1990. By March debt arrears were accumulating, and the zaire had depreciated precipitously, registering Z530 to $1, as against a parallel rate of Z700, clearly surpassing the desired IMF margin of 10 percent for the two rates.

The World Bank lending program was faring no better, and the frustrations of reform efforts were none too subtly revealed when it became publicly known that in mid-1989 perhaps as much as $400 million in foreign exchange earnings for 1988 could not be accounted for by IMF/World Bank experts.[31] Moreover, the Bank had been increasingly concerned with the Mobutu regime's misplaced priorities in budgetary spending—low allocations for areas such as agriculture and health compared to defense and the presidency (refer to Table 4.5). Consequently, after a joint World Bank/IMF mission to Kinshasa in March 1990, the Bank decided to curtail its 1990 lending program in Zaire significantly, withholding an estimated $100 million in nonproject structural adjustment loans and declining to release funds for new projects in the pipeline. The IMF took a similar position with respect to further tranches of its June 1989 standby due to noncompliance with performance criteria.[32]

A series of strikes throughout 1990 by civil servants, teachers, and mining workers forced the government to grant salary concessions, further increasing the government budget deficit. Increased deficit spending financed by an expansion in the money supply and increasingly scarce foreign exchange, along with a drop in mineral production levels, precipitated a massive free fall in the zaire in December 1990. At that time the zaire reached a rate of Z1,573 to $1 compared to a rate of Z455 to $1 in December 1989. Further depreciations occurred on a weekly basis in 1991. Between June and August 1991 the zaire fell from Z4,642 per dollar to Z7,393 per dollar. Currency depreciation had increased the local currency cost of debt service, while real GDP contracted by 2 percent in 1990 and was projected to contract by 4 percent in 1991. By August 1991 Zaire had implemented a package of monetary reforms including another massive devaluation to attract badly needed foreign exchange from the parallel market into official channels. At that time the parallel rate registered Z16,000 per dollar. These measures were dwarfed by political instability later in the year. Another free fall in the currency resulted in an official rate of Z54,000 per dollar, rising to Z142,000 by March 1992. The September riots resulted in a 2,000 percent pay increase in the minimum salary for civil servants and the military met by an expansion of the money supply, which further fueled inflation to surrealistic levels. As a result, early in 1992 government workers and the military were seeking to raise their minimum salaries from Z1.5 million per month to Z15 million simply to compensate for the higher cost of living. Political instability and political uncertainty have exacerbated financial indiscipline, and with inflation averaging more than 4,000 percent, parallel market estimates for the zaire ranged from Z700,000 = $1 to Z900,000 = $1 at the end of September 1992. By February 1993 the zaire had depreciated to Z2.6 million = $1, with further declines expected. This monetary crisis has produced a chronic shortage of cash; hence workers in both the public and private sectors are not being paid, and banks are barely operating, having had to limit customer withdrawals to the equivalent of $10 to $15 per month.[33] In a situation in which the economy is clearly out of control, additional reschedulings or adjustment programs will not be forthcoming from either the World Bank or the IMF.

Throughout the Zairian crisis the Mobutu regime has apparently been caught in the IMF/World Bank structural adjustment web. The situation is in fact more complex. The "debt game" in Zaire has really been one of mutual manipulation.[34] In the past the GOZ has been well aware of its importance to the West, and therefore it has been able to have some measure of autonomy with respect to external actors' reform efforts, playing on fears of the unthinkable consequences of the regime's collapse. Donors have differing views of the Zairian crisis and varying foreign policy objectives; hence the GOZ has found it advantageous to chip away at their efforts toward sustained cooperation on the debt issue. Over the years a familiar pattern has emerged: the GOZ consistently agreeing to implement economic reform and signing the necessary formalities, only to fail to follow through systematically on substantive restructuring owing to the political ramifications for the elite. The thinking has been that in the final analysis Zaire will not be allowed to fail. A more important reality is that the reforms strike at the heart of Mobutu's patrimonial system and will only serve to undermine patron-client networks, efforts to buy loyalty, and wealth-seeking strategies. Stabilization programs that are rational from a strictly economic point of view are therefore politically irrational, given the nature of the regime. In postcolonial states such as Zaire, where political rather than economic logic prevails, this lack of sustainability with respect to reform is by no means unique.

From the perspective of the World Bank and the IMF, Zaire stands as a challenge to the viability of the neoorthodox economic prescription. Success of an adjustment program in Zaire stands as proof that their policies work and that countries in similar straits can once again be "resuscitated" as fully functioning neocolonial states in the international system. Hence the true test has been to convince the government of the urgency of far-reaching reforms while systematically monitoring projects and programs and supplying administrative and technical support in key areas of the economy. Domestic constraints relating to the nature of the Zairian state and the regime have made it difficult to track economic performance, consistently prevent what is euphemistically called "foreign exchange leakage," and ultimately ensure program survival, even with expatriate teams in place in Kinshasa. In reality, the regime's attempts to circumvent the efforts of expatriate teams have been creative, persistent, and generally successful.

In spite of the GOZ's well-known pattern with respect to reform, over time donors have repeatedly come to Zaire's aid, regardless of their ultimate lack of confidence in the regime's sincerity. The massive devaluation and extensive liberalization measures to which the government agreed in 1983 were widely viewed as a positive step. It was felt in some circles, rather naively, that the GOZ was finally committed to effective change. In fact, Zaire managed to adhere to this program for three years, partly because Mobutu gave something of a free rein to expatriate teams and qualified technocrats within the Zairian government. Key officials who favored IMF-style reforms were in place at the Bank of Zaire and the prime minister's office. Scholars who understand Zaire maintain that reform efforts during this period occurred only because Mobutu sensed a narrowing of his options vis-à-vis the international community. Surrounded by donor ultimatums on all sides with respect to putting his house in order and faced with reduced foreign exchange due to a soft market for key commodity exports, the president saw no other recourse. As discussed in Chapter 2, free access to foreign exchange is crucial to the survival of the political elite. When Mobutu perceived that he stood on stronger ground in the face of higher copper prices and positive donor perceptions, he tried to reassert control over the reform process by unilaterally halting payments to the IMF. According to one U.S. official intimately involved in the Zairian economic reform process, Mobutu has tended to disregard the World Bank and the IMF during periods of strong export earnings. It is during these times that he perceives he has room to maneuver.[35]

Zaire's ultimate trump card vis-à-vis Western donors has been its strategic location and the fact that Mobutu has traditionally been viewed as a valuable ally opposed to the spread of communism in Sub-Saharan Africa. This anti-Communist argument played very well in the United States, for example, with Mobutu supporting American foreign policy objectives in areas such as Chad and Angola. As a result, there was often pressure from the U.S. government on both the Paris and London Clubs, as well as the World Bank and the IMF, to extend further credits to Zaire and to reschedule loans on favorable terms. Because of the apparent salience of the "Mobutu or chaos" thesis among Western governments, public pronouncements about "getting tough" with Zaire often yielded to quiet diplomatic maneuverings behind the scenes.

Things appear to have changed, however, in the aftermath of Mobutu's brief flirtation with structural reform from 1983 to 1986. In the late 1980s the configuration of international politics began to change dramatically, culminating in the prodemocracy movement in Eastern Europe in 1989, the ultimate breakup of the Soviet Union at the end of 1991, and the passing of the cold war era. In the aftermath of *perestroika*, economic hardship and political change in Russia and its relationship with the new Commonwealth of Independent States take precedence over any foreign policy objectives in regions such as Africa. As a result, Mobutu's perceived utility to the West has been irreparably undermined. With the anti-Communist argument gone, Western donors appear determined not to fall into the familiar Mobutu trap and have openly acknowledged the total lack of credibility of the Zairian regime with respect to reform.

Coincidentally, by March 1990 the rules of the debt and economic crisis "game" had again changed in favor of the World Bank and the IMF. Both organizations have taken a strong position and appear determined not to extend further structural adjustment and balance of payments funding to Zaire until there is sustained evidence of true government commitment to economic and political reform. So far, Zaire's leading bilateral creditors (Belgium, France, and the United States) have taken a similar stance. Unfortunately, donors have traveled this route before. According to sources in Washington, after the unraveling of the IMF/ World Bank initiative in 1990, the bank seriously considered withdrawing completely from Zaire, with all the accompanying political implications of such a move. In September 1991 the IMF formally suspended lending to Zaire, declaring it ineligible for further borrowing due to arrears of approximately $100 million. The IMF was astounded at Zaire's refusal to give it preferential treatment with respect to repayments, as is the norm with borrowing countries. World Bank projects, however, are still continuing as Zaire is not in arrears on World Bank loans, and there is therefore no legal rationale to halt project financing. The Bank is continuing ongoing projects in the social sectors and infrastructure but has refused to extend new loans. Early in 1990 there was some concern on the part of the World Bank that any efforts by the U.S. administration urging a softer stance on Zaire would undermine attempts to take a different approach with the regime.[36] However, it appears that this consensus among donors on structural reform will hold for the immediate future in the face of a crumbling economy and the lack of political will on the part of the government.

Infrastructure Disintegration and Agricultural Decline

In recent years agricultural production has consistently declined and local infrastructure fallen into disrepair despite continued external assistance targeted specifically for these areas. Given Zaire's large size and the existing structure of the economy, an efficient road, river, and rail system is crucial to the movement of agricultural and mineral products from the interior.

Overall, performance in the agriculture sector has not been encouraging, with increases in production of staple food crops falling well below estimated population growth since the early 1970s. As of 1992, except for products such as coffee, cocoa beans, and groundnuts, agricultural products have not reached preindependence production levels. Subsistence agriculture provides about 60 percent of the country's working population with a living. However, lacking adequate technology, Zairian small farmers have not been able to produce enough to satisfy the rising needs of the urban areas. The agricultural sector (commercial and subsistence agriculture) has experienced slow growth since independence. In 1970 the sector contributed 16.6 percent to GDP. By 1980 this figure had risen to 18.9 percent and by 1986 to 20 percent.[37] Nevertheless, agriculture is shrinking in real terms, given high inflation rates. Investment in the sector had been low; thus a country that has the capacity to be self-sufficient in food has been a massive importer for a number of years.

Austerity measures have made it difficult for the GOZ to meet the local-cost component of donor-financed agricultural projects. Nevertheless, as early as 1975 the World Bank was criticizing the government's lack of focus on agricultural investment and its emphasis on construction of new infrastructure rather than on maintenance of existing facilities. The government formulated a comprehensive recovery plan for the agricultural sector in 1982 (Plan de Relance Agricole, 1982–1984) with technical assistance from the World Bank. It was designed to increase food self-sufficiency, and measures were outlined for increased privatization of the sector, liberalization of pricing policies, improved marketing, and extension services. So far, price liberalization and increased private sector involvement in agriculture have been implemented on some level, largely because they were made preconditions for a 1983 IMF structural adjustment package. Since the agricultural plan was formulated, donors have been coordinating efforts to increase output from subsistence farms, funding farm-to-market road rehabilitation, and providing institutional support to the Ministry of Agriculture. Although there have been areas of success, mostly in the area of increased production, government allocations to the sector are still woefully inadequate; therefore, significant external assistance will be needed for some time to come.[38]

Problems in agriculture can be partially attributed to the local transport system, which has steadily deteriorated since independence. Ironically, during the colonial period the infrastructure in Zaire was reputed to be the best in Africa, although it was largely constructed to facilitate the export of primary products. Although significant damage occurred during the Congo Crisis, the Mobutu regime has not been able even to maintain the existing system. The three parastatals in charge of infrastructure—the Office des Routes (Bureau of Roads) responsible for road maintenance and construction, the Office National des Transports (ONATRA; National Transport Office), which maintains river services and ports, and the Société Nationale des Chemins de Fer du Zaire (SNCZ; Zairian National Railway Company) in charge of railways—have all suffered from severe foreign exchange shortages and inadequate budgets, as well as a lack of equipment and qualified staff.

The Office des Routes has been able to maintain only 25 percent of the estimated 145,000-kilometer network. Many Zairians estimate that the total usable roads has fallen to a mere 12,000 kilometers. It takes ten to fourteen days in a four-wheel-drive vehicle to make the 454-kilometer trip from Kinshasa to Lubumbashi.[39] Travel on the Voie Nationale— the road, rail, and waterway complex linking the mineral-rich Shaba province to the port of Matadi—is equally problematic. Although this is a major route for the export of Zaire's minerals, transport usually takes sixty days. There is no reliable road system between Kinshasa and eastern Zaire (Kivu), which is known for its agricultural production. As a result, foodstuffs from the region can arrive in Kinshasa only by air, and thus the capital cannot rely on Kivu to supply the local market. In an effort to improve river transport, the GOZ has eliminated ONATRA's monopoly, except for copper transportation, establishing free entry into the sector.

Air transport is also difficult. The national airline, Air Zaire— known in local circles as Air Peut-être (Air Maybe)—is highly unreliable. In the 1970s and early 1980s it was not unusual to have a flight canceled at the last minute because the plane was needed for a presidential trip out of the country. The French airline UTA signed a six-year agreement to run the airline in 1986 but had reneged on the contract by the end of 1989, allegedly overwhelmed by the company's problems. Expatriate and local businessmen prefer to purchase their own means of transportation— trucks, barges, aircraft—rather than to depend on state-owned arrangements. As a result of the poor state of the transport network and fuel shortages, transport costs are very high, often beyond the reach of subsistence farmers, and thus these farmers are isolated from local markets. This situation, in turn, results in higher agricultural prices for the Zairian consumer.

The World Bank and Western donors have made consistent efforts to facilitate rehabilitation of the transport sector, with no less than ten major cofinanced projects since 1975. However, project results have fallen far short of expectations. Overall, it has proven difficult to implement a large-scale maintenance and rehabilitation program involving several agencies with varying levels of expertise. There have also been other issues, such as persistent and creative forms of corruption, in addition to frequent policy differences with the government.

One bright spot is a private initiative in the area of air transport. Zaire's major private airline, Scibe-airlift, has been providing highly reliable cargo and passenger service. The airline is one of the many undertakings of a native Zairian, Bemba Saolona, president of the Scibe-Zaire business conglomerate. Scibe-airlift began ten years ago when Bemba needed reliable air transport for his trading and agricultural businesses. With the rapid deterioration of Air Zaire, domestic passenger service on Scibe began in 1982, and a Kinshasa-Brussels run was initiated three years later.[40]

Zaire is still overwhelmingly rural, with over 70 percent of the country's labor force involved in subsistence and plantation agriculture (see Table 4.8). Historically, economic development priorities of the central government have focused on the urban areas, leaving rural villages effectively marginalized and having to fend for themselves. The allocation of economic resources and operating funds begins with Kinshasa, the capital. It then extends to regional and subregional capitals, which in turn have to allocate funds to smaller towns and villages. In the current situation of economic scarcity, entire areas in the countryside operate without state assistance. This lack of financing has been underscored by government decentralization efforts, which include instructions to regions to provide their own funding.

To the rest of the country, Kinshasa and Lubumbashi, the second largest city, constitute two poles of development. Both receive the lion's share of goods and services. In the case of Lubumbashi, this status is attributable to the existence of the mining industry—the lifeline of the economy—and a considerable expatriate presence linked to GECAMINES. Rural dwellers throughout the country feel exploited. They provide agricultural produce for the urban centers and get precious little in return. Infrastructure has fallen into disrepair, and social services are inadequate. However, life in the urban areas has its own share of difficulties, and poverty is prevalent. In many instances, unemployment levels are high, with limited opportunities in the public sector and even fewer in the private sector. For those who are employed, wage differentials between the two sectors are quite stark, particularly in the face of inflation, devaluation, and economic decline in the larger economy. Table 4.9 gives an indication of public and private sector salary indices in Kinshasa for 1980 to 1988.

Economic austerity measures and the decline of subsistence agriculture, coupled with the state's inability to provide basic services, have exacerbated the plight of the average citizen. Consumer purchasing power has eroded because of devaluation and increasing prices. In an

TABLE 4.8
Employment in Zaire, 1965, 1985-1987, 1988

	1965	1985-1987	1988
Percentage of labor force in			
Agriculture	82.0	71.5	n.a.
Industry	9.0	12.9°	n.a.
Services	9.0	15.6	n.a.
Labor force (% of total population)	--	--	36.9
Women in labor force			
(% of total labor force)	--	--	35.9

Source: United Nations Development Program, <u>Human Development Report</u>, 1990
           (New York: Oxford University Press, 1990), table 15, p. 156.

TABLE 4.9
Public and Private Salary Indices, 1980-1988
(1980 = 100)

	1980	1981	1982	1983	1984	1985	1986	1987	1988
Consumer price index (CPI)[a]	100	135.4	184.5	326.7	497.4	615.9	903.6	1720.4	2855.0
Public sector									
Nominal	100	123.7	149.3	188.3	310.6	487.7	715.4	1194.6	1672.4
Real	100	91.4	80.9	57.6	62.4	79.2	79.2	69.4	58.6
Private sector									
Nominal	100	158.4	284.3	498.6	1186.0	1744.0	2591.5	5290.0	6900.6
Real	100	117.0	154.1	152.6	238.4	283.2	286.8	307.5	241.7
Minimum wage									
Nominal	100	117.5	148.1	376.8	1020.7	1020.7	1020.7	1020.7	1020.7
Real	100	86.8	80.3	115.3	205.2	165.7	113.0	59.3	35.7

[a] The CPI data is a weighted average of retail and market prices for Kinshasa in zaires, compiled by the National Institute of Statistics (INS) and similar series (base year, 1980) from the Institute for Economic Research (IRES) in Zaire.

Source: World Bank data, 1990.

effort to get by, Zairians have therefore developed various coping mechanisms, most of which are outside the formal sector in the second, or parallel, economy. Even though the actual size of the parallel economy is difficult to estimate, a 1986 household-budget survey in Kinshasa indicated that only about 25 percent of household income came from wages and salaries whereas about 29 percent came from unknown second-economy activities.[41] If these figures are typical of the rest of the country, official economic data on Zaire, such as GNP per capita, are highly deceptive.

The second economy encompasses an entire range of legal and illegal activities: black market transactions and smuggling, illicit production of commodities and services, the purchase and resale of goods for gain, middleman activity, theft of company time, and even legitimate activities of established companies (in trading, transport, construction, and manufacturing) that have gone underground to evade taxation. This system, with roots in the colonial period, has sophisticated networks for production, distribution, infrastructure, the purchase of foreign exchange, and importation. All these activities avoid state control and are frequently facilitated by family, kinship, and ethnic ties. Many individuals pursue underground activities to escape an oppressive, intrusive state and simply to survive on a daily basis. Others, however, use their privileged positions as state employees and members of the political elite to acquire resources to participate in this parallel economy purely for profit. Stealing

Children selling bread in Kinshasa.

from the formal economy thus often provides the resources for engaging in independent production.[42] Although the second economy is precarious, earnings from its activities are generally more lucrative than salaried employment.

Stories abound of smuggling—coffee, gold, diamonds—a practice that has an adverse impact on the official economy due to a loss of foreign exchange. Coffee has been particularly vulnerable, and in Haut Zaire, the center of production, as much as 40 percent of the output is smuggled across the Ugandan border and commonly exchanged for vehicles. With the meager wages of plantation workers and the artificially low prices paid to peasant producers, in spite of formal government policies touting price liberalization, it has not been uncommon for Zairians to sell illegally as much coffee as is exported legally. Food crops are smuggled across borders to take advantage of higher prices and to obtain commodities that are either unavailable or scarce in Zaire. In a situation rather reminiscent of precolonial times, a flourishing illicit trade in goods and services has developed between eastern Zaire and Uganda, Rwanda, and Burundi. This part of Zaire is virtually autonomous, as the disintegration of central government control has been aggravated by a poor—often nonexistent—transport system. A similar autonomy in Shaba has created ideal conditions for the trafficking of goods—mineral products and spare parts stolen from GECAMINES—to Zambia and South Africa in exchange for maize, foodstuffs, and fuel. Even though the production and sale of diamonds and gold were liberalized in 1983 to reduce illegal trade, nonetheless in 1988 diamonds and gold accounted for almost 94 percent of Belgian imports from Burundi and 88 percent of imports from Congo-Brazzaville. As neither country mines significant amounts of these products, the availability of these resources can be attributed only to smuggling across the border from Zaire. By some estimates, at the end of the 1980s the illegal mining and trafficking of diamonds in eastern and western Kasai were costing the Zairian government between Z30 million and Z80 million each month ($57,000 to $145,000 at 1989 exchange rates). Security measures cannot be effectively enforced, as the state-employed teams are often coconspirators with the Zairian and foreign (mostly West African) traders.[43]

The World Bank has recognized the importance of these informal activities and is seeking ways of quantifying or estimating the size of the second economy and studying its impact on development in countries such as Zaire. Given that most of these economic activities are largely illegal and questionable, this area is understandably a politically sensitive one.

Most individuals operate simultaneously in the formal and underground economies. Workers often keep jobs with established companies simply for the health benefits and subsidies that they provide. As long as economic decline persists unabated, the second economy will continue to grow, further diminishing the significance of legitimate activities.

Whether one examines the debt crisis or key sectors of the Zairian economy, it is clear that in spite of continued external support, the Zairian state has failed to improve the economic fortunes of its citizens even after more than two decades of "stability" under one leader. The colonial economic structure of the state with its overdependence on the mineral sector remains, and the majority of Zairians continue to be marginalized with respect to the formal sector. A strong argument can be made that on a fundamental level, the Zairian economic crisis, though it was precipitated by a fall in copper prices, was caused by a series of disastrous economic policies that were *politically* based. Since 1965 the perpetuation of such policies has formed a powerful element of continuity in the Zairian state. Accordingly, donor-inspired economic reform has lacked substance, and far-reaching changes have been rescinded as soon as the regime has had breathing room in the form of increased financial resources. Political expediency is also evident in Zaire's diplomatic maneuverings in the international arena, as will be seen in Chapter 5.

NOTES

1. Crawford Young and Thomas Turner, *The Rise and Decline of the Zairian State* (Madison: University of Wisconsin Press, 1985), pp. 33–34.

2. Under forced cultivation, export crops had to be sold at artificially low prices to the large agricultural companies that were given regional monopolies in the Congo such as Huilerie du Congo Belge (palm oil) and La Cotonco (cotton). This policy was complemented by forced recruitment of low-wage labor for the mines, plantations, and public works. Colonial economic policy was therefore designed to encourage the growth of the foreign enterprise and companies such as Union Minière were initially developed through labor intensive methods. Jean-Philippe Peemans, "The Social and Economic Development of Zaire Since Independence: An Historical Outline," *African Affairs* 74, no. 295 (April 1975), pp. 150–151.

3. Robert Cornevin, *Le Zaire* (Paris: Presses Universitaires de France, 1972), p. 71.

4. Roger Anstey, *King Leopold's Legacy* (London: Oxford University Press, 1966), p. 104.

5. Robert Cornevin, *Le Zaire*, p. 71.

6. Ibid., p. 104. The Congo accounted for 85 percent of total African production of cobalt and 64 percent of diamond production. Georges Brausch, *Belgian Administration in the Congo* (London: Institute of Race Relations, Oxford University Press, 1961), p. 1. On the structure of the colonial state in the 1950s, see Peemans, "Social and Economic Development," p. 153.

7. International Bank for Reconstruction and Development, International Development Association, *The Economy of The Republic of Congo-Leopoldville*, vol. II, July 1964, tables 3, 4.

8. Prior to independence 50 congolese francs were equivalent to $1. By 1962 the rate had increased fivefold to 250 congolese francs to $1. Crawford Young, *Politics in the Congo: Decolonization and Independence* (Princeton: Princeton University Press, 1965), pp. 353–355.

9. International Monetary Fund, *Surveys of African Economies*, vol. 4 (Washington, D.C.: IMF, 1971), pp. 12–17; Young and Turner, *Rise and Decline*, p. 279.

10. Young and Turner, *Rise and Decline*, pp. 296–298.

11. Ibid., p. 306.

12. For a detailed study of Zairianization, see Edward Kannyo, "Political Power and Class Formation in Zaire: The Zairianization Measures 1973–75," Ph.D. diss., Yale University, 1979. See also Michael Schatzberg, *Politics and Class in Zaire: Bureaucracy, Business and Beer in Lisala* (New York: Africana, 1980); Young and Turner, *Rise and Decline*, chap. 11.

13. See Wolf Radman, "The Nationalization of Zaire's Copper: From Union Minière to GECAMINES," *Africa Today* 25, no. 4 (October-December, 1978).

14. Winsome Leslie, *The World Bank and Structural Transformation in Developing Countries: The Case of Zaire* (Boulder: Lynne Rienner, 1987), p. 95. For background and the development of the mining industry in Zaire, see *Zaire: A Country Study*, 3d ed. (Washington, D.C.: American University, 1979), pp. 214–222; Ilunga Ilunkamba, *Propriété Publique et Conventions de Gestion dans L'industrie du Cuivre*

au Zaire (Kinshasa: Centre d'Étude et de Documentation [CEDAF], 1984); Gregory Kronsten, *Zaire to the 1990s: Will Retrenchment Work?* EIU, Special Report, no. 227 (London: Economist Publications, 1986), pp. 63–72.

Up until 1990 10 percent of Zaire's copper output had been produced in Shaba by the Société de Développement Industriel et Minier du Zaire (SODIMIZA). The company, originally established in 1969, was 15 percent government owned and 85 percent owned by a Japanese consortium. SODIMIZA was integrated with GECAMINES under the terms of a 1989 agreement.

15. Bank of Zaire, *Information Memorandum* (Kinshasa: Bank of Zaire, December 1981).

16. World Bank, *Zaire Report,* July 1986, p. 14; Confidential Interview, Washington, D.C., May 10, 1985.

17. Erwin Blumenthal, "Zaire: Report on Her International Financial Credibility," unpublished report, April 1982, p. 14; *Africa Economic Digest,* July 6, 1984, p. 14.

GECAMINES now consists of a holding company, GECAMINES Holding, and three affiliates: GECAMINES Exploitation, in charge of mining operations; GECAMINES Commercial, which has taken over marketing from SOZACOM; and GECAMINES Development, which runs the company's agricultural ventures. In April 1991 it was announced prematurely that GECAMINES Development had been sold to a South African firm. The government has in fact opted for privatization of the affiliate. EIU, *Country Report: Zaire,* no. 2 (1991), p. 20.

18. *Africa Economic Digest,* February 15, 1986, p. 12; Ibid., May 17, 1986, p. 13; Ibid., August 16, 1986; Ibid., January 24, 1987, p. 12; World Bank, *Zaire Report,* June 1989; *EIU Country Report: Zaire,* no. 2 (1991), p. 20; EIU, *Country Report: Zaire,* no. 4 (1991), pp. 19–20.

19. Jean-Claude Willame, *Zaire: L'Epopée D'Inga* (Paris: Éditions L'Harmattan, 1986), pp. 29–38.

20. Ibid., pp. 39–40, 43–44; Young and Turner, *Rise and Decline,* p. 299.

21. The Ex-Im Bank found itself in an untenable position with respect to Inga-Shaba. Without its continued financial support, Inga-Shaba could not be completed; if this were the case, it was felt in congressional circles that Zaire would not be able to increase GECAMINES' production to repay the loans. Nevertheless, there were Ex-Im Bank officials who rightly claimed that there were problems in the mining sector that additional electrical power would not solve, such as transportation difficulties and shortages of spare parts. For congressional testimony on Inga-Shaba see House Committee on Banking, Finance and Urban Affairs, *Oversight Hearing on the Export-Import Bank: Hearing Before the Subcommittee on International Trade, Investment and Monetary Policy,* 96th Cong., 1st sess., May 21, 1979; Senate Committee on Banking, Housing and Urban Affairs, Subcommittee on International Finance, *Hearings,* 96th Cong., 1st sess., May 24, 1979.

22. EIU, *Country Profile: Zaire, 1990–1991,* p. 5.

23. Ibid., p. 25.

24. U.S. Department of Commerce, International Trade Administration, *Foreign Economic Trends and Their Implications for the United States: Zaire,* 1990, p. 2.

The following section draws heavily on earlier research on the Zairian economy. See, in particular, Leslie, *Structural Transformation,* pp. 62–67; World Bank,

Zaire: Current Economic Situation and Constraints (Washington, D.C.: IBRD, 1979); World Bank, *The Economy of Zaire* (Washington, D.C.: IBRD, July 1975).

25. In 1975 1Z = $2; 1SDR = $1.15. See EIU, *Quarterly Economic Review: Zaire, Rwanda, Burundi,* Annual Supplement, 1975; World Bank, *Zaire: Current Economic Situation,* pp. 5, 13.

26. Jonathan Aronson, "The Politics of Private Bank Lending and Debt Renegotiations" in *Debt and the Less Developed Countries,* ed. Jonathan Aronson (Boulder: Westview Press, 1979), pp. 291–292; Jeffrey Garten, "Rescheduling Third World Debt: The Case of Zaire 1979–80," Ph.D. diss., School of Advanced International Studies, Johns Hopkins University, 1981, p. 35.

27. In 1982, before the devaluation, the official rate was Z6 = $1, against a parallel rate of Z30 = $1. After devaluation, the floating official rate registered Z35 = $1 at the beginning of 1984 and Z53 = $1 by November 1985, with the parallel rate varying between 8 percent and 15 percent of the floating rate.

28. U.S. Department of Commerce, *Foreign Economic Trends,* 1990, p. 4.

29. In May 1989 France broke with tradition in the Paris Club and decided to write off public sector debts to the world's poorest countries, including Zaire. Belgium followed suit in July, agreeing to cancel one-third of Zaire's $448 million in publicly guaranteed Belgian credits and about $126 million in bilateral loans. By the end of the year, an agreement had been signed with the United States for the cancellation of debts totaling $191 million in USAID credits, representing about 10 percent of the U.S. loan portfolio to Zaire. The first $53.9 million was to be written off immediately, with the remaining amount canceled in two phases, pending Zaire's acceptance of IMF/World Bank approved policies. Germany also agreed to cancel debts totaling $340 million. *FBIS Daily Report: Sub-Saharan Africa,* May 3, 1989, p. 2.; EIU, *Country Report: Zaire,* no. 1 (1990), p. 20; *Africa Economic Digest,* November 1989; ibid., July 24, 1990.

30. EIU, *Country Report: Zaire,* no. 1 (1990), p. 13. Unusually high export earnings were mainly attributable to the surprisingly high price of copper due to output constraints in Papua New Guinea and Peru. Prices peaked at $1.68 per pound in December 1988 and averaged $1.21 per pound for 1989. EIU, *Country Report: Zaire,* no. 3 (1989), p. 16.

31. Confidential interview, Washington, D.C., May 31, 1990. In December 1988 the official rate stood at Z274 = $1 but fell to Z455 = $1 one year later. EIU, *Country Report: Zaire,* no. 1 (1990), p. 14; *Africa Economic Digest,* July 31, 1989, p. 9; comments by Larry Saiers, Deputy Assistant Administrator for Africa, USAID; House Foreign Affairs Committee, *Foreign Assistance Legislation for Fiscal Years 1990–91,* part 6, *Hearings and Markup Before the House Subcommittee on Africa,* 101st Cong., 1st Sess., March 8, 1989, p. 104.

32. Confidential interview, Washington, D.C., May 31, 1990; *Wall Street Journal,* April 9, 1990, p. B5.

33. EIU, *Country Report: Zaire,* no. 1 (1990), p. 14; ibid., no. 4 (1990), p. 3; ibid., no. 2 (1991), pp. 3, 9; ibid., no. 3 (1991), p. 3; ibid., p. 17; *Africa Report* November-December 1991, p. 12; confidential interview, Washington, D.C., March 17, 1992; EIU, *Country Report: Zaire,* no. 1 (1992), p. 17; EIU, *Country Report: Zaire,* no. 2 (1992), pp. 14–15.

34. Thomas M. Callaghy, "The Ritual Dance of the Debt Game," *Africa*

Report, September-October 1984; Thomas M. Callaghy, "External Actors and the Relative Autonomy of the Political Aristocracy in Zaire," *Journal of Commonwealth and Comparative Politics* 21, no. 3 (November 1983), pp. 61–83.

35. Confidential interview, Washington, D.C., May 31, 1990.

36. At the time, there were those in the World Bank who held the view that a tough position on Zaire would convey a powerful message to Sub-Saharan Africa. It would demonstrate that the World Bank was prepared to effectively isolate those nations that were not interested in economic development and social welfare, more effectively linking continued multilateral aid to serious reform efforts. As one official pointed out, Zaire should not be entitled to the same levels of aid as those countries undertaking serious austerity measures. Confidential interviews, Washington, D.C., March 30, May 31, 1990; March 17, March 24, 1992.

37. Banque du Zaire Reports, 1975, 1980, 1989, table 5.

38. One such success story is a maize project in North Shaba, a USAID-funded project that began in 1977. USAID claims that over the ten-year life of the project maize yields increased by 100 percent to 300 percent through distribution of improved seeds and the training of farmers in better agricultural practices. Roads and bridges in the area were also rehabilitated to facilitate transport of maize production to market. The project was subsequently taken over by GECAMINES Development. However, the GOZ has been unable to maintain the infrastructure, and the project area has had to contend with illegal imports of maize flour from Zambia. As a result of these and other difficulties, GECAMINES Exploitation has assumed management of the operation. *Africa News*, April 4, 1988, p. 5; EIU, *Country Report: Zaire*, no. 2 (1989), p. 13; ibid., no. 2 (1991), p. 20.

39. USAID, "Country Development Strategy Statement, Zaire, FY 1986," January 1984. The Office des Routes is commonly known as the Office des Trous (Bureau of Potholes), indicating its inability to successfully undertake key maintenance projects.

40. *Africa Economic Digest*, June 21, 1986, p. 26.

41. Janet MacGaffey, "The African Underground Economy," in *Africa*, vol. 2, ed. Sean Moroney (New York: Facts on File, 1989), pp. 876–877.

42. For the complete argument, see Janet MacGaffey, "Fending for Yourself: The Organization of the Second Economy in Zaire," in *The Crisis in Zaire: Myths and Realities*, ed. Nzongola-Ntalaja (Trenton: Africa World Press, 1986), pp. 141–156.

43. *African Business*, January 1989, p. 43; *African Business*, April 1989, pp. 55–56; *African Business*, July 1989, p. 52. For an excellent analysis of second economy activities in various regions of Zaire, see Janet MacGaffey et al., *The Real Economy of Zaire: The Contribution of Smuggling and Other Unofficial Activities to National Wealth* (Philadelphia: University of Pennsylvania Press, 1991).

5

Zaire in the
International Arena

Several themes that need to be examined in any discussion of Zaire's maneuverings in the international arena are touched on in the following official statement of Zaire's foreign policy:

> Positive non-alignment, or indiscriminate openmindedness to the world, is a fundamental feature of Zaire's foreign policy. To this end, we are exerting ourselves in a bid to promote genuine cooperation among all countries that are willing to accept Zaire for what it is. . . . The debacles that Zaire has faced and continues to face in various areas—colonization, alienation, exploitation, secession, rebellion—are due to the imperialistic policies of the superpowers who have assumed the right to govern the world. Thus, we do not want to be involved directly or indirectly in any attempt to subjugate a state or group of states.[1]

Nonalignment, the notion of Zaire as victim in the superpower game, and nonintervention in the affairs of other states are issues that have been touted by the Mobutu regime since 1965. The reality is that in many respects the tone of Zaire's current foreign policy was established in the chaotic period immediately after independence, when the Congo was news and the international community became intimately involved in the affairs of the new state. Similarly, international criticism against Leopoldian excesses in the Congo Free State at the end of the nineteenth century had brought it sharply into focus on the world stage, resulting in annexation of the territory by Belgium. Historically, Zaire has been seen as either a prize, a crisis area, or a strategic location vital to Western interests, but there are strong indications that it has declined in relative importance in the 1990s.[2]

In this chapter I will examine the many facets of Zaire's relationship with other states over the years—its strategic value and its crucial dependence on external support, the desire for recognition as a "legitimate"

137

regional political force, and its flirtation with nonalignment—all against a background of the Machiavellian statecraft of the Mobutu regime.

EARLY CHAOS AND INTERNATIONAL RESCUE: ESTABLISHING A LASTING PATTERN

The international diplomatic maneuverings during the Congo Crisis, resulting in external intervention to restore the status quo in the Zairian state, set a precedent for foreign involvement in the country's domestic affairs that has lasted to the present day. Since independence, international assistance in both the political and economic realms has been crucial to state preservation, consolidation, and ultimately, in the Mobutu era, regime survival. This connection is clearly illustrated by the immediate postindependence events between 1960 and 1965, the two Shaba invasions, and Zaire's economic and debt crises. Some have viewed the more recent international rescue efforts, in both the economic and political realms, as a recolonization process in which Zaire is reverting to de facto foreign control.[3] Nevertheless, although Zaire is a dependent state, the Mobutu regime cannot be regarded as either a puppet or a pawn in its foreign relations.

During the Congo Crisis the country was seen in strategic terms against the background of the cold war. Accordingly, the Congo soon became the focus of a series of high-level UN Security Council debates that culminated in foreign intervention in the form of a UN peacekeeping force conveniently drawn from African and nonaligned nations. Three key members of the Security Council—the United States, the Soviet Union, and Great Britain—provided logistical support for the operation. The United Nations and, more specifically, the United States played a leading role in the subsequent course of events—Lumumba's murder, in which the CIA was implicated, and the end of the Katanga secession in 1963. With the subsequent rebel capture of Stanleyville (Kisangani), Prime Minister Tshombe once again appealed for international assistance. Western powers mounted the Stanleyville Rescue, with the United States supplying transport and aircraft to carry Belgian troops into the area to evacuate the European population. Throughout the initial crisis from 1960 to 1963—even though actual Soviet support consisted largely of posturing at the UN—Belgian intervention and secessions in Katanga and Kasai made the Congo a potential battleground for a U.S.-Soviet confrontation.

The need for international rescue has continued under the Mobutu regime with the two invasions of Shaba province by the FLNC from bases in Angola and Zambia in 1977 and 1978. In contrast to the Congo Crisis, where foreign intervention gave external actors license to restructure politics in Leopoldville, the Shaba incidents were effected to maintain the status quo—that is, the survival of the Mobutu government. In Shaba I, Mobutu played the Communist card, citing evidence of Cuban and Soviet involvement in the attack in order to reaffirm Zaire's strategic importance and justify the need for Western intervention. Mobutu himself spent several weeks at the front in Kolwezi to indicate the seriousness of the situation from the government's perspective. It was clear that some members of the international community bought into the geopolitical argument, as during that time at least twenty-three countries either dispatched supplies to Zaire or sent senior officials to Kolwezi or Kinshasa.[4] The United States, however, kept a relatively low profile. It was not convinced of Cuba's role in the invasion; and because of President Jimmy Carter's new foreign policy focus on human rights, the administration had become more critical of the Mobutu government. As a result, the United States stuck to a pattern already established in the Congo Crisis, providing nonlethal military aid—radio equipment and spare parts, for example—rather than committing forces to the operations. The FLNC's efforts were ultimately thwarted by Moroccan troops with French logistical support.

Shaba II, in 1978, was a more devastating attack, in that the copper mining town of Kolwezi was actually seized and Europeans as well as locals were killed. Not only was this invasion sufficient to elicit a swift international response; it prompted the United States to give more credence to Mobutu's allegations about a Communist connection. Fidel Castro admitted to knowing about the planned incident about a month before it occurred. Although Castro denied involvement, saying that he had actually tried to stop the attack,[5] from the U.S. perspective the hint of Cuban complicity underscored Zaire's importance as a likely target for Communist influence. Unlike the response to Shaba I, Moroccan troops played no role in this second rescue. The French Foreign Legion and Belgian paratroopers retook Kolwezi, with the United States providing air transport. Overall, the general incompetence of the Zairian troops in the face of the two attacks was viewed by the West as yet another indication that Zaire was in need of fundamental political and economic reform. As a result, the events in Shaba proved to be a turning point, as they precipitated future large-scale Western involvement in the affairs of the Zairian state.

Late 1991 saw foreign troops once again on Zairian soil. In the midst of widespread dissatisfaction with Mobutu's efforts to thwart the democratization process, growing internal dissent, and ongoing workers' strikes, several army units protesting low wages seized Kinshasa's airport on September 22. They systematically looted and burned businesses, warehouses, and other commercial properties in the capital. Citizens, deprived of basic consumer staples because of ongoing economic hardship, joined the rioting, emptying the capital of food supplies, medicine, and most consumer items. Residences and businesses of wealthy Zairians were particular targets. At one point, the crowds marched down Kinshasa's main street waving the blue and red flag of the Congo Democratic Republic, as Zaire was known in the 1960–1965 period, further indicating a rejection of Mobutu's rule.[6]

Even as the violence began spreading to other regions, including traditional centers of anti-Mobutu sentiment such as Shaba and Kivu, foreigners began to flee to neighboring Congo-Brazzaville and Zambia. They described widespread destruction in Kinshasa, Kolwezi, and Kisangani and indiscriminate shootings by soldiers, resulting in an estimated 100 dead and 1,500 wounded. In a situation strangely reminiscent of the foreign intervention after the army mutiny that triggered the Congo Crisis, France and then Belgium quickly secured Mobutu's approval to airlift troops into Zaire to protect the European population. Within two days about 2,000 French and Belgian paratroopers were arriving in Kinshasa from Brazzaville to take control of the airport and other strategic points around the city. With U.S. logistical support, about 10,000 expatriates were evacuated according to a detailed plan devised by the

French paratroopers in front of the American Consulate, September 24, 1991. Moments after this photograph was taken, a French soldier was killed here in a drive-by shooting. French and Belgian troops were brought in from Brazzaville to protect expatriates in response to widespread looting by the FAZ. Photo courtesy of Learned Dees.

UFERI supporters at a funeral for a party member killed when armed men attacked the party headquarters. Banner on the left reads, "Union Sacrée in mourning; dictatorial assassination continues." Placard on the right reads, "Union Sacrée in mourning; Mobutu has murdered it." Photo courtesy of Learned Dees.

Europeans in Kinshasa in 1990 after the massacre of students in Lubumbashi. France, Belgium, and the United States also sent emergency food supplies and medicine through private voluntary organizations operating in the country.[7]

The Union Sacrée—the coalition of opposition groups—initially condemned the intervention by foreign troops as an effort to save the Mobutu regime and preserve the status quo. Nevertheless, subsequent looting and large-scale destruction in Lubumbashi in October 1991 and additional evacuations of expatriates from Shaba resulted in opposition appeals to Belgium and France to leave their troops in place to prevent civil war. Apparently the incident began with disgruntled soldiers ransacking homes and offices, but it quickly grew into clashes between pro-Mobutu forces and the opposition over the dismissal of Tshisekedi as prime minister, as well as confrontations between rival opposition groups. The United States, France, and Belgium had closed their consulates by early November, and the foreign troops were withdrawn after additional evacuations, bringing the total to 20,000 foreigners transported out of the country.

Western governments led by Belgium, France, and the United States used the 1991 incidents to insist on democratic reform in the interest of political stability. Mobutu was urged in the strongest terms to allow the formation of a transition government acceptable to the opposition as a precursor to free and fair elections leading to a Third Republic. Indeed, the responses of Western governments to Zaire's political crises over the years have been due as much to individual bilateral interests as to the perception of the country as an important point of stability in the region. These interests have, in turn, affected Zaire's foreign policy and given Mobutu some room to maneuver.

RELATIONS WITH OTHER STATES

Belgium: A Stormy Relationship

Since Zaire's independence, its relationship with Belgium has been symbiotic yet volatile and marred by periodic disagreements. As the former colonial power, Belgium is still Zaire's major trading partner (refer to Table 4.7), and investment ties remain strong. Several of the large conglomerates established in Zaire in the early 1900s continue to have significant holdings and thus indirect influence in the local economy. Société Générale de Belgique (SGB) is directly or indirectly involved in all sectors of the economy, although since 1988 majority shares of the company have been held by France's Suez Group. Important SGB investments include a 25 percent interest in the largest and most important Zairian bank, Banque Commerciale Zairoise (BCZ), and a 20 percent holding in the only diamond company, Miba. More significantly, about half of Zaire's copper is processed in Belgium at the plant of an SGB subsidiary, Metallurgie d'Hoboken Overpelt (MHO). The Groupe Empain has a 72 percent interest in Sominki, a tin mining company. Unilever holds majority shares in Plantations Lever au Zaire (PLZ)—which cultivates and processes palm oil, rubber, and cotton—and Marsavco, a manufacturing company producing soap, margarine, and cooking oil. Marsavco also owns a chain of supermarkets. Four of the five largest textile companies (Groupe Hassan et Frères, Solbena, Amato Frères, and Sotexki) are Belgian owned. In 1983 Belgian private investment was estimated at $875 million, but by 1992 this figure had fallen to an estimated $100 million.[8]

Zaire's dependence on Belgian foreign aid is quite extensive. Belgium alone accounts for one-third of total bilateral loans and grants. Ties with Belgium have been reinforced by a local Belgian community of as many as 20,000 in Zaire as of 1989, mostly linked to commercial interests, technical assistance, top-level appointments in government parastatals, and development projects. Approximately an equal number of Zairians reside in Brussels. The community is so well established that the Zairian quarter has been christened Matonge after a district in Kinshasa.[9]

In spite of this apparent closeness, there have been periodic outbursts of friction, characterized by much grandstanding on both sides. Over the years disagreements between Zaire and Belgium have centered on several contentious issues. First, Mobutu has repeatedly claimed that Belgium has a moral debt to Zaire and should compensate the country financially for colonial exploitation. In addition, Belgian Catholic organizations and members of the Belgian Socialist party have been consistently drawing attention to the GOZ's human rights abuses. Such blatant criticism of the Zairian regime has been widely publicized in the Belgian press. Finally, the president has never been comfortable with the fact that in the past Belgium has served as a haven for groups opposed to his regime and that some of these political exiles' activities were encouraged by Belgian politicians.[10] Several so-called coup attempts over the years have allegedly originated in Brussels with the active support of Belgian officials.

The question of compensation developed into open confrontation in 1988 over Zaire's repayment of debts owed Belgium. A debt rescheduling offer made by Belgium in November that year was flatly rejected by the Zairian government as inadequate on the basis of the years of Belgian exploitation of Zaire's resources. Belgium had offered to cancel Bf1 billion ($25 million) of an estimated Bf40.7 billion in Zairian debt. From the perspective of the Mobutu regime, existing relations and formal agreements between the two countries did not reflect postcolonial realities. Although this argument had some merit, the "crisis" came at a time when Mobutu was disturbed by his declining influence with the ruling political group in Brussels (the Socialist party) and angered by constant berating in the Belgian press.[11] To indicate its dissatisfaction, the GOZ implemented drastic measures, ordering all Zairians living in Brussels to leave with their assets by the end of the year. Zaire's ruling party (the MPR) announced that the government would not be using the Belgian airline, SABENA, or the Belgian shipping company, Compagnie Maritime Belge. Mobutu himself claimed that he had transferred his own assets in Belgium to Zaire. Further, it was announced that the Brussels offices of nine Zairian parastatals would be moved to other European capitals.

The Belgian government initially offered a low-keyed response to Mobutu's threats, with top officials—including foreign minister Leo Tindemans—visiting Zaire to maintain a dialogue. At this point, the announcements seemed to lack substance. Certainly there was no massive exodus of Zairians from Brussels. But Mobutu took the situation even further, canceling debt service on private and public debt owed to

Belgium and declaring the 1960 Friendship Treaty and a 1976 Cooperation Accord between the two countries null and void. In addition, he announced the government's intention to diversify the refining of GECAMINES' copper production away from Brussels to other countries in Europe. These new developments now struck at the heart of Belgian economic interests, and Brussels retaliated with a decision to halt all new development projects in Zaire and to seek legal recourse in reaction to the GOZ's suspension of SABENA's flights to Kinshasa. According to a March 1989 article in the Belgian journal *Le Soir*, Zaire had much to lose in the continuing feud—an estimated Z100 million per month.[12] But the crisis was resolved by mid-1989, when Zaire and Belgium signed the Rabat Protocol, the culmination of several months of mediation efforts by King Hassan of Morocco, a longtime ally of Mobutu. The focus of the agreement was Belgium's partial cancellation of Zaire's public and publicly guaranteed debts, part of a program covering thirteen African countries.[13]

The tenuous truce between the two countries was once again shattered in May 1990, this time over the sensitive issue of human rights. The Belgian press widely publicized the massacre by government forces of university students in Lubumbashi protesting Mobutu's rescinding of political liberalization measures announced in April. It was claimed that at least fifty students were killed by the army, who fired on them at point-blank range. The students were supposedly buried in a mass grave. By contrast, official GOZ reports stated that only two students died. Following a visit to Lubumbashi by the Belgian ambassador, Belgium called for an international commission of inquiry into the killings. In addition, planned balance of payments support funds to the GOZ for 1990 as well as its overall aid program (including technical assistance) were suspended, and preparations for a Belgian-Zairian Joint Cooperation Commission were abandoned. The suspension of aid put several cofinanced local projects in jeopardy. In response to what it termed blatant interference in its internal affairs, the GOZ renounced the Belgian debt relief package signed in 1989; announced the closure of three of the four consulates in Zaire, including those in Lubumbashi and Kinshasa; reduced SABENA's flights from five to two a week; and expelled Belgian development workers in Zaire being paid by their government. Belgium, in turn, warned of the dangers of breaking formal relations.

Since the 1980s Belgium has been diversifying its economic interests away from Zaire. Following the Zairianization measures and the lack of government compensation, Belgian businessmen had begun to look at opportunities elsewhere in Africa. Furthermore, the publication of the Blumenthal report in 1982, alleging that Mobutu was siphoning off portions of the Zairian budget for personal use and linking several Belgian officials to Zairian corruption, caused the Belgian government to re-examine its relationship with Zaire. Accordingly, Belgium embarked on a policy of strengthening economic ties with other nations in Africa—Algeria, Nigeria, South Africa, and Egypt. In 1983 Zairian-Belgian relations hit a new low over precisely this issue, as Mobutu had interpreted such moves to mean that Zaire would no longer have its privileged status. Nevertheless, by June 1985 Zaire's relations with Belgium were as good as they ever were when King Baudouin and Queen Fabiola attended the official celebrations marking the twenty-fifth year of Zaire's independence.

It is likely that the stormy relationship between the two countries will persist. Belgium will remain critical of and cool toward Zaire for the indefinite future unless substantial political and economic change takes place. It is felt that Mobutu himself was implicated in the Lubumbashi incident and that such an atrocity was all the more blatant in view of his alleged commitment to democracy. After the September and October 1991 disturbances and subsequent evacuations, about 1,000 Belgians remained in Zaire in March 1992, including 800 missionaries. Since these incidents the Belgian government has stated openly and categorically that Mobutu must relinquish power. Accordingly, it has taken the lead in suspending further economic aid unless Mobutu permits an orderly and *sustained* transition to democratic government. Furthermore, on the economic front, Belgium has genuine cause for concern, with Zaire's financial and economic system in shambles and the GOZ in arrears on its bilateral debt by an estimated $1 billion.

In reality, under Mobutu's leadership, Zaire has been critically dependent on Brussels in economic terms and does not seem anxious to lose its privileged status. Nevertheless, Zaire apparently wants aid without strings—namely, absence from censorship and scrutiny. This applies equally to Zaire's relationship with the United States.

The United States: Strategic Interests

The U.S.-Zaire relationship has flowed from the perceived pivotal location of Zaire in Central Africa. Bordering nine other African countries, leading all nations in exports of industrial diamonds, and producing between 60 percent and 70 percent of the world's cobalt and 5 percent to 7 percent of its copper, Zaire is considered vital to the West. Further, since his takeover in 1965, Mobutu's consistent pro-Western stand served to underscore Zaire's strategic importance in view of U.S. perceptions of a renewed Soviet interest in Africa in the 1960s and 1970s. It was hoped that under Mobutu's leadership, Zaire could be the focal point for U.S. foreign policy objectives in Sub-Saharan Africa in much the same way that Brazil was in Latin America. As a result, except for

President Carter, because of his strong human rights policy, successive U.S. presidents have chosen to ignore Mobutu's heavy-handed oppressive moves to consolidate his power at home. The focus instead has been on his pro-Western stand and his support on key U.S. foreign policy issues such as Angola.

In 1987 Zaire made headlines in U.S. newspapers over precisely this subject. It came to light that Mobutu was permitting U.S. covert military aid to be funneled through Zairian territory to support the U.S.-backed União Nacional para Independência Total de Angola (UNITA; Union for the Total Independence of Angola) guerrillas. Movements of arms were occurring even as Mobutu himself was beginning his role as official mediator between UNITA and the government of the Movimento Popular de Libertação de Angola (MPLA; Popular Movement for the Liberation of Angola). The United States was granted access to the military base at Kamina (in north-central Shaba) for the transshipments. Kamina was built by the Belgians during the colonial period and was used extensively by foreign troops during the Congo Crisis and the two Shaba invasions. It is ideally situated as it permits U.S. planes to travel from the base to any point in Africa and to return without refueling. U.S. Army Special Forces have frequently held joint military maneuvers with Zairian troops there. According to several accounts, U.S. covert aid to UNITA was initially carried out without congressional approval and was subsequently facilitated by Israel and South Africa. It was further revealed that the Pentagon was pressing the administration of Ronald Reagan to negotiate a formal access agreement to Kamina so that it could undertake a $2 million renovation scheme.[14]

Regardless of this strategic component, the U.S.-Zaire relationship has ebbed and flowed over the years, with an ever-widening gap developing between Congress and the administration over support to the Mobutu regime. The Zairian president made three official trips to the United States during the Reagan years and was the first African head of state to visit the White House after George Bush's inauguration. Nevertheless, the positive reception by the administration in each case contrasted with the skepticism of Congress, which consistently reduced White House allocations for economic and military aid to Zaire. In a series of hearings on Capitol Hill in 1983, members of a congressional study mission to Zaire stated that U.S. policy appeared to be attached to Mobutu personally. Although in principle the United States seemed to be urging major economic reform, little or no attention was being focused on the political system sustaining corruption and economic mismanagement.[15]

U.S. administration aid requests for Zaire (Economic Support Funds [ESF], food aid, development assistance, and military assistance) have been large by Sub-Saharan African standards, averaging $60 million to

$85 million in the 1980s.[16] However, at the start of the Bush presidency, campaigns on Capitol Hill to severely limit aid to Zaire accelerated because of repeated reports of corruption, misappropriation of U.S. aid funds, and consistent human rights abuses over the years. Congressional efforts focused on the House Subcommittee on Africa and were supported by local interest groups such as the Rainbow Lobby and the U.S.-Congo Friendship Committee. After hearings in March and April 1989 on foreign assistance for fiscal 1990/91, a bill was introduced by Congressman Ronald V. Dellums, chairman of the Congressional Black Caucus, eliminating military aid and Economic Support Funds and restricting aid to amounts channeled through private voluntary organizations operating in the country. In addition, the bill stipulated that congressional approval would be required before any U.S. aid could be spent.[17] Subsequently the House Appropriations Foreign Operations Subcommittee formulated legislation capping military aid at $3 million and eliminating ESF. The original Dellums bill was passed by Congress in November 1990, denying the administration's request for $4 million in military aid and channeling the estimated $40 million in economic aid through PVOs.

Ironically, all this occurred at the same time that the White House chose to focus on Mobutu as "friend" and the statesman who was instrumental in peacekeeping efforts in Africa—particularly in Angola. The following year Zaire provided invaluable support for U.S. foreign policy objectives in the Desert Storm operation against Iraq, when Zaire's representative served as president of the UN Security Council at the time of the U.S-led invasion in January 1991. This was yet another example of the support Zaire has given intermittently over the years to the U.S. position in international forums.

In the wake of attempts by Mobutu's security forces to intimidate the opposition movement in Zaire in the midst of abysmal economic conditions, the Bush administration consistently pressed the Zairian leader to permit political pluralism. In March 1990 Secretary of State James Baker visited Zaire en route from Namibia's independence celebrations. At that time Mobutu was encouraged to initiate a democratic process in the country in view of similar trends elsewhere on the continent. A month later, Mobutu reversed his decision against a Zairian *perestroika* and came out in favor of a multiparty system.

Clearly concerned about his image and future aid prospects, Mobutu began aggressively cultivating a domestic constituency in the United States. Undoubtedly, sweeping democratic changes in Eastern Europe and the end of the cold war, together with the withdrawal of Cuba and the former Soviet Union from Africa, have made countries in the region strategically less relevant, causing Zaire to decline in relative importance. Accordingly, in 1989 Mobutu hired two public relations firms in Wash-

Mobutu Sese Seko of Zaire at the United Nations in 1991. Photo courtesy of Africa News Service.

ington, D.C., to step up lobbying efforts on Zaire's behalf on Capitol Hill. Coincidentally, one of these firms, van Kolberg & Associates, had also conducted lobbying efforts on behalf of Romania. Nicolae Ceausescu, the Romanian dictator, was an ally and personal friend of Mobutu before the Romanian's violent overthrow and death. In addition, a Zairian-American Research Institute (ZARI) was established at the same time in Washington, funded by prominent Zairian businessman Bemba Saolona, president of the Scibe-Zaire industrial group. Until its closure in 1991,

ZARI sought to promote a better understanding of the country and its leader in order to counter the efforts of Mobutu's most vocal critics in the United States.

Mobutu's attempts to sabotage the democratic process in Zaire, though paying lip service to the need for political and economic reform, come at a time when Zaire's usefulness in a strategic sense has declined. These efforts have apparently left U.S. administration officials short on solutions with respect to an effective Zaire policy. Congress concurs with the Belgian position that genuine political and economic reforms as well as an effective transition government are not possible with Mobutu on the scene. Many individuals in the administration have acknowledged privately that ultimately Mobutu must go. However, the official U.S. view has been that in order to ensure stability, Mobutu must remain a part of any transition until elections can be held, given the fact that he controls key elements of the security forces—the DSP and the Civil Guard. Under the U.S. plan, Mobutu should retain control of foreign policy and the army but turn over control of the economy to the transition government.

U.S. economic interests in Zaire are significantly less than are those of Belgium. In October 1988 private investment was in the range of $200 million to $250 million, and there were twenty companies either fully or partially U.S.-owned operating in Kinshasa in areas such as motor vehicle assembly (General Motors), petroleum exploration (Mobil Oil), banking (Citibank), tire manufacturing (Goodyear), and hotel management (Intercontinental). Nevertheless, the looting and destruction in fall 1991 have resulted in a major decline in the American presence. Many American operations were partially or completely destroyed. The General Motors plant, with significant ownership by Zairian interests, was beyond repair, and the company immediately sought $30 million in insurance compensation under an Overseas Private Investment Corporation arrangement. Zaire Gulf Oil, the offshore petroleum exploration consortium including Chevron, was not significantly affected by the riots and continues to operate. The United States and Zaire signed a bilateral investment treaty in 1984, guaranteeing U.S. investors national treatment status and unrestricted repatriation of profits, among other provisions. New investment under the program has not materialized. U.S.-Zaire trade favors Zaire, largely because of mineral imports of copper and cobalt for U.S. stockpiles. Over the years U.S. assistance to Zaire has included food aid under the PL 480 program, Development Fund for Africa grants, as well as small amounts of military aid.[18] In June 1991 Zaire was one year in arrears on its bilateral debt to the United States. According to Brooke Amendment requirements, all development assistance therefore had to be suspended. By December 31, 1991, military and economic development funds one year in arrears totaled $30 million, and PL 480 arrears were $26.2 million. USAID terminated its country program at that time and began the process of "de-obligating" funds previously committed to Zaire.

France: A New Friend

In contrast to Zaire's relationships with Belgium and the United States, its close relationship with France has developed more recently. The Mobutu regime began to court the French in the early 1970s, during the period of relative economic strength, when Zaire wanted to look beyond its traditional alliances with Belgium and the United States. With the election of Valéry Giscard d'Estaing in 1974, both France and Zaire took concerted steps to strengthen their relationship. Prior to this time, France and Zaire had established ties in the context of the French-dominated Organization Commune Africaine et Malgache (OCAM; African and Malagasy Community Organization).[19] Zaire ultimately withdrew from OCAM in 1972, accusing the French of dominating the organization.

As the largest French-speaking African state, Zaire has always been attractive to France. On his part, Mobutu deliberately courted the French in an effort to counterbalance the relationship with Belgium. In the past, Mobutu has enjoyed a close personal relationship with French president François Mitterrand and has supported French foreign policy aims in Sub-Saharan Africa. To underscore France's commitment to Zaire, the first Franco-African Summit was held in Kinshasa in 1982. Twice in the early 1980s Zairian troops were sent to Chad in response to Libyan aggression, and Chadian army battalions have received training in Zaire. In 1986 Zairian troops intervened in a joint military operation in Togo after riots erupted there. In turn, France has been instrumental in the training of various Zairian parachute divisions, the 31st Parachutist Brigade in particular, viewed as one of the most reliable army units.

French ties with Zaire were consolidated during the Giscard d'Estaing regime. The French president went on a state visit to Zaire in 1975, and shortly thereafter several agreements were signed for French participation in various major commercial projects in Zaire. The French agreed to fund and develop a national telecommunications system at the Voice of Zaire, which was completed in 1980 at a cost of over $500 million. Interestingly, a cousin of the French president, Phillipe Giscard d'Estaing, was head of Thompson CSF International, the major contracting firm for the project; and another cousin, François Giscard d'Estaing, was chairman and chief executive officer of the Banque Française du Commerce Extérieur, which provided most of the financing. During this period France also became Zaire's chief supplier of military transport vehicles—

Mirage jets, tanks, and helicopters. Subsequently, French military support for the Mobutu regime during the Shaba invasions further solidified the relationship.[20]

By 1989 France had become Zaire's second largest aid donor, after Belgium, in the area of economic development loans (refer to Table 4.6). Further, in 1989 Zaire was included in the list of countries that France targeted for writing off public sector debts totaling $2.35 billion. Subtle rivalry between France and Belgium with respect to aid and, by extension, power and influence with the GOZ has worked to Mobutu's advantage in the past. However, the friendship between the two countries has since cooled. At the 1990 Franco-African Summit, President Mitterrand, echoing the United States and other major donors, indicated that future aid to Africa would be linked to progress toward democracy. In the uncertain Zairian political environment, French aid pledges as well as disbursements by the Caisse Centrale de Coopération Economique (CCCE) and the Fonds d'Aide et de Coopération (FAC) have been suspended pending concrete steps toward representative government. The fourth Franco-African Summit was switched from Kinshasa to Paris, largely because of the 1991 turmoil and rioting, Zaire's poor human rights record, and the fact that Zaire requested $50 million in aid to organize the event. Nevertheless, the French position on Zaire has seemed to be less clear than that of either Belgium or the United States. It is interesting to note that French troops arrived in Kinshasa to evacuate foreigners in the September riots a day before their Belgian counterparts. Allegedly out of concern for the safety of expatriates, President Mitterrand took the initiative before Belgium did to secure clearance from Mobutu for intervention. This action was initially seen by anti-Mobutu groups as an attempt to preserve the status quo, as had been the case with the Shaba invasions. Officially, after the riots France advocated the notion of "cohabitation," in which Mobutu would bring key members of the Union Sacrée into a transition government. In fact, French negotiations with both Mobutu and the opposition were partly responsible for Tshisekedi's appointment as prime minister. Tshisekedi's quick dismissal within a week of assuming office in October 1991 led France to halt its aid program, becoming the last major bilateral donor to do so. Policy differences over Zaire have become evident within the French government, with the Foreign Ministry adopting the Belgian position on the need for Mobutu's departure.[21]

The Soviet Union and China:
Antagonism and Friendship

On the whole, Zaire's relationship with the former Soviet Union was always tenuous and strained, given Mobutu's pro-Western stand.

Because of Soviet support for Lumumba during the Congo Crisis, albeit mostly verbal, and then the backing of the Stanleyville rebels in 1963–1965, Mobutu was not anxious to normalize relations after he assumed power. However, a rapprochement with the Soviet Union was necessary in order to project Zaire's nonaligned image and to counter the perception of the state as a client of the West, in general, and the United States, in particular. In 1968 the Soviets were permitted to establish an embassy in Kinshasa, although Zaire supported the U.S. condemnation of the Soviet invasion of Czechoslovakia. Soviet-Zairian relations remained cool throughout the 1970s. In 1970 four Soviet diplomats were expelled on charges of subversion, and the following year about twenty Soviet-bloc officials were declared persona non grata for complicity in student demonstrations at Lovanium University in Kinshasa.[22] Interestingly, Mobutu has never visited Moscow, even though he did accept an invitation in 1974. The trip was canceled and finally postponed indefinitely. Soviet trade with Zaire historically has been low, reaching approximately $15 million in 1986.[23]

Chinese policy toward Central Africa was previously motivated by Sino-Soviet rivalry for Third World support. As a result, the People's Republic of China (PRC) and the United States have had similar goals—namely, a desire to minimize Soviet influence in Zaire. In the first few years of Congolese independence, the People's Republic of China sent modest amounts of aid to rebel groups in the face of Soviet wooing of Lumumba. China was also driven in its efforts by a desire to frustrate U.S. policy in the Congo because of Washington's recognition of Taiwan. The PRC was one of the few countries that recognized the Gizenga regime in Kisangani as the legitimate government of the Congo in 1963.

By 1964 Mao Tse-tung viewed the Congo as the key to the ideological conquest of Africa. Apparently the country's strategic location and the position it occupied in the forefront of international news made it a test case for the export of the Chinese revolution. It was felt that popular discontent already existed among the Congolese and that only proper revolutionary training was necessary.[24] Nevertheless, modest efforts in this regard—the circulating of Communist pamphlets and books—failed to bring about the anticipated Maoist revolution in the Congo.

By the early 1970s the Chinese had shifted their policy and were working to expand their influence by establishing more conventional ties with Zaire through trade and various aid agreements. It had become apparent by then that the People's Republic would be admitted to the United Nations. Therefore, the support of revolutionary groups and subversion in Third World countries—in Africa, in particular—no longer seemed appropriate. Mobutu himself saw advantages in encouraging a change in Chinese strategy: Recognizing the PRC would not only project Zaire's nonaligned status but would also neutralize Chinese support for the PRP, the internal opposition group operating in eastern Zaire. Accordingly, the Mobutu regime formally recognized the PRC on November 25, 1972, in the aftermath of President Richard Nixon's new China policy.[25]

A subsequent visit to China by Mobotu produced several agreements for projects in the agricultural and health sectors and secured promises of military assistance. The Chinese also agreed to provide funds for the construction of a huge cultural center (the People's Palace) in Kinshasa at an estimated cost of $24 million. Finally, Mobutu adopted several Chinese concepts, including the emphasis on work and discipline. Shortly after returning from China, he announced a new policy of "voluntary" labor called *salongo*, which would focus on collective work to promote national development.[26]

Because of increasing Russian support for the MPLA in neighboring Angola, the PRC also began to funnel aid to the rebel UNITA movement through Zaire. During the first Shaba invasion, China was one of the countries that rushed to Mobutu's aid, sending small arms, antiaircraft guns, and field artillery to the Zairian army.[27] China's relations with Zaire have continued to be cordial. A Chinese-Zairian joint commission was established in the late 1980s to facilitate economic, military, and technical assistance to Zaire. A Chinese delegation visited Kinshasa in March 1989 to follow up on initial discussions held in Beijing in November 1988 at the second session of the joint commission. At that time new loan agreements were expected with respect to the operation of Lotokila Sugar Company in Haut Zaire, the Agricultural Equipment Factory of Zaire (UMAZ), and the construction of the Kamanyola Stadium in Kinshasa.[28] Chinese aid tends to focus on agriculture—rice cultivation, vegetable farming, and livestock production.

Israel and the Arab States: Shifting Political Orientations

In 1992 Zaire is enjoying a quite profitable relationship with Israel. Aid is primarily in the military area, with Israel supplying the FAZ with helicopters, tanks and equipment, light arms, radar systems, and Israeli-made pilotless planes. Israel is also responsible for training the elite Presidential Guard and the Kamanyola Division based in Shaba province.

This era in Zaire-Israeli relations is rather reminiscent of an earlier period in 1960–1973 when Israel assisted with military training and funded agricultural and educational projects. At that time Israel also provided medical personnel under the auspices of the United Nations. Nevertheless, trade and technical assistance to Zaire was small compared to Israeli involvement elsewhere on the African continent.[29]

Shortly after attending the Afro-Asian Non-Aligned Summit in Algiers in 1973, Mobutu suddenly announced before the UN General Assembly that he was breaking diplomatic relations with Israel. This announcement came during a period of economic strength and occurred shortly before Mobutu was due at the White House for an official visit with President Nixon.[30] The reasons for the break were allegedly the Israeli occupation of Egyptian territory (the Sinai) and Israel's close relationship with South Africa. The announcement caught the United States by surprise and attracted considerable attention, most noticeably in Africa. Not only was Zaire the first "moderate" African state to take such a position, but it had traditionally had close ties with Israel. However, Mobutu apparently had less principled motives for the move—namely, the desire to demonstrate Zaire's independence of the West in foreign policy and to set the tone for a nonaligned-nation strategy toward Israel.

The significance of Mobutu's break with Israel was not lost on the Arabs, and Mobutu was the only black African leader invited to the Arab summit in November 1973. Shortly after the summit, Mobutu followed with visits to major Middle Eastern states—Egypt, Saudi Arabia, Kuwait, the United Arab Emirates, and Libya. This trip coincided with the start of the oil crisis, and it is said that Mobutu hoped to secure agreements for a guaranteed oil supply at concessionary prices. This deal failed to materialize. Nevertheless, Libya did make a significant investment commitment to Zaire in 1975, helping to fund GECAMINES' second expansion program. During Shabas I and II, Egypt and Morocco provided military assistance to the Mobutu regime, and Saudi Arabia financed the airlift of troops. These countries were acting out of what they viewed as a direct Soviet threat in Africa. Further, King Hassan evidently saw parallels between Mobutu's problems with the Katangan rebels and his own difficulties with the Frente Popular para la Liberación de Saguia el-Hambra y Rio de Oro (POLISARIO; Popular Front for the Liberation of Saguia el-Hambra and Rio de Oro) in the Western Sahara.[31]

Even though formal ties had been broken, the Mobutu regime still continued to tacitly support Israel in international forums. Zaire abstained from supporting the UN resolution equating Zionism with racism and did not take the Arab position on the question of Palestine.[32] Technical assistance and commercial relations between Zaire and Israel also continued unofficially. On its part, Israel began to strengthen its ties with South Africa in reaction to the setback in Zaire. At the time, Mobutu had quite substantial dealings of his own with South Africa.

By 1982 Mobutu had again switched sides in the Arab-Israeli game. In May he announced a resumption of ties with Israel, alleging that with the return of the Sinai to Egypt and the emergence of diplomatic relations between Israel and Egypt, the rationale for Zaire's action in 1973 was no longer present. Saudi Arabia immediately responded by breaking diplomatic relations with Zaire. The Israeli government viewed this Mobutu strategy as a diplomatic coup. Since the 1970s various Israeli leaders had been anxious to reestablish ties with Sub-Saharan Africa. Gaining a foothold in a strategic African country at the center of the continent could serve as the precursor for relations with other states. The Zaire connection also facilitated the transfer of Israeli aid to UNITA forces in Angola.[33]

Subsequently several high-level Israeli delegations visited Zaire to discuss the parameters of military and investment agreements between the two countries, and a five-year military cooperation pact was signed in 1983. In addition to supplying about $8 million in equipment, Israel agreed to expand Zaire's air force and to reorganize and train several Zairian battalions, including the Kamanyola Division, and the Special Presidential Brigade, which was increased from 3,000 to 7,500 men. Mobutu rejected an Israeli offer to reorganize the entire army, preferring not to rely on a single foreign source in the crucial area of defense.[34]

Aside from the obvious economic benefits to be gained from bilateral cooperation with Israel, Mobutu's motives for the move were political. Israel had indicated its willingness to act as a pro-Zaire lobby in the U.S. Congress, which had become increasingly hostile in criticizing Mobutu's regime. Two days before his announcement concerning Israel, Congress had voted to reduce U.S. military aid to Zaire from $20 million to $4 million and to eliminate ESF funds completely. Needless to say, Mobutu had spurned this American package because of the congressional condemnation of his regime. As of 1992, Zaire's ties with Israel remain strong, and its relations with the Arab states have been reestablished. Unfolding events in the Middle East—namely, Iraq's invasion of Kuwait in August 1990—have worked to Mobutu's advantage. Zaire's position as a member of the UN Security Council in 1991 brought that country into the heart of the UN debate. Zaire's vote for the U.S.-sponsored plan for the recapture of Kuwait led to the Mobutu government's regaining the support of key Arab states. Shortly after the end of the crisis, ties were reestablished with Kuwait, Saudi Arabia, and the United Arab Emirates.

Africa: Proclamations of Unity and Persistent Tensions

Zaire initially sought recognition and legitimacy as a nonaligned country from fellow African nations, particularly in the context of the Organization for African Unity (OAU). An attempt was made to stress the nationalist thrust of the new Mobutu regime through symbolic moves such as the recasting of Lumumba as a national hero, the breaking of diplomatic relations with Portugal because of its continued colonization of Angola, and the establishment of a program of "authenticity" and economic nationalism. This strategy apparently paid off when Zaire was chosen as the site of the 1967 OAU summit.

Over the years, Mobutu has come to be recognized as an elder statesman, and he has been asked to mediate several disputes between OAU members. In the 1970s he was included in the group of OAU leaders appointed to negotiate an end to the Israeli occupation of the Sinai. He also played a role in the settlement of the border dispute between Burundi and Tanzania.[35] His good offices were requested in 1990 by the OAU and Egypt in the civil war in the southern Sudan. In 1991 he was appointed mediator by the OAU in talks between the Rwandan government and rebel troops who invaded the country in 1990.

Notwithstanding these efforts, Mobutu has often been at odds with the OAU over matters of policy. In 1984, articulating dissatisfaction with the domination of the radical states, Mobutu proposed the creation of a new organization of black African states to solve the OAU deadlock over Chad and the Western Sahara. The GOZ subsequently withdrew from the OAU in November 1984 as a sign of solidarity with Morocco, following the organization's decision to recognize POLISARIO. King Hassan and Mobutu had a long association reinforced by Morocco's assistance in Shaba I. Zaire's resumption of relations with Israel also sharply divided African states, particularly in view of Israel's growing ties with South Africa. Finally, the OAU members were displeased at Mobutu's attempt to project himself into the midst of efforts to free Nelson Mandela, the imprisoned head of the antiapartheid African National Congress, meeting with two South African presidents, P. W. Botha in 1988 and Frederik W. de Klerk in 1990, when Zaire had not been in the forefront of the antiapartheid campaign. When Mobutu met with Mandela a few months after his release in February 1990, the African National Congress expressed the view that Mobutu might actually have delayed Mandela's release by announcing that he had secured Mandela's freedom during Botha's visit.[36]

Zaire's relations with its nine neighboring states have sometimes been tenuous. Mobutu's alliance with the United States and South Africa in support of UNITA severely damaged Zaire's image in the OAU and has been a key variable in Zaire's exclusion from the economic organization of Southern African states (Southern African Development Coordination Conference [SADCC]). During the Shaba I conflict OAU members were sharply divided. The more moderate francophone states came out in support of the Mobutu regime, whereas other states such as Zambia and Tanzania openly accused Mobutu of deliberately internationalizing the conflict. In 1986 Zaire and Burundi were at odds over a growing Zairian presence in Burundi's private sector. The central government in Bujumbura objected to the lack of commitment of these "foreigners" to Burundi's national development. Such disagreements could threaten the already fragile Communauté des États des Grands Lacs (CEPGL; Economic Community of the Countries of the Great Lakes).[37]

Zaire-Zambian relations have been shaped by an arbitrary colonial territorial division between the two countries, which resulted in both the Lunda and Bemba ethnic groups straddling the border. Northern Zambia is divided by a narrow strip of Zairian territory in Shaba known as the "pedicle." As a result, during the colonial period interdependent links developed between northern Zambia and Zaire's Shaba province. In the late nineteenth and early twentieth centuries Zambia provided labor and vital food supplies for Zairian copper mines. The Zambia railway also became a vital link between Elisabethville (now Lubumbashi) and South Africa. During the Katanga secession, the United National Independence Party (UNIP), the leading Zambian party, opposed Tshombe's initiative; consequently, during his tenure as prime minister, Zaire was not given formal recognition by Zambia.[38]

Economic interdependence between the two countries has persisted. Zaire and Zambia dominate the world production of cobalt, accounting for about 70 percent of total output. However, border incidents have consistently been a problem, a situation that was aggravated when Zambian territory was used by FLNC forces during the second Shaba incident. Zambian border villages were accidentally bombed during Shaba I. In 1984 tensions flared openly when Zaire announced that it was deporting Zambians from the Shaba region in reaction to the Lusaka government's expulsion of Zairian immigrants. High levels of illegal trading across the border have also been an issue due to decline in state capacity in Zaire and suspension of formal networks in the early 1980s because of deteriorating economic conditions in Zambia. Zaire subsequently created a civil guard to patrol the border. Not surprisingly, Zambian nationals traveling through the pedicle are persistently harassed by the Zairian security forces. Similar border issues and problems with smuggling exist with Uganda, the Sudan, and Congo-Brazzaville.

Traditionally, Congo and Zaire have been close. The two capitals—Brazzaville and Kinshasa—were twinned in 1988, and several cooperative agreements are in place, as well as a joint security commission. However, December 1991 saw strains in the relationship when hundreds of Zairians living in Congo were expelled as part of a more general policy directed at all foreigners. The Zairian population there had increased to 750,000 when many Zairian citizens fled to Brazzaville in the wake of the September 1991 riots and devastation in Kinshasa. According to the Congolese government, those expelled were all illegal immigrants. Furthermore, officials feared that Congolese parties would fraudulently enlist the Zairian population to win upcoming elections.[39]

In 1986 Zambia, Mozambique, and Angola—three of the frontline states in SADCC—held a series of meetings with Mobutu on the economic situation in Southern Africa. The discussions focused on efforts to develop alternative trade routes that would exclude South Africa, thereby reducing Southern Africa's export vulnerability. With the closure of the Benguela railway by Angolan rebels, much of Zaire's copper had to pass through Zambia and Zimbabwe to South African ports. It was hoped that the prospect of joining SADCC in this transport venture would entice Mobutu to end his support for UNITA. The talks failed, and Zaire's support remained a sensitive issue between Zaire and the states in question.

Angola: Foreign Policy Disaster and Attempted Reconciliation

Mobutu made his most serious foreign policy blunder with respect to Angola. As with Zambia, Zaire and Angola have been linked historically because of the existence of the same ethnic group (the Kongo) on either side of the Angolan-Zaire border. Prior to Zaire's independence, Kongo people often migrated from northern Angola into the Bas Zaire region in search of economic opportunities. Shortly after the start of Angola's liberation struggle in 1961, Zaire came out in support of the FNLA, partly because of a close friendship between Holden Roberto, head of the FNLA, and Mobutu attributable to their respective links to the Central Intelligence Agency (CIA) and to familial ties. Mobutu's first wife and Roberto's second wife were from the same village.

With the military coup in Portugal in 1974 and the prospect of immediate Angolan independence, Zaire took a strategic position, officially endorsing an OAU formula calling for a coalition government consisting of the three independence movements—the MPLA, UNITA, and the FNLA. In reality, Zaire wanted a government that excluded the Marxist-oriented MPLA based in Congo-Brazzaville. It was thought that a more right-wing government would be more supportive of Zaire's regional aspirations. In addition, Zaire saw the prospect of gaining control of the oil-rich enclave of Cabinda, which was technically under Angola's jurisdiction but was cut off from it by Zairian territory.[40]

By 1975 the OAU compromise had broken down into civil war, and covert aid for all three players in the Angolan scenario began to accelerate. Soviet, Eastern European, and Cuban aid and military expertise flowed in for the MPLA, whereas Chinese animosity toward the Soviets triggered support in the form of supplies and equipment to the FNLA. U.S. aid also came in for the FNLA. As hostilities escalated, Zaire made a tactical decision to intervene militarily in Angola to support the FNLA. By midyear the first units had entered the country, and within a few months FAZ units had invaded Cabinda, together with members of the Frente do Libertação do Enclave de Cabinda (FLEC; Front for the Liberation of the Enclave of Cabinda).[41] A military invasion by South African troops in support of UNITA added another dimension to the crisis.

Mobutu's support continued when the FNLA formed a coalition with UNITA, with Zaire quickly becoming the conduit for funneling arms to UNITA. Support for UNITA was also pragmatic, as the movement controlled most of the Benguela railway—Zaire's chief export route for copper—during the Angolan conflict. South African and U.S. covert and overt support for UNITA caused other African states to throw their support behind the MPLA, leaving Zaire the only state in Sub-Saharan Africa to be identified with the apartheid regime and openly recognized as a client of the United States. The MPLA victory in 1975 and the subsequent presence of Cuban and Soviet forces in Angola increased Zaire's role, from the American perspective, as a bulwark of pro-Western stability against communism.

Up to the Angolan settlement and the signing of the Bicesse Accords in May 1991 (if not beyond), Zaire continued to allow its territory to be used as the transit point for arms and military supplies to UNITA guerrillas. Official public statements from the GOZ denied these reports, as this action was in direct violation of a nonaggression pact signed between Zaire and Angola in 1985. Understandably this was cause for concern on the part of Zaire's neighbors, the frontline states in particular, who saw Zairian complicity as undermining any peace efforts. Over the years Zaire and Angola had made several half-hearted attempts to normalize relations: Zaire pledged to end support for UNITA, and Angola agreed to cease providing sanctuary for the FLNC. These agreements were never upheld, as political imperatives took precedence over cooperation.

In true Mobutuist fashion the Zairian president took a new position with respect to Angola in 1986. As part of a renewed effort to project himself as a senior African statesman and to portray a positive image of Zaire abroad, he sought to foster negotiations between the MPLA and UNITA. He met with Angolan President Jose Eduardo dos Santos in October 1986 even while there was speculation about Zaire being used as a transshipment point for U.S. arms to UNITA. Talks between Mobutu and the frontline states on precisely this issue seemed to bear fruit when, in March 1988, President Kenneth Kaunda of Zambia announced that Zaire would no longer allow the United States to ferry arms to UNITA through its territory.[42] Nevertheless, the shipments continued.

April 1989 witnessed a tripartite meeting between Zaire, the Congo, and Gabon to discuss the situation in Southern Africa and the prospects of national reconciliation in Angola. These three states emerged as key players in subsequent negotiations, but Mobutu consistently claimed the leading role, ensuring that key meetings took place in Zaire. As an indication of "good faith" vis-à-vis Angola, Mobutu announced that he intended to ask the United States to stop aid to UNITA and to resume normal diplomatic relations with Angola. All of this activity was occurring in the midst of international negotiations on Cuban withdrawal from Angola and independence for Namibia.

The real diplomatic coup for Mobutu came in June 1989, when he successfully staged a meeting of twenty African heads of state in Gbadolite (his native town in Équateur province), bringing delegations from UNITA and the MPLA together in negotiations for the first time. By the end of the conference, Jose Eduardo dos Santos and Jonas Savimbi had agreed to a cease-fire as of June 24, ending the fourteen-year-old civil war. UNITA agreed to recognize dos Santos as the legitimate Angolan leader and consented to a two-year self-imposed exile for Savimbi. The MPLA committed itself to national reconciliation and amnesty for UNITA members. The peace process was to be supervised by a three-nation commission consisting of Mobutu and the presidents of Gabon and the Congo.[43] By March 1990 this arrangement had become academic. The terms of the treaty were disputed on both sides almost immediately, and African support for Mobutu's mediation efforts waned, in view of continued U.S. arms shipments to UNITA. Fighting resumed between the Angolan government and the rebels, with the government launching offensives against key UNITA military installations. President dos Santos subsequently indicated that his government no longer accepted Mobutu's mediation. Furthermore, when the MPLA and UNITA signed their historic peace agreement in May 1991, Mobutu played no role in the final settlement.

South Africa: Public Condemnation but Quiet Dealings

Zaire's duplicitous policy on Angola has also extended to South Africa. Rhetorical and routine condemnation in public forums has been equally matched by significant ties. In a speech before the UN General Assembly in 1973, Mobutu evoked the provocative image of Africa as a revolver, with the trigger located in Zaire and South Africa serving as the barrel. This was meant to illustrate that Zaire would be taking the initiative to fight colonialism and racism on the continent, particularly the apartheid system in South Africa.[44]

Subsequently, Mobutu maintained his public condemnation of the apartheid system and in the latter half of the 1980s undertook a strategy to involve Zaire in the debate with respect to constructive change in South Africa and the rest of Southern Africa. Although Zaire is not a frontline state, Mobutu acted unilaterally in 1988 and held formal talks with South African President P. W. Botha. Discussions focused on Angola, prospects for Namibian independence, and an end to apartheid in South Africa. Botha's announcement two months after that meeting about the easing of restrictions on Nelson Mandela and the reprieve of the Sharpeville Six was viewed by Mobutu as a triumph of his diplomacy, and he said that this announcement justified his unilateral initiative.[45] Similar claims were made after South Africa agreed to the independence of Namibia and the release of Mandela. Mobutu had met with South African president Frederik de Klerk in 1989 and discussed these issues.

The two countries had no formal diplomatic relations until June 1991, when the official exchange of ambassadors took place. Prior to this time, however, economic and trade ties were strong. Indeed, a South African trade office was established in Kinshasa in 1989 to further facilitate a growing economic relationship. Business links with South Africa are expanding. Metro, a South African supermarket chain, opened a store in Kinshasa in 1990 at a cost of $20 million, and as of 1991 there were plans to expand to two additional locations. At the same time, visits to South Africa have been organized by Air Zaire and the Association Nationale des Enterprises Zairoises (ANEZA; National Association of Zairian Enterprises) to explore economic and trade contact as well as joint venture agreements. Finally, a major Zairian bank, the Banque Commercial Zairoise (BCZ), has opened an office in Johannesburg to exploit growing ties.[46]

Zaire's economic dependence on South Africa began with the closing of the Benguela railway. Zaire had to rely on a southern route through Zambia to South African ports. Although some copper and other products travel on the Voie Nationale—the rail-river-road network from Shaba to the port of Matadi—the South African route is faster and South African facilities are more efficient. Equally important, Zaire imports about 40 percent of its food, much of which comes from South Africa. Ironically, because of chronic internal transportation problems, it is easier to import from South Africa than to obtain supplies from Kivu and elsewhere in Zaire. Nevertheless, according to one expert, the inordinate size of this trade is directly due to the nature of the regime. As a result, Zaire has become South Africa's fourth most important trading partner in Africa (after Zimbabwe, Zambia, and Mauritius). The extent of Zaire's import dependence is graphically portrayed in Table 4.7. In Shaba, South African equipment is used in the copper mines, and the shops are stocked with South African products.[47] Some products are smuggled into Zaire, and in turn, mineral products from GECAMINES move illegally from Zaire into South Africa. Several airlines—TAP (Portugal), UTA (France),

SABENA (Belgium), and Swiss Air—fly regularly between Kinshasa and Johannesburg, and the South African airlines fly weekly between Lubumbashi and Johannesburg.

The most important economic link between Zaire and South Africa lies in the area of investment. The Anglo-American Corporation, headed by Harry Oppenheimer until 1982—with extensive holdings in DeBeers, Société Générale de Belgique, and Union Minière—has been indirectly involved in Zaire's mining sector since the colonial period. Anglo-American has used Mobutu's friend and business partner, Maurice Templesman, to arrange investment in copper and cobalt mining operations.[48] More specifically with reference to DeBeers, the company controlled the sale of all Zaire's diamond production until 1981, when Mobutu severed the relationship. SOZACOM, the Zairian parastatal in charge of marketing mining products, was given control of diamond sales in order to secure higher revenues for the Zairian government. After some relative success, Zaire returned to the fold, signing a two-year contract with DeBeers allowing it to market all the production of the Miba mine, the largest source of supply.

Irrespective of how events develop in Southern Africa, the Zaire–South Africa link is likely to be strengthened, although current instability in Zaire will undoubtedly deter likely investment. For the moment, as long as he remains in power and has control over foreign policy, Mobutu will continue to defy the efforts of the frontline states to ease their economic dependence on South Africa if such moves go against his economic and political interests. This position in turn will undermine Mobutu's credibility with the states involved and prevent Zaire from joining SADCC.

MOBUTU AS THIRD WORLD LEADER: REVOLUTIONARY RHETORIC BUT CONSERVATIVE STATECRAFT

Mobutu's foreign policy has been governed by political pragmatism— hence, for example, the strategy of simultaneously cultivating American, South African, and Israeli connections while striving to play a meaningful role in Angola. Like many pro-Western postcolonial states, Zaire's foreign policy choices are somewhat limited by dependent relations with the former colonizer, in particular, and the West, in general. Nevertheless, within these limited parameters Mobutu has managed to pursue his own foreign policy goals, notably in times of economic strength at home, supporting pro-Western positions when they coincided with his regional or global aims and extracting quid pro quos for overt expressions of support.

The Zairian president came to power with the blessing and assistance of the United States, establishing himself as firmly anti-Communist and a reliable ally of the United States. This conservative position has been a consistent theme throughout his tenure, even in times of revolutionary rhetoric or "displeasure" at U.S. criticism of his domestic policies. Successive U.S. administrations have considered Zaire a friend, largely because of its support of U.S. foreign policy positions in public forums such as the UN. As a case in point, following the U.S. lead, Zaire condemned the Soviet invasion of Afghanistan, supporting the UN resolution calling for a complete Soviet withdrawal, and was the first African state to refuse to participate in the 1980 Olympic Games in Moscow. In 1990, in its capacity as a member of the UN Security Council, Zaire fully endorsed the U.S. position on Iraq's invasion of Kuwait, calling for the use of force if Iraq refused to withdraw. Later, as president of the Security Council, Zaire supported the American-sponsored plan for the recapture of Kuwait and the counterattack on Iraq.

Ultimately Mobutu sought to be recognized as a respected Third World leader and head of what is potentially the most powerful country in Africa. After a few years of political consolidation on the home front following independence, Mobutu actively embarked on this strategy during the early 1970s, at the height of Zaire's economic ascension. Part of this strategy involved pursuing an independent course in foreign policy and diversifying international linkages. Proclaiming a policy of non-alignment, he traveled extensively overseas courting Western countries as well as the Eastern bloc, the People's Republic of China, and North Korea, spending the equivalent of about half a year out of the country in 1973.[49] Relative stability at home and apparent economic strength fostered these goals. Another step in this regard was the formation of a "regional" organization—the Economic Community of the Countries of the Great Lakes—with Rwanda and Burundi.

However, Mobutu's illusions of grandeur were soon shattered when in 1974 Zaire began to experience serious economic difficulties and Zaire's image became tarnished overseas because of the corrupt and repressive practices of the regime. Zaire became more overtly pro-Western, particularly with respect to U.S. foreign policy positions. At that time, the regime's anti-Communist proclamations played well in the United States, given Soviet direct and covert incursions into Sub-Saharan Africa—Ethiopia and Angola. The hope was that, in turn, the United States would intervene for Zaire in crucial areas, particularly in negotiations with the IMF, World Bank, and bilateral donors concerning its debt crisis. This strategy was only partially successful.

In the latter part of the 1980s, Mobutu sought to assume a preeminent role on the regional stage once again, partly in an effort to whitewash Zaire's tarnished image overseas—hence his efforts to take the leading role in an Angolan solution. Several countries, including the United States, bought into Mobutu's good faith in the negotiating process. Countries such as Mauritania and Mozambique requested that he mediate their respective disputes, and Secretary of State James Baker paid a special visit to Zaire early in 1990 after attending Namibia's independence celebrations. In the area of foreign policy, Mobutu has proved to be the consummate politician over time, exploiting differences in foreign policy goals and priorities between Western allies and, in the process, attracting a wide range of support. Throughout the 1970s and 1980s this ability was illustrated clearly in the area of debt, where he skillfully took advantage of the varying interests of the actors involved—the banks, Western governments, the IMF, and the World Bank. According to one observer:

> Mobutu's personalized style of diplomacy has been amazingly efficient: taking aggressive stands and using nationalist claims as weapons, practicing unexpected tactical offensives and then strategical withdrawals, seizing all opportunities to trigger contradictions between his collaborators, compelling decisionmakers to take responsibilities that they did not wish to assume, using foreign "friends" to defend Zaire's case or to spy on opponents abroad.[50]

We have also seen these strategies utilized in relationships with various African states on such issues as Angola and South Africa. Mobutu's maneuverings and rhetoric have created suspicion among the more "radical" states in the OAU and, in turn, have undermined his aspirations to continental leadership. In the past foreign policy moves have deflected attention away from political imperatives at home. As of 1992 Mobutu's options in the foreign policy arena have diminished. Key Western allies are no longer willing to render unequivocal support. It remains to be seen to what extent Mobutu will ultimately be forced to relinquish control of foreign policy strategies in response to demands for democratization amidst popular discontent in his own country.

NOTES

1. Mobutu Sese Seko, quoted in *Voices of Zaire: Rhetoric or Reality*, ed. Jeffrey M. Elliot and Mervyn M. Dymally (Washington, D.C.: Washington Institute Press, 1990), p. 51.

2. Edouard Bustin, "The Foreign Policy of the Republic of Zaire," *Annals of the American Academy of Political and Social Science* 489 (January 1987), p. 64.

3. Galen Hull, "Zaire in the World System: In Search of Sovereignty," in *Zaire: The Political Economy of Underdevelopment*, ed. Guy Gran (New York: Praeger, 1979), p. 263.

4. Elise Forbes Pachter, "Our Man in Kinshasa: U.S. Relations with Mobutu, 1970–1983," Ph.D. diss., Johns Hopkins University, 1987, p. 260; Kenneth L. Adel-

man, "Zaire: Old Foes and New Friends," *Africa Report*, January-February 1978, pp. 5–10.

5. Pachter, "Our Man in Kinshasa," p. 274.

6. *FBIS Daily Report: Sub-Saharan Africa*, September 23, 1991, p. 2. For a description of the events, see the *Washington Post*, September 28, 1991, p. A11; *New York Times*, September 29, 1991, p. 3; "Belges Fondent sur Kinshasa" and "Les Troupes de la 'paristroïka,'" *Liberation*, September 25, 1991, p. 3.

7. The evacuation plan called for the intervention of French troops, in the event of serious riots, to take control of the airports at N'Djili and N'Dolo and the port in Kinshasa, allowing the link with Brazzaville to be maintained. Belgian soldiers were later airlifted in aboard U.S. C-141 aircraft. Simultaneous assembly points in Kinshasa were created so that those foreigners who wanted to leave could be escorted to the harbor or airports by Belgian and French soldiers. According to the Brussels paper *Le Soir*, Belgian paratroopers had been on alert for at least two weeks prior to the army attacks. *FBIS Daily Report: Sub-Saharan Africa*, September 23, 1991, p. 3; ibid., September 25, 1991, p. 5.

8. Gregory Kronsten, *Zaire to the 1990s: Will Retrenchment Work?* (London: Economist Intelligence Unit, 1986), p. 12; confidential interview, Washington, D.C., March 19, 1992.

9. EIU, *Country Report: Zaire*, no. 1 (1989), p. 9.

10. *FBIS Daily Report: Sub-Saharan Africa*, March 2, 1989, p. 3.

11. EIU, *Country Report: Zaire*, no. 1 (1989), p. 9.

12. Ibid., pp. 8–9; Yojana Sharma, "Zaire and Belgium Count the Cost of Friendship" (London: Gemini News Service, 1983); *FBIS Daily Report: Sub-Saharan Africa*, April 4, 1989, p. 3; "Back to Katanga: The U.S. and the Crisis in Zaire," *International Bulletin* 4, no. 6 (March 28, 1977), p. 1.

13. Zaire's public debts totaling Bf5 billion ($123 million) as well as Bf5.9 billion ($145 million) of its publicly guaranteed debt were canceled. The estimated Bf11 billion remaining in publicly guaranteed commercial debt plus interest arrears was rescheduled over twenty-five years. Current interest is to be paid in zaires and then rechanneled back into development projects. *FBIS Daily Report: Sub-Saharan Africa*, July 27, 1989; EIU, *Country Report: Zaire*, no. 3 (1989), p. 20.

14. Michael Schatzberg, "Zaire Under Mobutu: The Consistencies and Contradictions of U.S. Policy," in *Friendly Tyrants: Contemporary Cases*, ed. Adam M. Garfinkle and Daniel Pipes (New York: St. Martin's, 1990), p. 26; *New York Times*, February 22, 1987; *The Washington Times*, March 2, 1987; *New York Times*, February 1, 1987; *Africa Report*, May-June 1987, p. 5; *Africa Confidential*, August 5, 1987; *New York Times*, July 27, 1987. Continued U.S. covert aid to Angola precipitated the repeal of the Clark Amendment in 1985, which had prohibited U.S. assistance to any faction in the Angolan civil war since 1976.

15. *Africa News*, March 7, 1988, p. 10.

16. House Foreign Affairs Committee, "The Impact of U.S. Foreign Policy on 7 African Countries," Report of a Congressional Study Mission to Ethiopia, Zaire, Zimbabwe, Ivory Coast, Algeria, and Morocco, August 6–25, 1983, and a Staff Study Mission to Tunisia, pp. 35–36.

17. U.S. Congress, H.R. 1899, *To Establish Conditions on United States Assistance for Zaire*, 101st Cong., 1st sess., April 13, 1989.

18. Confidential interviews, Washington, D.C., March 17, March 24, 1992. Note that U.S. military aid for fiscal 1988 and fiscal 1989 was $4 million each year, compared to $8.4 million for 1985 and 1986. U.S. Dept. of Commerce, *Foreign Economic Trends Report,* September 1989, p. 2; ibid., May 1990, p. 2.

19. The French had encouraged Moise Tshombe to bring the Congo into the organization in 1965 and had in fact backed Tshombe during the Katanga secession. OCAM was not viewed favorably in Sub-Saharan Africa, being seen as a vehicle for the perpetuation of French influence in the region and thus a source of factionalism within the OAU. It is therefore not surprising that participation in OCAM hampered Tshombe's efforts to have the Congo recognized as a full member of the OAU. Bustin, *Foreign Policy,* pp. 67, 70.

20. Crawford Young and Thomas Turner, *The Rise and Decline of the Zairian State* (Madison: University of Wisconsin Press, 1985), pp. 374–375.

21. *FBIS Daily Report: Sub-Saharan Africa,* May 2, 1989, p. 5; ibid., May 31, 1989, p. 2; EIU, *Country Report: Zaire,* no. 2 (1991), p. 16; *FBIS Daily Report: Sub-Saharan Africa,* February 13, 1991, p. 8; "Zaire: Disunity on the Western Front," *Africa Confidential,* November 8, 1991, p. 3.

22. Young and Turner, *Rise and Decline,* p. 370.

23. Pachter, "Our Man in Kinshasa," p. 188. In the 1980s the USSR imported timber from Zaire and purchased Zairian tin and cobalt on the international market. *FBIS Daily Report: Sub-Saharan Africa,* September 22, 1986, p. S4.

24. Warren Weinstein and Thomas H. Henriksen, *Soviet and Chinese Aid to African Nations* (New York: Praeger, 1980), p. 47.

25. Najib Hakim and Richard Stevens, "Zaire and Israel: An American Connection," *Journal of Palestine Studies* 12, no. 3 (Spring 1983), p. 46; Pachter, "Our Man in Kinshasa," p. 187.

26. Some establish a connection between *salongo* and the corvée labor of the colonial period. See Thomas M. Callaghy, *The State-Society Struggle: Zaire in Comparative Perspective* (New York: Columbia University Press, 1984), pp. 299–303.

27. Weinstein and Henriksen, *Soviet and Chinese Aid,* pp. 163–164.

28. *FBIS Daily Report: Sub-Saharan Africa,* March 29, 1989, p. 5.

29. Hakim and Stevens, "Zaire and Israel," p. 44. The two countries signed a formal military assistance agreement in 1971.

30. Pachter, "Our Man in Kinshasa," p. 177.

31. Bustin, *Foreign Policy,* p. 71. Designed to bring copper production from 470,000 metric tons to 570,000 tons by 1980, the GECAMINES project was estimated at $460 million, $200 million of which came from foreign loans, including $100 million from Libya. Winsome J. Leslie, *The World Bank and Structural Transformation in Developing Countries: The Case of Zaire* (Boulder: Lynne Rienner, 1987), p. 96; Young and Turner, *Rise and Decline,* p. 369. POLISARIO is a liberation movement fighting Morocco for self-determination and control of the Western Sahara, which the group considers its territory.

32. Hakim and Stevens, "Zaire and Israel," p. 51.

33. Pachter, "Our Man in Kinshasa," p. 352.

34. Hakim and Stevens, "Zaire and Israel," p. 42; J. Coleman Kitchen, Jr., "Zaire and Israel," Center for Strategic International Studies (CSIS), *Africa Notes,* no. 10 (March 21, 1983).

35. Bustin, *Foreign Policy*, pp. 69–71.

36. EIU, *Country Report: Zaire*, no. 4 (1990), p. 16.

37. *Africa News*, October 13, 1986.

38. The following section draws heavily from Sam Kongwa, "Relations Between Zambia and Zaire," *Africa Insight* 17, no. 2 (1987), pp. 102–106.

39. *FBIS Daily Report: Sub-Saharan Africa*, November 25, 1991, p. 4, and December 9, 1991, p. 3.

40. Bustin, *Foreign Policy*, p. 72.

41. Young and Turner, *Rise and Decline*, p. 377.

42. *FBIS Daily Report: Sub-Saharan Africa*, March 28, 1989, pp. 3–4; ibid., April 27, 1989, p. 2; ibid., May 2, 1989, p. 3.

43. *FBIS Daily Report: Sub-Saharan Africa*, June 23, 1989, pp. 1–6.

44. To date, very little has been written about Zaire's relationship with South Africa, as this is a sensitive issue. One writer, however, has succinctly outlined the various aspects of this liaison. See Thomas Callaghy, "Absolutism and Apartheid: Relations Between Zaire and South Africa," in *South Africa in Southern Africa: The Intensifying Vortex of Violence*, ed. Thomas M. Callaghy (New York: Praeger, 1983), pp. 371–403.

45. *FBIS Daily Report: Middle East and Africa*, November 28, 1988, p. 4.

46. EIU, *Country Report: Zaire*, no. 4 (1990), p. 20; *FBIS Daily Report: Sub-Saharan Africa*, February 19, 1991, p. 2; EIU, *Country Report: Zaire*, no. 3 (1991), p. 17.

47. Callaghy, "Absolutism and Apartheid," pp. 381–382; *New York Times*, February 8, 1987, and October 2, 1988; EIU, *Country Report: Zaire*, no. 2 (1991), p. 18.

48. Callaghy, "Absolutism and Apartheid," p. 378.

49. Young and Turner, *Rise and Decline*, p. 369.

50. Jean-Claude Willame, "Political Succession in Zaire, or Back to Machiavelli," *Journal of Modern African Studies* 26, no. 1 (March 1988), p. 42.

6

Plus Ça Change . . .
Zaire and the Future

THE NEW COLONIAL STATE

Overall, the image of the Zairian state outlined in the preceding chapters has not been a positive one. The second independence that Zairians called for in the 1964 revolts has failed to materialize under the Mobutu regime. The basic continuities between the contemporary state and its past have already been stressed. The reality is that Mobutu has perpetuated and institutionalized the worst aspects of the Belgian economic and political legacy, producing a kind of postcolonial colonialism. Relative political stability has been achieved at the cost of repression and political control. Personal rule has been the norm, and interesting parallels can be drawn between the Leopoldian and Mobutu eras. Both rulers have considered the state their personal domain.

A pervasive, intrusive state in the political arena exists in tandem with weakened state capacity with respect to economic and social welfare. State institutions cannot deliver basic services; therefore, citizens increasingly improvise and fend for themselves outside the system. In many rural areas life is just as harsh as during colonial times. Ironically, however, there is one crucial difference that Zairians freely admit: Under the Belgians, there was working infrastructure, and consumer goods were generally available. Indeed, the difficulties of day-to-day existence constitute another form of oppression. For the majority of Zairians, life in Zaire today is simply to be endured. In an atmosphere of clientelism and corruption, a significant *productive* class capable of leading the nation has not emerged.

On the economic front, Zaire remains an open, dependent state with a modern mineral sector intimately linked with international markets that has developed at the expense of agriculture, as is the case in many other states in Sub-Saharan Africa. Attempts to alter the colonial economic structures and gain effective control over the country's resources have

169

failed, partly because of the limits imposed by the government's crucial dependence on primary-product exports for foreign exchange. The country is still firmly entrenched in the world economy as a producer of minerals and will be for some time to come. Any serious attempts at economic diversification by a new regime will have to take second place to large-scale and sustained economic reconstruction.

Finally, the international system has been a crucial source of support for the Mobutuist state. Beginning with the Congo Crisis, Western powers have sought to maintain internal stability as well as Zaire's territorial integrity because of the country's strategic importance and Mobutu's value as an ally. International rescue of the Mobutu regime—or the preservation of the status quo on both political and economic fronts—has frustrated possibilities for regime change. Indeed, because of past patterns Belgian and French intervention in the fall 1991 riots and violence was initially perceived by many Zairians as yet another example of attempts to support and protect a repressive government. In reality, Zaire's leading allies—Belgium, France, and the United States—evacuated their citizens, virtually eliminated their diplomatic presence in the country, and suspended aid in view of escalating political and economic instability and Mobutu's failure to appoint a credible and legitimate transition government. In the 1993 incidents, French marines took the lead in evacuating over one thousand expatriates. Belgian paratroopers were not permitted by Mobutu to enter the country from Brazzaville, perhaps because of Belgian officials' consistent calls for Le Guide to leave the political scene.

Under Bush, the United States continued to see a role for Mobutu in any transition, acknowledging his right to participate in the democratic process—in effect, a form of indirect support. After a February 1992 visit to Zaire by Assistant Secretary of State for African Affairs Herman Cohen, there was a subtle shift in the official perspective. The administration released an official statement proposing that Mobutu become a "titular" president, in effect a "figurehead," and that a "neutral" transition government be appointed, headed by someone affiliated with neither the Union Sacrée nor the Forces Démocrates Unies and with no interest in running for president when elections take place. Belgium has stated categorically that Mobutu must go; but given that direct intervention has been ruled out, there are no ideas on how this should be achieved. At the same time, France's position has been less coherent. Initially, in 1990 and 1991 the official approach closely approximated that of the United States. After the cancellation of the National Conference by Prime Minister Nguza Karl-i-Bond in January 1992, the French government apparently adopted the view of the Foreign Ministry, focusing on the need for Mobutu's departure. France and Belgium have been on the

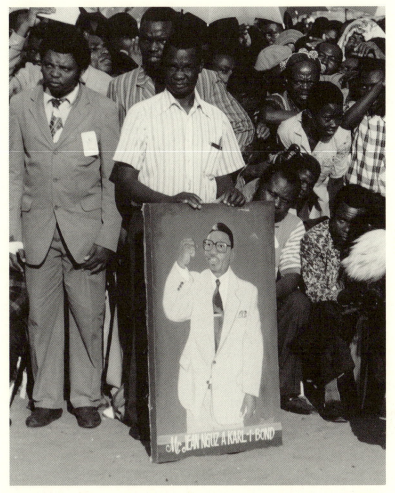

Supporters of Nguza Karl-i-Bond holding a picture of him at a UFERI
rally in May 1991. Photo courtesy of Learned Dees.

same side with respect to political change in Zaire, with the United States
taking a more conservative and cautious approach. This position has led
to Mobutu's accusing Belgium and France of plotting to overthrow him.
Up to the 1993 riots, these key allies could not agree on a common position, saying they no longer had "leverage." As of February 1993, the
United States, Belgium, and France are in agreement and have formally
demanded that Mobutu yield power to avert further violence. Zairians
see the current political situation as partly the responsibility of external
forces. They have not responded positively to the Mobutuist rhetoric for
some time now. In effect, the regime has lost its legitimacy.

PROSPECTS FOR REFORM

Zaire is poised to enter yet another phase in its history, and the future remains uncertain. President Mobutu's strategic decision to permit political pluralism ushered in the beginning of the third postindependence regime. Mobutu appears determined to retain control regardless of which government eventually leads the Third Republic. Repeated calls for his resignation have produced cosmetic concessions: five transition governments since April 1990 appointed by him to guide the democratization process, half-hearted attempts at a National Conference, and a vague timetable for legislative and presidential elections. Many see these measures as designed to placate the international community, while troops from the Special Presidential Brigade and the Civil Guard employ terrorist tactics against the opposition and the population at large. This internal unrest coupled with the mass departure of expatriates who controlled much of the commercial sector has virtually destroyed an already weak economy.

By April 1992, the National Conference had reconvened and unilaterally declared itself sovereign. Its suspension in January had been widely seen as unconstitutional by the United States and the European Community, and Prime Minister Nguza Karl-i-Bond's proposal to replace the conference with a small National Roundtable based on equal regional representation was flatly rejected by both the Union Sacrée and Zaire's key allies. Obvious parallels were drawn by the opposition to the Roundtable Conference held with Belgium on the eve of independence in 1960. The political impasse was further complicated in February when DSP troops violently suppressed a mass protest by opposition members and church groups calling for a resumption of the conference. It is estimated

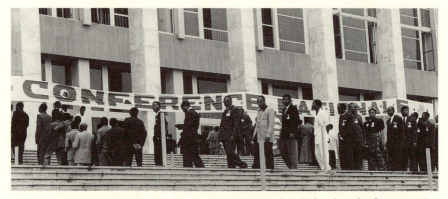

Delegates on the steps of the Palais du Peuple (People's Palace) at the first opening of the National Conference in May 1991. Photo courtesy of Learned Dees.

that at least thirty-two people were killed in the incident. The reconvening of the conference came only after French, Belgian, and U.S. ambassadors, conference Chairman Monsignor Laurent Monsengwo Pasinya, and Prime Minister Nguza Karl-i-Bond had a series of separate meetings with President Mobutu. In these discussions Mobutu took the position of final arbiter, distancing himself from the apparent conflict between the Nguza government and the opposition. In April 1990 this role was the one that Mobutu indicated he would assume in the Third Republic, and in the context of the conference, it was clearly an attempt to ensure his political survival.

Opposition groups have clearly recognized the inherent contradictions in Mobutu's flawed process of political liberalization. But in the face of international pressures to compromise with the regime, the Union Sacrée has found it difficult to be consistently cohesive. Almost on cue, ethnic and regional rivalries have once again emerged with political liberalization. Some Zairians are already dismayed at the apparent Luba domination of one of the most popular groups, the UDPS. In this vein a November 1990 conference on the prospects for democracy in Zaire held in Washington, D.C., was criticized as being pro-UDPS with the Luba disproportionately represented. There are ethnic cleavages in the Union Sacrée itself. Even before his appointment as prime minister, Nguza and his Lunda-dominated UFERI party based in Shaba had distanced themselves from Tshisekedi and the UDPS, with its strong Luba support in Kinshasa and Kasai Oriental. This development effectively divided the Union Sacrée into two opposing factions, as both Nguza and Tshisekedi held leadership roles in the organization. It appears that Zaire has taken this route before; parallels can be drawn with the immediate preindependence period, when a myriad of political parties emerged and political mobilization occurred within the context of existing ethnic cleavages.

By August 1992 the Sovereign National Conference had drafted La Chartre de la Transition (Transition Charter) to replace the constitution. The charter provided the framework for political transition, including the creation of a 359-member Haut-Conseil de la République (High Council of the Republic). The council is in effect a parliament, responsible for executing the Transition Charter, and has control over the government and, ultimately, the president himself. Under the charter, Mobutu loses control of state finances, foreign affairs, and defense. Furthermore, in a direct challenge to Mobutu's rule and Nguza Karl-i-Bond's government, the conference voted overwhelmingly to reinstate Etienne Tshisekedi to the position of prime minister. The ouster of Nguza has provoked ethnic violence in Shaba, his native region, between his Lunda tribe and Tshisekedi's Luba tribe. Lubas have fled in large numbers to neighboring Kasai. Nguza further fueled tensions by stating that Shaba would not

Etienne Tshisekedi, reinstated as prime minister by the Sovereign National Conference in August 1992, in a campaign photo.

recognize Tshisekedi's authority. In a development strangely reminiscent of the Congo Crisis, local leaders in Shaba have demanded independence from the central government. The challenge facing the Tshisekedi transition government is the imperative of attracting and maintaining broad-based support while mitigating ethnicity in the interest of effective and enduring political change. The appointment of political unknowns from many opposition parties in the Union Sacrée and the selection of Paul Bandoma, a native of Équateur, as minister of defense are attempts to garner both internal and external support.

Mobutu's initial acceptance of Tshisekedi's government was hailed by the United States and the European Community as a positive step toward democracy. In Belgium's formal statement, Willy Claes, the new foreign minister, indicated that Belgium would be willing to resume cooperation and would use its efforts to secure international aid for the interim government if human rights and democracy were respected by this new regime. Nevertheless, the new government was destined to be short-lived. The 1993 riots by the army precipitated another crisis between Tshisekedi and Mobutu. After soldiers and merchants in Kinshasa refused to accept the Z5 million notes. Tshisekedi declared them illegal and called for foreign military intervention to oust Mobutu. Taking issue with the Transition Charter, Mobutu in turn has called on the transitional parliament to elect a new prime minister, blaming Tshisekedi for the violence. The Parliament and Tshisekedi himself have refused to recognize what in effect has been his dismissal. On their part, the United States, France, and Belgium are seeking ways to force Mobutu's departure. There is talk of seizing his personal assets overseas as well as other political and economic sanctions. At this juncture, however, it is not altogether clear whether these measures will be seriously attempted or, more importantly, whether they will work.

It is clear that political liberalization will move forward and that elections in some form will take place. The national dialogue in January 1990 unleashed a process that cannot be stopped, short of another Mobutu coup, owing to Zairians' rising expectations. The conference had discussed the possibility of holding local, parliamentary, and presidential elections within eighteen to twenty-four months from August 1992. However, Prime Minister Nguza Karl-i-Bond had created an election commission during his tenure, with Mobutu's blessing, to establish a much shorter timetable. The actual date of elections therefore remains elusive. If Mobutu attempts to turn back the clock, the costs will be high, given the risk of internal revolt, fragmentation, and international censure.

At this stage it is not clear whether a united opposition, divorced from Mobutu's influence, will be allowed to emerge. The free press in Zaire has already accused the president of funding new opposition groups and resorting to the now-familiar strategy of dividing the opposition by talking selectively with various political groups. Further flying in the face of popular protest, Mobutu has announced his candidacy for the next presidential elections, effectively staying on as president without a mandate even though his seven-year term officially expired on December 4, 1991.

Although outcomes are difficult to predict at this juncture, three scenarios are possible with respect to possibilities for political reform. In the first, Mobutu manipulates the current situation and manages to remain in control, in spite of the "free" electoral process. In reality, Mobutu's staying power to date has clearly demonstrated the limits of attempts by external powers to engineer political reform, even with a cut-off in aid. In the second scenario, a party with ties to the old Mobutu regime wins the elections; and although technically outside the system, Mobutu continues to direct politics in Zaire. With both of these possibilities, the status quo remains, with disastrous results on state capacity as well as economic and social welfare.

In the final scenario, a popular party such as the UDPS wins with a mandate to create a new Zaire. Many prominent members of the opposition, however, including Tshisekedi himself, have ties to the old politics of the Mobutu era, generating fears among some Zairians of politics as usual. Even under the best of circumstances, such a party will face a herculean task, given the characteristics of the new colonial state already described and the complication added by the economic devastation in 1991 and 1993. The process of nation building will be a long one. Old norms and values grounded in the patrimonial, authoritarian state have to be unlearned, and this takes time. Given the current salience of ethnicity and regionalism, transferring lofty democratic ideals into reality will demand strong legitimate leadership. Ultimately, if progress is to occur, national interest will have to take precedence over ethnic and regional concerns. Furthermore, the age-old question of centralization versus federalism that plagued the early 1960s will have to be effectively resolved if the country is to move forward.

On the economic front, several challenging issues must be dealt with: the unmanageable debt crisis, the dual nature of the economy, corruption, the rapid growth of the second economy, infrastructural decline, and abysmal living standards. Even if Zaire takes the first few positive steps toward truly representative government, there is no guarantee that economic development will follow. In 1993, however, thirty-three years after independence, there is, in addition to abundant natural resources, a cadre of qualified personnel who can contribute effectively to the development process. Unfortunately, under Mobutu many of these technocrats have been demoralized in their efforts to do their jobs effectively and expectations have been lowered. Whether a new regime will be able to motivate and inspire changes in attitudes is another question.

Life has been hard, and the flourishing underground, or second, economy must be seen in this light. Although corruption—*le mal zairois*—has been firmly entrenched in society, it can at least be mitigated to the extent that opportunities for economic advancement can be provided that do not depend on access to political office. It is for this reason that Zaire's fledgling business class, which ironically has developed out of the second economy, must be nurtured and permitted to grow within formal channels.

By and large, the international community seems to be adopting a wait-and-see attitude with respect to political outcomes in Zaire. Rapidly unfolding events in Europe, the Middle East, Russia, and the new Commonwealth of Independent States as well as internal imperatives are occupying national leaders. Therefore, Zaire has declined in relative importance. This apparent lack of interest from the rest of the world, if sustained, may be ideal. Zairians would then have to rely on their own initiatives to change their future. Ideally, the electoral process in Zaire will permit a new regime to emerge, but even then there is the very real danger that the existing structural weaknesses in the state will remain. The reality is that Zaire may not be able to mitigate the effects of its historical and Mobutuist legacies for some time to come.

Acronyms

ABAKO	Alliance des BaKongo (BaKongo Alliance)
AIDS	acquired immune deficiency syndrome
ANC	Armée Nationale Congolaise (Congolese National Army)
AND	Agence National de Documentation (National Documentation Agency)
ANEZA	Association Nationale des Enterprises Zairoises (National Association of Zairian Enterprises)
AZAP	Agence Zaire-Presse (Zaire Press Agency)
BCK	Compagnie du Chemin de Fer du Bas-Congo au Katanga
BCZ	Banque Commerciale Zairoise
BIS	Bank for International Settlements
CCCE	Caisse Centrale de Coopération Economique
CCIZ	Centre Commercial International Zairois (Zairian International Trade Center)
CEPGL	Communauté des États des Grands Lacs (Economic Community of the Countries of the Great Lakes)
CFA	francs de la Coopération Financière en Afrique
CFL	Chemin de Fer du Congo Supérieur aux Grands Lacs
CIA	Central Intelligence Agency
CLC	Comité pour la Liberation du Congo-Kinshasa
CND	Centre National de Documentation (National Documentation Center)
CNL	Comité Nationale de Libération (National Liberation Committee)
CNRI	Centre National de Recherche et d'Investigation (National Center for Research and Investigation)
CONACO	Convention National Congolaise (National Congolese Assembly)
CPM	*contribution personnelle minimum* (head tax)
CRISP	Centre de Recherche et D'information Socio-politiques
CVR	Corps des Volontaires de la République (Volunteer Corps of the Republic)
DCRL	Department of Citizens' Rights and Liberties

179

DM	deutsche marks
DSP	Division Spéciale Presidentielle (Special Presidential Brigade)
ECZ	Église du Christ au Zaire (Church of Christ in Zaire)
EFF	Extended Fund Facility
EJCSK	Église de Jésus-Christ sur Terre par le Prophète Simon Kimbangu
ESF	Economic Support Funds
FAC	Fonds d'Aide et de Coopération
FAZ	Forces Armées Zairois (Zairian Armed Forces)
FBEI	Fonds du Bien-Être Indigène (Native Welfare Fund)
FCD	Front Congolais pour la Restauration de la Démocratie (Congolese Front for the Restoration of Democracy)
Fenadec	Fédération Nationale des Démocrates Convaincus (National Federation of Conservative Democrats)
FLEC	Frente do Libertação do Enclave de Cabinda (Front for the Liberation of the Enclave of Cabinda)
FLNC	Front pour la Liberation Nationale du Congo (Front for the National Liberation of the Congo)
FNLA	Frente Nacional de Libertção de Angola (Front for the National Liberation of Angola)
Forminière	Société Internationale Forestière et Minière
GECAMINES	Générale des Carrières et des Mines
GECOMIN	Générale Congolaise des Minérais
GNP	gross national product
GOZ	government of Zaire
IMF	International Monetary Fund
JMPR	Jeunesse du Mouvement Populaire de la Révolution (Youth of the Popular Movement of the Revolution)
MHO	Metallurgie d'Hoboken Overpelt
MNC	Mouvement National Congolais (National Congolese Movement)
MNC-L	Mouvement National Congolais—Lumumba (National Congolese Movement–Lumumba)
MPLA	Movimento Popular de Libertação de Angola (Popular Movement for the Liberation of Angola)
MPR	Mouvement Populaire de la Révolution (Popular Movement of the Revolution)
MPR	Mouvement Populaire pour le Renouveau (Popular Movement for Renewal)
NGO	nongovernmental organization
OAU	Organization for African Unity
OCAM	Organization Commune Africaine et Malgache (African and Malagasy Community Organization)
OFIDA	Office des Douanes et des Accises (Customs and Excise Office)
OGEDEP	Office de Gestion de la Dette Publique (Office of Debt Management)
ONATRA	Office National des Transports (National Transport Office)
PALU	Parti Lumumbiste Unifié (United Lumumbist Party)

PLZ	Plantations Lever au Zaire
PNP	Parti National du Progrès (National Progressive Party)
POLISARIO	Frente Popular para la Liberación de Saguia el-Hambra y Rio de Oro (Popular Front for the Liberation of Saguia el-Hambra and Rio de Oro)
PRC	People's Republic of China
PRI-Fenadec	Parti des Républicans Indépendants–Fédération Nationale des Démocrates Convaincus
PRP	Parti Révolutionnaire du Peuple (Revolutionary People's Party)
PSA	Parti Solidaire Africain (African Solidarity Party)
PSZ	Parti Socialiste Zairois (Zairian Socialist Party)
PVOs	private voluntary organizations
RDR	Rassemblement des Démocrates pour la République
SADCC	Southern African Development Coordination Conference
SARM	Service d'Action et de Renseignements (Military Action and Intelligence Service)
SCP	Société Commerciale Petrozaire
SDRs	Special Drawing Rights
SGB	Société Générale de Belgique
SGM	Société Générale des Minérais
SNCZ	Société Nationale des Chemins de Fer du Zaire (Zairian National Railway Company)
SNI	Service National d'Intelligence (National Intelligence Service)
SODIMIZA	Société de Developpement Industriel et Minier du Zaire
SOZACOM	Société Zairoise de Commercialisation des Minérais
SOZIR	Société Zairo-Italienne de Raffinage
UDPS	Union pour la Démocratie et le Progrès Social (Union for Democracy and Social Progress)
UFERI	Union des Fédéralistes Républicains Indépendants (Party of Independent Republican Federalists)
UGEC	Union Générale des Étudiants Congolais (General Union of Congolese Students)
UMAZ	Agricultural Equipment Factory of Zaire
UMHK	Union Minière du Haut-Katanga
UNAZA	Université Nationale du Zaire (National University of Zaire)
UNECRU	Union National des Étudiants du Congo et du Ruanda-Urundi (National Union of Students of the Congo and Ruanda-Urundi)
UNESCO	United Nations Educational, Scientific, and Cultural Organization
UNICEF	United Nations Children's Fund
UNIP	United National Independence Party
UNITA	União Nacional para Independência Total de Angola (Union for the Total Independence of Angola)
UNTZA	Union National des Travailleurs Zairois (National Union of Zairian Workers)
UPEZA	Progressive Union of Zairian Students and Pupils
USAID	U.S. Agency for International Development
ZARI	Zairian-American Research Institute

Selected Bibliography

THE HISTORICAL SETTING

Anstey, Roger. *King Leopold's Legacy.* London: Oxford University Press, 1966.

Belgian Ministry of the Belgian Congo and Ruanda-Urundi. *Public Health in Belgian Africa.* Brussels: Infor Congo, 1958.

Brausch, Georges. *Belgian Administration in the Congo.* London: Oxford University Press, 1961.

Buisseret, M. A. "The Policy of Belgium in Her Overseas Territories." Address by M. A. Buisseret to the House of Representatives in Brussels, June 26, 1957. Brussels: Information and Public Relations Office for the Belgian Congo and Ruanda Urundi, 1st Directorate, 1957.

Bustin, Edouard. *Lunda Under Belgian Rule: The Politics of Ethnicity.* Cambridge: Harvard University Press, 1975.

Chatterjee, D. N. *Storm over the Congo.* New Delhi: Vikas House, 1980.

Cornevin, Robert. *Histoire du Congo: Des origines préhistoriques à la Republique Démocratique du Congo.* Paris: Éditions Berger-Levrault, 1970.

Fetter, Bruce. "Changing War Aims: Central Africa's Role, 1940–41, as Seen from Leopoldville." *African Affairs: Journal of the Royal African Society* 87, no. 348 (July 1988).

First, Ruth. *The Barrel of a Gun.* Penguin Press, 1970.

Hodgkin, Thomas. *Nationalism in Colonial Africa.* New York: New York University Press, 1957.

Kalb, Madeleine G. *The Congo Cables.* New York: Macmillan, 1982.

Kanza, Thomas. *The Rise and Fall of Patrice Lumumba.* Cambridge: Schenkman, 1977.

Lefever, Ernest W. *Crisis in the Congo: A United Nations Force in Action.* Washington, D.C.: Brookings Institution, 1965.

Lefever, Ernest W., and Joshua Wynfred. *United Nations Peacekeeping in the Congo, 1960–64: An Analysis of Political, Executive and Military Control.* 4 vols. Washington, D.C.: Brookings Institution, 1966.

Lemarchand, René. *Political Awakening in the Belgian Congo.* Berkeley: University of California Press, 1964.

Reed, David. *111 Days in Stanleyville.* New York: Harper & Row, 1965.

Slade, Ruth. *King Leopold's Congo.* London: Oxford University Press, 1962.

U.S. Congress. House Committee on Foreign Affairs, Subcommittee on Africa. *Staff Memorandum on the Republic of the Congo.* August 24, 1960. Washington, D.C., 1960.

Vanderlinden, J., ed. *Du Congo au Zaire, 1960 to 1980.* Brussels: Centre de Recherche et d'Information Socio-politiques (CRISP), 1980.

Van Lierde, Jean, ed. *Lumumba Speaks: The Speeches and Writings of Patrice Lumumba, 1958–61.* Translated from French by Helen R. Lane. Boston: Little, Brown, 1972.

Vansina, Jan. *Introduction à L'ethnographie du Congo.* Éditions Universitaires du Congo. Brussels: CRISP, 1966.

Wagoner, Fred E. *Dragon Rouge: The Rescue of Hostages in the Congo.* Washington, D.C.: National Defense University Research Directorate, 1980.

Willame, Jean-Claude. "The Congo." In *Students and Politics in Developing Nations,* pp. 37–63, edited by Donald K. Emmerson. New York: Praeger, 1968.

Young, Crawford. *Politics in the Congo: Decolonization and Independence.* Princeton: Princeton University Press, 1965.

_____. "Rebellion and the Congo." In *Protest and Power in Black Africa,* pp. 969–1011, edited by Robert I. Rotberg and Ali A. Mazrui. New York: Oxford University Press, 1970.

THE ZAIRIAN POLITY

Adelman, Kenneth Lee. "The Church-State Conflict in Zaire: 1969–1974." *African Studies Review* 28, no. 1 (April 1975).

Callaghy, Thomas M. "State-Subject Communication in Zaire: Domination and the Concept of Domain Consensus." *Journal of Modern African Studies* 18, no. 3 (1980), pp. 469–492.

_____. *The State-Society Struggle: Zaire in Comparative Perspective.* New York: Columbia University Press, 1984.

Elliot, Jeffrey M., and Mervyn M. Dymally. *Voices of Zaire: Rhetoric or Reality.* Washington, D.C.: Washington Institute Press, 1990.

Gould, David. "The Administration of Underdevelopment." In *Zaire: The Political Economy of Underdevelopment,* pp. 87–107, edited by Guy Gran. New York: Praeger, 1979.

_____. *Bureaucratic Corruption and Underdevelopment in the Third World: The Case of Zaire.* Elmsford, N.Y.: Pergamon Press, 1980.

Gould, David, and Mushi-Mugumorhagerwa. "La multi-rationalité et le sous-développement: Écologie du processus decisionnel dans l'administration locale zairoise." *Canadian Journal of Political Science* 10, no. 2 (June 1977), pp. 261–285.

Gutteridge, William. "Africa's Military Rulers: An Assessment." *Conflict Studies,* no. 62 (October 1975).

Jackson, Robert, and Carl Roseberg. *Personal Rule in Black Africa.* Berkeley: University of California Press, 1982.

Kazadi, F.S.B. "Zaire: Mobutu, MPR, and the Politics of Survival." *Africa Report* 23, no. 1 (January-February 1978), pp. 11–15.

Lawyers Committee for Human Rights. *Zaire: Repression as Policy—A Human Rights Report.* New York, August 1990.

Nguza Karl-i-Bond. *Mobutu ou L'incarnation du Mal Zairois.* London: Rex Collings, 1982.

Nzongola-Ntalaja. "The Continuing Struggle for National Liberation in Zaire." *Journal of Modern African Studies* 17, no. 4 (1979), pp. 595–614.

Schatzberg, Michael G. "Fidelité au Guide: The J.M.P.R. in Zairian Schools." *Journal of Modern African Studies* 16, no. 3 (1978), pp. 417–431.

_____. *Politics and Class in Zaire: Bureaucracy, Business and Beer in Lisala.* New York: Africana, 1980.

_____. "Le Mal Zairois: Why Policy Fails in Zaire." *African Affairs* 81, no. 324 (July 1982), pp. 337–349.

_____. *The Dialectics of Oppression in Zaire.* Bloomington: Indiana University Press, 1988.

Vengroff, Richard. *Development Administration at the Local Level: The Case of Zaire.* Syracuse: Maxwell School of Citizenship and Public Affirs, Syracuse University, 1983.

Willame, Jean-Claude. "Zaire: Système de Survie et Fiction d'Etat." *Canadian Journal of African Studies* 18, no. 1 (1984), pp. 83–88.

_____. "Political Succession in Zaire, or Back to Machiavelli." *Journal of Modern African Studies* 26, no. 1 (March 1988), pp. 37–49.

Young, Crawford, and Thomas Turner. *The Rise and Decline of the Zairian State.* Madison: University of Wisconsin Press, 1985.

SOCIETY AND CULTURE

Ahluwalia, Rashim, and Bernard Mechlin, eds. *Traditional Medicine in Zaire: Present and Potential Contributions to the Health Services.* Ottawa, Ont.: International Development Research Centre, 1980.

Asch, Susan. *L'Église du Prophète Kimbangu.* Paris: Éditions Karthala, 1983.

Bergman, Billy. *Goodtime Kings: Emerging African Pop.* New York: Quill, 1985.

Biebuyck, Daniel. *The Arts of Zaire.* Vol. 1, *Southwestern Zaire.* Berkeley: University of California Press, 1985.

Bobb, F. Scott. *Historical Dictionary of Zaire.* African Historical Dictionaries, no. 43. Metuchen, N.J.: Scarecrow Press, 1988.

Botombele, Bokonga Ekanga. *Cultural Policy in the Republic of Zaire.* Paris: UNESCO Press, 1976.

Callaghy, Thomas M. *Politics and Culture in Zaire.* Monograph in Politics and Culture series. Ann Arbor: University of Michigan, Center for Political Studies, Institute for Social Research, 1987.

Cornevin, Robert. *Le Zaire.* Paris: Presses Universitaires de France, 1972.

Davis, Joseph M., ed. *Congo Profile, 1965: A Study of Historical and Socio-economic Factors Influencing the Development of the Church in the Democratic Republic of the Congo.* World Division of the Board of Missions, Methodist Church, 1965.

Davis, W., Jr. "An Ethical Evaluation of the Development Goals and Achievements of the Government of the Republic of Zaire from 1965 through 1971." Ph.D. diss., Boston University, 1974.

Davison, Jean, ed. *Agriculture, Women and Land: The African Experience.* Boulder: Westview Press, 1988.

Ettinger, David. "Media-Government Relations in Zaire: A Case Study in Comparative Perspective." Ph.D. diss., Columbia University, 1986.

Gould, Terri F. "A New Class of Professional Zairian Women." *Africa Review* 7, nos. 3, 4 (1977), pp. 92–105.

———. "Value Conflict and Development: The Struggle of the Professional Zairian Woman." *Journal of Modern African Studies* 16, no. 1 (March 1978), pp. 133–139.

Gran, Guy, ed. *Zaire: The Political Economy of Underdevelopment.* New York: Praeger, 1979.

Lukoschak, Edettraud C. *Zaire: A Study in Ideology and Social Change.* Ph.D. diss., University of California, Berkeley, 1977.

MacGaffey, Janet. "Evading Male Control: Women in the Second Economy in Zaire." In *Patriarchy and Class: African Women in the Home and Workforce,* edited by Jane Parpart and Sharon Strichter. Boulder: Westview Press, 1987.

MacGaffey, Wyatt. "The Policy of National Integration in Zaire." *Journal of Modern African Studies* 20, no. 1 (1982), pp. 87–105.

———. *Modern Congo Prophets: Religion in a Plural Society.* Bloomington: Indiana University Press, 1983.

———. *Religion and Society in Central Africa.* Chicago: University of Chicago Press, 1986.

Markowitz, Marvin D. *Cross and Sword: The Political Role of Christian Missions in the Belgian Congo, 1908–1960.* Stanford: Hoover Institution Press, 1973.

Mukohya Vwakyanakazi. "Small Urban Centers and Social Change in South-Eastern Zaire." *African Studies Review* 31, no. 3 (December 1988), pp. 85–94.

Newbury, M. Catharine. "Ebutumwa Bw'Emiogo: The Tyranny of Cassava: A Women's Tax Revolt in Eastern Zaire." *Canadian Journal of African Studies* 18, no. 1 (1984), pp. 35–54.

Nzongola-Ntalaja, ed. *The Crisis in Zaire: Myths and Realities.* Trenton: Africa World Press, 1986.

Over, M., et al. "The Direct and Indirect Cost of HIV Infection in Developing Countries: The Cases of Zaire and Tanzania." In *The Global Impact of AIDS,* edited by Alan F. Fleming et al. New York: Liss, 1988.

Schoepf, Brooke Grundfest, and Claude Schoepf. "Land, Gender and Food Security in Eastern Kivu, Zaire." In *Agriculture, Women and Land: The African Experience,* pp. 106–113, edited by Jean Davison. Boulder: Westview Press, 1988.

Sklar, Richard. "The Nature of Class Domination in Africa." *Journal of Modern African Studies* 17, no. 4 (December 1979).

Stewart, Gary. *Breakout: Profiles in African Rhythm.* Chicago: University of Chicago Press, 1992.

———. "Soukous: Birth of the Beat." *Beat* 8, no. 6 (1989), pp. 18–21.

Turner, Thomas. "Clouds of Smoke: Cultural and Psychological Modernization in Zaire." In *Zaire: The Political Economy of Underdevelopment,* pp. 69–82, edited by Guy Gran. New York: Praeger, 1979.

United Nations. Economic Commission for Africa. *Le Droit et la Condition de la Femme au Zaire.* Addis Ababa, 1985.

Vansina, Jan. "Mwasi's Trials." *Daedalus* 3, no. 2 (Spring 1982), pp. 49–70.

Verhaegen, Benoît. *Femmes Zairoises de Kisangani: Combats pour la Survie.* Paris: L'Harmattan, 1990.

Verheust, Thérèse. *Portraits de Femmes: Les Intellectuelles Zairoises.* Vol. 6, no. 1, of *Les Cahiers du CEDAF.* Brussels: CEDAF, 1985.

Winternitz, Helen. *East Along the Equator.* New York: Atlantic Monthly Press, 1987.

Young, Crawford. *The Politics of Cultural Pluralism.* Madison: University of Wisconsin Press, 1976.

_____. "Patterns of Social Conflict: State, Class and Ethnicity." *Daedalus* 3, no. 2 (Spring 1982), pp. 71–98.

Zaire: A Country Study. 3d ed. Washington, D.C.: American University, 1979.

ECONOMICS, POLITICS, AND INTERDEPENDENCE

Aronson, Jonathan. "The Politics of Private Bank Lending and Debt Renegotiations." In *Debt and the Less Developed Countries,* edited by Jonathan Aronson. Boulder: Westview Press, 1979.

Bank of Zaire. *Information Memorandum.* Kinshasa: Bank of Zaire, December 1981.

_____. *The Republic of Zaire: Recent Economic and Financial Developments.* Kinshasa: GOZ, June 1982.

Blumenthal, Erwin. "Zaire: Report on Her International Financial Credibility." April 7, 1982.

Callaghy, Thomas M. "The Ritual Dance of the Debt Game." *Africa Report,* September-October 1984, pp. 22–26.

_____. "The Political Economy of African Debt: The Case of Zaire." In *Africa in Economic Crisis,* edited by John Ravenhill. London: Macmillan, 1986.

_____. "Lost Between State and Market: The Politics of Economic Adjustment in Ghana, Zambia and Nigeria." In *Economic Crisis and Policy Choice: The Politics of Adjustment in the Third World,* pp. 257–319, edited by Joan Nelson. Princeton: Princeton University Press, 1990.

Cornevin, Robert. *Histoire du Congo: Léopoldville-Kinshasa.* Paris: Éditions Berger-Levrault, 1966.

_____. *Le Zaire.* Paris: Presses Universitaires de France, 1972.

Garten, Jeffrey. "Rescheduling Third World Debt: The Case of Zaire, 1979–80." Ph.D. diss., School of Advanced International Studies, Johns Hopkins University, 1981.

Gran, Guy. "The Sociology of World-System Stabilization: The IMF in Zaire, 1978–80." Chap. 5 in *Development by People: Citizen Construction of a Just World,* pp. 117–143. New York: Praeger, 1983.

Ilunga, Ilunkamba. *Propriété Publique et Conventions de Gestion dans l'Industrie du Cuivre au Zaire.* Kinshasa: Centre d'Étude et de Documentation (CEDAF), 1984.

International Monetary Fund. *Surveys of African Economies.* Vol. 4. Washington, D.C.: IMF, 1971.

Jewsiewicki, Bogumil. "Zaire Enters the World System: Its Colonial Incorporation as the Belgian Congo, 1885–1960." In *Zaire: The Political Economy of Underdevelopment,* pp. 29–51, edited by Guy Gran. New York: Praeger, 1979.

_____. "African Peasants in the Totalitarian Colonial Society of the Belgian Congo." In *Peasants in Africa: Historical and Contemporary Perspectives,* pp. 45–75, edited by Martin A. Klein. Beverly Hills: Sage, 1980.

Kabwit, Ghislain C. "Zaire: The Roots of the Continuing Crisis." *Journal of Modern African Studies* 17, no. 3 (1979).

Kannyo, Edward. "Political Power and Class Formation in Zaire: The Zairianization Measures, 1973–75." Ph.D. diss., Yale University, 1979.

Kronsten, Gregory. *Zaire to the 1990s: Will Retrenchment Work?* Economist Intelligence Unit, Special Report no. 227. London: Economist Publications, 1986.

Leslie, Winsome J. *The World Bank and Structural Transformation in Developing Countries: The Case of Zaire.* Boulder: Lynne Rienner, 1987.

MacGaffey, Janet. *Entrepreneurs and Parasites: The Struggle for Indigenous Capitalism in Zaire.* New York: Cambridge University Press, 1988.

MacGaffey, Janet, et al. *The Real Economy of Zaire: The Contribution of Smuggling and Other Unofficial Activities to National Wealth.* Philadelphia: University of Pennsylvania Press, 1991.

Makala-Lizumu and Mwana Elas, "Modernization and Urban Poverty: A Case Study of Kinshasa." In *Zaire: The Political Economy of Underdevelopment,* pp. 108–121, edited by Guy Gran. New York: Praeger, 1979.

Newbury, M. Catharine. "Dead and Buried or Just Underground: The Privatization of the State in Zaire." *Canadian Journal of African Studies* 18, no. 1 (1984), pp. 112–114.

Northrup, David. *Beyond the Bend in the River: African Labor in Eastern Zaire, 1865–1940.* Athens: Ohio University Center for International Studies, 1988.

Peemans, Jean-Philippe. "The Social and Economic Development of Zaire Since Independence: An Historical Outline." *African Affairs* 74, no. 295 (April 1975), pp. 148–179.

Radmann, Wolf. "The Nationalization of Zaire's Copper: From Union Minière to GECAMINES." *Africa Today* 25, no. 4 (October-December 1978).

U.S. Department of Commerce. International Trade Administration. *Foreign Economic Trends and Their Implications for the United States: Zaire.* Washington, D.C., September 1989.

Willame, Jean-Claude. *Zaire: L'Épopée D'Inga.* Paris: Éditions L'Harmattan, 1986.

World Bank. *The Economy of Zaire.* Washington, D.C.: IBRD, July 1975.

_____. *Zaire: Current Economic Situation and Constraints.* Washington, D.C.: IBRD, 1979.

Young, Crawford. "Zaire: The Unending Crisis." *Foreign Affairs* 57, no. 1 (Fall 1978), pp. 169–185.

_____. "Zaire: Is There a State?" *Canadian Journal of African Studies* 18, no. 1 (1984), pp. 80–82.

_____. "Zaire: Prospects for the Future." Paper presented at U.S. State Department Conference on Zaire, Washington, D.C., August 24, 1982.

_____. "Zaire: Old Foes and New Friends." *Africa Report* 23, no. 1 (January–February 1978), pp. 5–10.

ZAIRE IN THE INTERNATIONAL ARENA

Bayart, Jean-Francois. *La politique africaine de François Mitterrand.* Paris: Éditions Karthala, 1984.

Bustin, Edouard. "The Foreign Policy of the Republic of Zaire." In *International Affairs in Africa.* Annals of the American Academy of Political and Social Science, vol. 489 (January 1987). Edited by Gerald J. Bender. Newbury Park: Sage, 1987.

Callaghy, Thomas M. "External Actors and the Relative Automony of the Political Aristocracy in Zaire." *Journal of Commonwealth and Comparative Politics* 21, no. 3 (November 1983), pp. 61–83.

_____. "Absolutism and Apartheid: Relations Between Zaire and South Africa." In *South Africa in Southern Africa: The Intensifying Vortex of Violence,* pp. 371–403, edited by Thomas Callaghy. New York: Praeger, 1983.

Hakim, Najib J., and Richard P. Stevens. "Zaire and Israel: An American Connection." *Journal of Palestine Studies* 12, no. 3 (Spring 1983), issue 47.

Hull, Galen. "Zaire in the World System: In Search of Sovereignty." In *Zaire: The Political Economy of Underdevelopment,* pp. 263–281, edited by Guy Gran. New York: Praeger, 1979.

Kongwa, Sam. "Relations Between Zambia and Zaire." *Africa Insight* 17, no. 2 (1987), pp. 102–107.

Lemarchand, René, ed. *American Policy in Southern Africa: The Stakes and the Stance.* Washington, D.C.: University Press of America, 1978.

Mobutu Sese Seko. *Dignity for Africa: Interviews with Jean-Louis Remilleux.* Paris: Éditions Albin Michel, 1989.

Pachter, Elise Forbes. "Our Man in Kinshasa: U.S. Relations with Mobutu, 1970–1983." Ph.D. diss., Johns Hopkins University, 1987.

Schatzberg, Michael. *Mobutu or Chaos? The United States and Zaire, 1960–1990.* New York: University Press of America, 1991.

USAID. *Congressional Presentation, Fiscal Year 1990.* Annex 1, Africa.

U.S. Congress. House. Committee on Foreign Affairs. *Foreign Assistance Legislation for Fiscal Years 1990–91.* Part 6, *Hearings and Markup Before the House Subcommittee on Africa.* 101st Cong., 1st Sess., March 8–9, April 25, 1989.

U.S. General Accounting Office. The Comptroller General. Report to the U.S. House, Committee on Foreign Affairs, Subcommittee on Africa. *Search for Options in the Troubled Food For Peace Program in Zaire.* Washington, D.C., February 1982.

Weinstein, Warren, and Thomas H. Henriksen, eds. *Soviet and Chinese Aid to African Nations.* New York: Praeger, 1980.

Young, Crawford. "Zaire: The Politics of Penury." *SAIS Review* 3, no. 1 (Winter–Spring 1983), pp. 115–130.

About the Book and Author

Crisis has marked the history of Zaire, from its inception as the Congo Free State and its later restructuring as the Belgian Congo through the period of chaos and secession in the early 1960s and the establishment of the authoritarian rule of President Mobutu Sese Seko in 1965. The author begins by describing the historical setting, then focuses on economic and political developments during the Mobutu era. She examines in detail the corrupt and closed political system, with its roots in the colonial state and precolonial political patterns, arguing that although Mobutu has survived by shrewdly manipulating the nation's strengths and weaknesses in the global arena, internal political strife has destroyed his aspirations for a leading role in African and Third World affairs.

Despite vast resources, crisis has also plagued Zaire on the economic front. Leslie illustrates why the country has fallen deeply into debt, economic growth has stagnated, and inflation and unemployment have escalated. Her discussion of Zairian society looks in particular at the impact of ethnicity, emerging classes, Western-style education, and religion on traditional patterns of life in Zaire. Finally, the author assesses the long-term impact of the Mobutu legacy in view of halting efforts, initiated since 1990 by Mobutu himself, to introduce a multiparty system.

Winsome J. Leslie is adjunct professor of African studies at The Johns Hopkins University School of Advanced International Studies and Adjunct Professor in Residence at The American University.

Index

DATE DUE

NOV 24 '99

BRODART, CO.

Cat. No. 23-221-003